The Church in Brazil
The Politics of Religion

Latin American Monographs, No. 56
Institute of Latin American Studies
The University of Texas at Austin

The Church in Brazil
The Politics of Religion

by Thomas C. Bruneau

University of Texas Press, Austin

Library of Congress Cataloging in Publication Data

Bruneau, Thomas C.   1939-
    The church in Brazil.

    (Latin American monographs / Institute of Latin American
Studies, the University of Texas at Austin)
    "This book is in many respects a logical continuation of
The political transformation of the Brazilian Catholic
Church, published in 1974"—Pref.
    Bibliography: p.
    Includes index.
    1. Catholic Church—Brazil. 2. Brazil—Church history.
I. Title. II. Series: Latin American monographs (Univer-
sity of Texas at Austin. Institute of Latin American Studies)
BX1466.2.B77   282'.81   81-16391
ISBN 0-292-71071-2   AACR2

Requests for permission to reproduce material from
this work should be sent to:
    Permissions
    University of Texas Press
    P. O. Box 7819
    Austin, Texas 78712

For Bruce and Jennifer

Contents

Tables

Map

Preface

This book is in many respects a logical continuation of *The Political Transformation of the Brazilian Catholic Church,* published in 1974. That work described and analyzed change in the Catholic church from an institutional and historical perspective, and whereas there was some consideration of religious beliefs and practices in this earlier volume, the main emphasis was on the institutional church in a political context. I argued that the church had changed significantly in the past twenty years, and that the explanation for such change lay in the church-society relationship as facilitated or restrained by the Holy See and the Brazilian state. Institutional dynamics are clearly important and require detailed analysis, yet a complete approach to any religious system must consider the degree to which the institution influences the beliefs and practices of its members. This book is, to the best of my knowledge, the first study to attempt to measure or gauge religious influence in Latin America and the first anywhere to link institutional features to beliefs and practices.

The Introduction establishes my general approach to analysis and how it relates to methods employed by other scholars with similar interests. The body of the book begins with a brief review of the institutional history of the Brazilian church, with emphasis on the weakness of the early institution and, consequently, its slight impact on a dispersed population in a huge country. The literature on religious beliefs and practices in Brazil is reviewed and the findings synthesized. This synthesis is then compared with the findings from my sample survey, and types of religiosity (patterns of religious beliefs and practices) are defined and described. The history of the post-World War II church is briefly reviewed, pointing out how some sectors of the institution adopted progressive sociopolitical roles which are intricately related to the nature of the social, economic, and political regime in Brazil. A description of this regime in its present-day configuration is followed by an update of church responses to the regime since 1974. Recently there has been an important process of definition and consolidation taking place, which has projected the Brazilian church to the forefront of sociopolitical criticism and activism to a degree unknown elsewhere in the Catholic church.

Although developments and activities at the national level are extremely important, the church is still based on the diocese, and it is at this level that most implementation of new sociopolitical roles does (or does not) take place. Chapter 6 describes and analyzes change in the eight dioceses which were studied in depth and shows the nature of the new orientation concerning sociopolitical matters. Change in dioceses and parishes is then related to the patterns of religiosity defined in Chapter 2 so that the church's potential level of influence can be understood. Patterns of religious beliefs and practices are related to sociopolitical attitudes and the matter of religion as an independent variable is further clarified. Chapter 8 looks at a new strategy of influence, the Basic Christian Community (Comunidade Eclesial de Base, or CEB), both as an organizational form and as a means to reorient church influence. The Conclusion examines institutional change in light of survey results and discusses the role of the church in future Brazilian development.

Certainly the Brazilian church deserves further study. It is located in a context of an evolving dictatorial government—the oldest "newest military regime" in Latin America—and one which has served as a model for regimes in Argentina, Chile, and Uruguay. It is a regime in which economic growth is promoted to the detriment of the means of distribution and in which industrialization takes place under state auspices but without subsequent modifications in class structures. The church in Brazil actively criticizes this political and economic model and has encouraged the formation of grass-roots organizations—the CEBs—which in many ways undermine the regime. Thus this historic institution, which under other circumstances might have been a pillar of the government, militates for change in, or even replacement of, that government. At the macro-level the church clearly has an impact, if only by advocating other socioeconomic models and encouraging independent groups and organizations to oppose the regime. In a repressive state which discourages pluralism this function in itself is important.

However, to analyze fully the impact of change in the church, it is necessary to measure the influence it has on its members. It is frequently stated that Brazil is the largest Catholic country in the world, with more than 90 percent of its 120 million population formally members of the Catholic church. Paradoxically, this country is also the home of various

Spiritist movements, including Candomblé, Umbanda, Batuque, and Kardecism, and a wide literature exists on Brazil's nonspecific (that is, non-Spiritist) but historic "peasant Catholicism." Brazil is considered by many Protestant fundamentalist sects, as well as by the Mormons, to be a particularly promising area for conversions. There is ample reason, therefore, to question the amount of influence the Catholic church really wields in such a varied religious context. Does institutional change within the church occur because of the church's influence among the population or because the church lacks such influence and hopes to achieve it by taking on another role, such as that of sociopolitical critic? This question will be dealt with, as well as that of whether or not religion is the "opium" of the people and under what conditions the church can turn religion into a stimulant.

The research for this book was carried out in Brazil during most of 1974–1975, with a one month follow-up visit in 1978. Eight dioceses located in four regions of the country were the main field sites, and the techniques used to gather information included a sample survey, in-depth interviews, participant observation, and a review of relevant primary and secondary documentation. Although a study based on eight dioceses is not claimed to be representative of the entire country, linking the results from the four regions with evidence from the national level should offer a fairly balanced view of the overall situation in Brazil. (For a description of the field study and the data analysis, see the appendices.)

Initial work on this study began in 1972 with support from the Social Science Research Committee of McGill University. The field research was supported by the Canada Council and the International Development Research Centre of Ottawa. I extend my appreciation to these bodies for their generosity and patience. In Brazil I was assisted by almost everyone with whom I came in contact, but must mention particularly D. Ivo Lorscheider and Pe. Virgílio Rosa Netto of the Conferência Nacional dos Bispos do Brasil (National Conference of Brazilian Bishops—CNBB), Pe. F. B. de Avila and Pe. Paulo Menezes of the Instituto Brasileiro de Desenvolvimento (Brazilian Institute for Development—IBRADES), and Waldo César of the Centro de Estudos, Pesquisa e Planejamento (Center for Study, Research and Planning—CENPLA).

A large project requires extensive cooperation, and I received it in good measure. If willingness to assist research and an openness of spirit are any indication of a changing institution, then the Catholic church in Brazil is indeed that. Daniel Levine and Thomas Sanders have provided ongoing support and criticism, for which I am most appreciative. I also thank three McGill University graduate students: Gary Firestone was most helpful in the fieldwork stage; Edmund Horka, in the data analysis; and Mary Mooney, for her general comments and criticisms. Professors Jerome Black and J. O. Ramsay, also of McGill University, were most helpful in assisting me with the interpretation of the data. Kim Reany and Judith Sabetti typed various parts of several drafts, and I am most grateful for their continuing cooperation and good will.

The Church in Brazil
The Politics of Religion

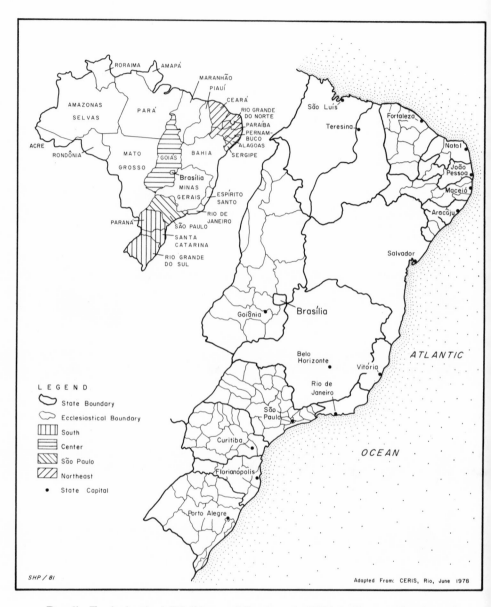

Adapted From: CERIS, Rio, June 1978

Brazil: Ecclesiastical Divisions of Regions in Which Survey Conducted

Introduction

The primary purpose of this book is to integrate analysis of the Catholic church with an analysis of religious beliefs and practices in Brazil. To accomplish this one must understand how the church changes, the impact of this change on religiosity, and the implications of this impact for the individual and society. Up to now, the literature on Brazil and on Latin America as a whole has not integrated the two main levels of analysis. Study of the church has remained in the sphere of historians and political scientists, and religious beliefs and practices have been dealt with primarily by sociologists and anthropologists. In other words, structures and organizations are considered one field of study, beliefs and practices another. Even extensive research projects, such as that carried out by the Centro de Estatística Religiosa e Investigações Sociais (Center of Religious Statistics and Social Investigation—CERIS) between 1966 and 1970, have not systematically tried to relate the church's structure to actual beliefs and practices, nor to integrate a study of popular religiosity with a study of church groups and structures.[1] However, if the significance of change in the church is to be fully understood, these relationships must be so analyzed and tested.

Prominence has been given to study of the institution of the church partly because religious beliefs and practices are affected by change in the church, and thus it is logical that this change be fully described. Equally important is the fact that Catholicism views the institution as central— indeed necessary—to its primary goal, salvation. Personal salvation is the ultimate objective of church membership, is mediated through the church, and is impossible without the church.[2]

Various approaches have been employed to study the Catholic church in Latin America, sometimes resulting in vastly different interpretations. It is not always obvious what level or sector is being discussed, let alone what overall conclusions can be drawn from a particular work. Charles Glock and Phillip E. Hammond have pointed out that in studies of church and religion, there has been little accumulation and consolidation of concepts and methodology.[3] Even though some writers have advocated particular aproaches to the study of the church and of religion in Latin America, there is so far no general consensus.

One way to view the church has been in the context of party politics: religion is analyzed in terms of its electoral implications, or seen in terms of a political party (such as a Christian Democratic party) over which the church is presumed to exert some influence. The Christian Democrats have been studied in some Latin American countries, most notably Chile. However, Chile no longer has a functioning electoral system, the Christian Democratic party in Venezuela (Comité de Organización Política Electoral Independiente—COPEI) is only tangentially related to the church, and in the other Latin American countries there are either nondemocratic systems or no Christian Democratic party. Surveys have been conducted in Latin America which include items on religion, and articles have appeared on religion and politicization, but these articles fail to relate attitudinal data to structural variables nor do they differentiate religion from general cultural characteristics.[4] Consequently, such works are unable to evaluate the impact of the church-as-institution on either the individual or on society. Evaluating this is even more difficult when the church is changing. Thus it does not seem particularly useful to study the church by means of either analysis of political parties or by means of general surveys.

One may also view the church as a pressure group seeking to influence other groups and the state. A substantial literature exists in which sectors within the church are shown to attempt to affect state, society, and other groups. The pressure-group literature includes Lucy C. Behrman's and Thomas Sanders's and Brian Smith's work on Chile, George W. Grayson's on Peru, Sanders's on all of Latin America, the studies of priests' groups by Carlos Astiz, and Michael Dodson, and Emanuel de Kadt's work on Brazil.[5] The chief drawback of this approach is its noncomprehensiveness, which frequently tends toward an assumption of a rough balance among groups. This approach also tends to disregard the special characteristics of the church-as-institution and its unique position in Latin American society.

The use of attitude surveys or content analyses of documents such as pastoral letters which pertain to the church elite (primarily the bishops) is a third approach to the study of the Latin American church. Content analysis of a wide range of documents was the basis for a book by Frederick C. Turner and an article by Hubert Schwan and Antonio

Ugalde; Thomas G. Sanders and Daniel Levine have conducted attitude surveys.[6]

It is interesting to discover what the Catholic elite say, or how they feel, about a series of topics or issues, but whereas some studies, such as Levine's, are better than others, there remains the problem of relating attitudes to action. This approach tends to be somewhat abstract, since situations arise in which immediate demands easily override stated attitudes and lead to unanticipated behavior.

The organizational approach to the study of the church is subject to two main interpretations, one of which is more flexible. The organizational approach employed in the Rand Corporation study conducted by Luigi Einaudi and in David Mutchler's book adheres to a very rigid view, that of an organization so constrained by multiple internal and external factors that it can barely function, let alone respond and change. Mutchler misperceived the churches in Chile and Colombia and predicted a takeover by foreign-trained priest-sociologists. Of course nothing of the sort happened, a fact which highlights his fundamental misunderstanding of the church-as-institution. The Rand Corporation study foresaw a continuing reliance on the state and a lack of internal coherence, which would weaken the church's orientation toward change.[7] Because of ideological changes in the church, poorly understood in the Rand study, church reliance on the state is increasingly less feasible and internal coherence, if anything, tends to be greater than in the past. Such short-sighted organizational approaches often see problems where none exist and demonstrate little appreciation of church dynamics.

A more flexible and fruitful approach is suggested by Rowan Ireland, Daniel Levine, Lars Schoultz, Brian Smith, and Kenneth Westhues, whose works are useful and informative for describing, and possibly explaining how the church operates and what can reasonably be expected of it in changing societies.[8] The problem, however, is that the church is not just any organization, and its long history, its Latin American peculiarities, international scope, and singular message combine to produce very particular dynamics, which can act as impediments to change or as propelling factors, depending on poorly understood internal and external variables. It must always be remembered, as Ernst Troeltsch has argued and so skillfully illustrated, that the history of the Christian ethos appears as a constant process of compromise, and, at the same time, as a constant opposition to the spirit of compromise.[9] We must make an effort to understand when compromise, characteristic of all "normal" organizations, stops and when opposition begins. None of these approaches, not even the organizational, can fully contend with the special characteristics of the church, even though many of their proponents demonstrate great understanding of how the church functions.

An approach must be sought which takes into consideration factors basic to the church's dynamics and role in society, that is, the simultaneous founding of church and state in Latin America, the linkages between all levels of church and state, the implied significance that change in one has for the other, the international legitimation and control of the church, its transcendental message, its reliance on nonmaterial coercion for implementation, and church membership based on faith. Without including at least these points in any analysis, it is impossible to understand change in the church, much less to evaluate the impact this change has on the individual and society. An approach employing some of these basic components has been used by myself, Levine and Alexander Wilde, Sanders and Smith. Such an approach, however, was initially stated and elaborated most fully by Ivan Vallier.[10] By examining the key elements and limitations of his approach, it is possible to build on his framework and refine the institutional approach employed in this book.

Vallier's view removes the church from the exclusive realm of history or theology and treats it as an institution, one with the special characteristics noted above. He sees the church as a complex system capable of perceiving and responding to external threats. He argues that it has played a conservative role in the history of Latin America not because of its theology, but, rather, because of its particular linkage with society, a linkage which has become institutionalized. Therefore, in Vallier's view, the chief problem confronting the church today is how to extract itself from these linkages and commitments, how to refrain from compromise and links with other groups or classes, and how to reenter society at a higher level of abstraction and specialization. Vallier describes the nature of church-state linkages and the structural features of the church, from parish to the Vatican, from which might come an understanding of the church's dynamic. It is his contention that the church's most recent changes are due to international legitimation combined with the church's perceived threats to influence. He outlines a model of change for the church, in which church operations are studied in a historical perspective, followed by an interpretation of its new role in society, a role which is part of his larger, evolutionary view of society, which presupposes institutional specialization and differentiation.

Vallier has undoubtedly produced the most valuable analytical model of the Latin American church. However, his prediction for the role of the "new church" was rather far afield and indicates the main limitation in his analysis. He believed the new church would, and should, provide specialized involvement at the cultural and associational levels, as well as normative integration at a more general level—a direction toward which he felt the church in Chile was tending in 1972. He also argued strongly against repoliticization of the "extracted" church, a move that would short-circuit the whole specialization and differentiation process that he found so important. In my view, the chief drawback to this model is that Vallier allowed his general evolutionary model (differentiation and specialization) to affect his analysis of what, specifically, the church could do and how it could do it. He could not conceptualize politics as an autonomous sphere and thus failed to include it as a key variable in analysis of the church.

In fact, rather than an increasing complexity and differentiation in society in the context of which the church could distinguish itself and specialize according to more modern views of theology, Latin America has seen a certain paradoxical, nonevolutionary development process in which economic and societal changes do occur, but without fundamentally affecting most existing social structures. This pertains to most key institutions and most certainly to those in the political realm, where democraticization is the exception rather than the rule. This situation may be self-limiting, but it is more likely a characteristic of modernization in the late-industrialization pattern.[11]

In this situation of little group formation, repression, and injustice, it is difficult for the church to extract and insulate itself from the rest of state and society. With its history of linkages and commitments to other segments of society, as amended by internal ideological or theological shifts, anything the church says or does has political implications, as Troeltsch argued six decades ago, and as the proponents of the Theology of Liberation argue today.[12] Furthermore, as dictatorships have become more pervasive and consolidated and intolerant of opposition and criticism, the church, as a large, internationally legitimated institution, emerges as the main organized force with which opposition elements can ally themselves. Thus, to the detriment of Vallier's analysis, the Theology of Liberation (for which he had harsh words) is accurate in its analysis, if not in its prescriptions; that is, the political factor must be introduced as a key consideration in determining the church's ability to act in its present Latin American context.

The most useful way to analyze the church, then, is to regard it as an institution historically linked with state and society in Latin America. Sociologists of organizational behavior, such as Phillip Selznick, Daniel Katz, Robert Kahn, and James Thompson, point out that an institution is a product of social needs and pressures and remains a responsive and adaptive organism.[13] This differs from the view which holds that an organization is a technical instrument for mobilizing human energies and directing them toward set goals. Obviously, the difference is a question of degree, and Selznick, for example, sees the infusion of values inherent in the institution and held by a majority of its members as critical.

It is clear that the church, as the oldest continuing institution or corporate entity in western civilization, has had to change in order to survive, and, by surviving, has lent its precepts to other present-day institutions which were based on the model provided by the church or which grew in the spaces provided by it in society. This is certainly the case with Brazil; the church and state together founded the society, and the church has evolved with society over a period of 480 years and has all the while affected its make-up. My approach, then, is broad and all-encompassing: it regards the institution within its social and political context and treats it as a responsive, adaptive organism.

It might seem initially that this is an unreasonably large and unmanageably complex topic. I argue that it cannot be analyzed in bits and pieces; as the church has been integrated historically with the state and religion with Latin American culture, so must it be analyzed and treated comprehensively. In order to begin analysis, I will focus on the setting and implementation of the goals of this continually dynamic institution, locked as it is into its environment. Goals are essentially statements about or definitions of the relationship of an institution to its environment.[14] Goals indicate how the environment is perceived, what purpose an institution serves in the environmental context, and the means or instruments by which the institution relates to its environment. Obviously, as the environment changes, goals must be implemented in different ways, even if the goals themselves do not change.

The goal of the church is to influence men and society, or, more specifically, to lead men and, by implication, society, to salvation. As noted earlier, the institutional church is central to this process. Various strategies to accomplish this goal have been employed with greater or lesser enthusiasm over the past two thousand years. As societies changed, tactics were modified, but the essential goal—influence—has persisted. As Thomas O'Dea points out, the Second Vatican Council (1962-1965) represented an attempt by the church to update an approach to influence which had been on the wane since the Renaissance.[15]

In order to work with a definition of the goal as influence, several areas must be clarified beforehand. The formation of this goal in a specific context must be noted, as well as the church's perception of the environment and the tasks it intends to undertake in order to realize the goal. The sectors of society to be focused on must be identified and the church's relationship to them indicated. The instruments or mechanisms by means of which the church exercises influence and generates commitment must be defined. Because of the particular history of church and society in Latin America, there are severe constraints on the church's setting and implementation of its goal, constraints aggravated by the development process. Church-society linkages constrain the church's field of action considerably and, because of its long-standing integration with the state, there has been a tendency to equate religious influence with political power. The church's difficulty in avoiding dependence on the state for various resources decreases its independence with respect to goals that much more. This seeking of independence in goal definition is further complicated by the fact that the church has relied on some sectors of society for support and almost completely ignored others (such as the urban and rural poor). One cannot tacitly assume, therefore, that the majority religious culture is necessarily based on ecclesiastical doctrine; the institutional church's historical links with most of the population are tenuous indeed. Yet, because of particular relations with the Brazilian state, because of encouragement from the Holy See, and stimulated by perceived threats in the environment, interpretation of church goals in the period since World War II has changed.

As Troeltsch argued, the basic beliefs in the Gospel are revolutionary, for they press beyond any one society to an ideal religious unity.[16] For reasons to be analyzed later, large sectors of the Brazilian church have adopted as their primary, immediate role (originating from the goal of influence) the denunciation of the present state and economic model and the offering of alternative, utopian models of society. What is more, these sectors are encouraging the formation of grass-roots communities by means of which the centralizing and authoritarian state can be undermined as the people begin to participate in politics and to act on their own initiative. As the lower classes become more politically active, the church loses the resources of those classes to which it has traditionally directed its influence. Moreover, the very model of development in Brazil implies secularization and a certain marginalization of the church in society. The church, therefore, in its approach to influence, is changing in Brazil and has no option but to continue to change. However, it is severely constrained both by its historical lack of influence among those classes it seeks out today and by its nature as a part of the universal Church, with its center in Rome.

Thus far, we have dealt with what might be loosely termed a "national church" when, in fact, the Roman Catholic church does not recognize national churches per se but, rather, aggregations of dioceses located in specific national units. The recent proliferation of national episcopal conferences and international councils might lend some credence to the idea of national churches—and the CNBB does claim to speak for all Brazilian bishops—but cooperation among the members of the church hierarchy in terms of goal implementation comes down to the actions of the individual bishop. All sources emphasize and canon law confirms that he has absolute power in his diocese; only the pope is superior.[17] If a national church seems to emerge and adopt new approaches to its goal, this does not necessarily mean that all the bishops are likely to fall into line. There are almost three hundred bishops in Brazil in some 222 ecclesiastical divisions; some favor the idea of a national church and others oppose it with varying degrees of vehemence. It is necessary, therefore, to look to the individual dioceses, whose respective bishops, for the most part, set the tone for the approach to influence. It was for this reason that eight dioceses were selected for intense study, the results of which will be joined with information drawn from previous studies and other sources of information to explain change in the church at the local level. Thus change in the national church will be related to change at the local level and an integrated view of the Brazilian church suggested.

Even this is not enough, however, for, as noted earlier and as demonstrated in the next chapter, the influence of the Brazilian church historically has been low. The question of how much influence the changing (or nonchanging) church can generate is, thus, an empirical one, one which will be analyzed by considering the results of the two-thousand-question survey conducted in the eight dioceses. The main argument, or hypothesis, if you will, of this book is that the church lacks influence among the general and predominantly lower-class population of Brazil and as it changes will lose influence among the more-favored classes as well. Since its structures have evolved in accordance with its involvement with these favored classes, it must develop new structures in order to reach the lower classes. It is in this context that the Basic Christian Community becomes important, for its purpose is to allow the church to penetrate sectors of society hitherto neglected and to stimulate the organization and awareness of a people as yet unorganized and unaware.

A combination of national- and local-level institutional variables and survey results provides a comprehensive view of the church and the religious situation in Brazil. This comprehensive view makes possible the evaluation of the role of the church and religion in Brazilian development and allows speculation on the future of the centralized and authoritarian state and the socioeconomic model it has promoted.

1. History of the Church in Brazil

The manner in which the church was established in Brazil was to have far-reaching implications in terms of the church's approach to influence, in addition to affecting the level of influence it eventually attained. The church, because of its integration with the colonial and, later, Brazilian state, did not develop independently as an institution and was unable to make much of a specific imprint on the overall society. Largely because of these structural factors, its influence (discussed in more detail in Chapter 2) was amorphous and generally weak. It is necessary to review this historical background, if only briefly, in order to understand later changes in the church and in its approach to influence.[1]

The discovery and settlement of colonial Brazil was a joint endeavor of the Portuguese crown and the Catholic church, the two mutually reinforcing and legitimating one another. Portugal's maritime discoveries and subsequent colonization of new lands were viewed as a continuation of the Reconquest of the Iberian peninsula, in global terms, as the crown and the church brought new lands and souls into the "One True Faith" at a time when much of Christendom remained under Islamic control. This was seen as further proof that Portugal, vanquisher of the Moors in Europe and North Africa, could be counted on to defend the Faith and, with the continuing assistance of the church, would uphold and spread Catholicism throughout a world being discovered and colonized. This attitude was further reinforced by Portugal's reaffirmation of loyalty to Rome during the Reformation, when it was felt that "the discovery of America [was] a provident fact of God's industry to compensate and balance the losses that Protestantism had caused the church, giving to Pedro Alvares Cabral a divine mission; making, then, of Brazil a new area given to Christianity."[2] This type of observation was common at the time and a vivid description is provided by the famous Antônio Vieira, whose interpretations of the founding and settling of Brazil were based on the premise that "the Portuguese are a people chosen by God to establish his kingdom in this world. Every Portuguese inherits a special vocation which is different from the vocations of other people."[3] That sense of divine mission lives on in the current saying, "God is a Brazilian"—a sentiment that is thoroughly engrained in the national psyche and from which the church may well never recover.

In order to share in the enterprise of discovering and colonizing new lands, the Holy See ceded tremendous rights of patronage to the Portuguese crown, to which it was already favorably disposed for having fought against the Moors. Papal bulls gave the crown virtual control of the new church by granting it basic powers: the crown appointed the bishops and other high-level clergy; the crown collected and administered the tithes; churches were built by the state and by private groups; communications were sent first to Lisbon and only then on to Rome; and the crown had to approve all ecclesiastical documents. As J. Lloyd Mecham observed for all of Latin America, "Never before or since did a sovereign with the consent of the Pope so completely control the Catholic Church within his dominions."[4] This was certainly the case in Brazil: "The real leader of the church, and consequently of the mission enterprise, was the king and not the Pope."[5] In addition to the formal grants specified in the bulls, informal privileges evolved from the exercise of patronage. These included the right of recourse to the crown in ecclesiastical courts, which effectively denied the church control of internal discipline; the placet, or right of the crown to censor all ecclesiastical letters, bulls, and other documents prior to publication in the colony; and the right to determine the quantity and, indirectly, the quality of missionaries allowed in Brazil.

Such an arrangement hindered the church's development as an institution with a distinct identity, for it was almost totally reliant on the state for its infrastructure and the processes for exercising influence. However, at that time such considerations were unimportant because the goals of church and crown were virtually identical: total coverage of the society. The environment was one of exploration and conversion, and the tasks were to bring in resources for the crown and souls for the church. All of society was to be included in the church. The colonists had to be Catholic, Indians were baptized by the missionaries, and, later, Negro slaves were baptized before landing in the colony. Although the church did maintain some institutions of its own, such as churches and schools, in most instances these were supported by the crown from the tithe, and generally it was the joint structure of crown and church that imposed the religion: the king was Catholic, therefore, so were all his subjects. With adherence to the religion guaranteed, not to say imposed, there was no need to have the faithful develop a personal sense of commitment or belief. Because of this church-state integration, the church enjoyed more than two hundred years of formal prominence in the colony and was present in all aspects of life. As Eduardo Hoornaert declares, "By means of convents, parishes, brotherhoods, and confraternities there was formed a society in which nobody avoided the need to rely on religious institutions: to find work, borrow money, guarantee burial, arrange a dowry for a daughter wanting to marry, buy a house, and secure medicine."[6] It should also be noted that only in this period did vocations to the priesthood flourish in Brazil.

However, even then this initial positive perspective on the church gave indications of certain problems to come. First of all, patronage meant that the real direction of religious activity was not under the control of the church. Most of the time the state's goals were identical to those of the church, but when this was not the case, the crown's took precedence, as exemplified by abuses in church-state finances during colonial times. The crown levied the 10 percent tax, or tithe, on everything produced in Brazil, ostensibly to provide for church support. However, the crown soon became accustomed to setting aside the greater part of the tithes for state use, after providing what the king deemed sufficient for the needs of the church. Abuses of this nature were common but presumably not flagrant enough, in the context of Christendom, to prompt the Brazilian church to define a more independent position vis à vis the state either by strengthening its shaky structures or by elaborating its ties with the Holy See.

Second, concessions to the state were regarded as necessary and, from the beginning, religious influence was neither specifically defined nor pursued. Because of the integration of the two institutions, the desire for total conversion, and the lack of autonomy and religious commitment, the church tended to confuse political power with religious influence. Because the Catholic ruler guaranteed the faith and the state passed out the tithes, it is not surprising that the church saw itself in this light. However, what influence it would normally have secured on the bases of belief, faith, and personal commitment gave way in Brazil to political power, which guaranteed conversions, spread the Word, and financed the institution.

A third point follows from the second and concerns the church's failure to develop a membership with any depth of personal commitment. The obligatory nature of the religion meant that conversion was rarely an individual matter, nor, indeed, was religious observance much more than a *pro forma* affair. Because the church could rely on the state, it had no need (and, in all events, probably little opportunity) to create its own independent infrastructure. As a result, it was never forced to develop a committed laity whose church membership was based on personal conviction rather than on social norms.

It should be noted that the Catholic church was not alone in leaving a broad but amorphous imprint on society. All observers of Brazilian colonial life note that it was decentralized and rural and that the colony could hardly be termed a state simply because of the crown's presence there. The colony was in essence a patrimonial system. At the center was the crown in Portugal, representing the focus of personal and arbitrary power, but the bureaucratic system to make it effective was lacking everywhere but in the few administrative centers. The colonization of Brazil was mainly rural in nature; the colony lacked a great center like Mexico City, Puebla, or Lima. "The whole life of the country gravitated completely around the country estate; the city was practically, if not totally, a mere appendage of the latter."[7] The rural families with their sugar mills, slaves, and dependencies became the great colonizers and dominant institutions of society, as Gilberto Freyre has so forcefully argued.[8] Attached to them, perhaps as part of the family, and usually in the pay of the landowning families, were the priests. The few cities which did spring up (Olinda, Salvador, Ouro Preto, Rio de Janeiro) did not weaken the influence of the rural families or develop a central church authority. The dominant religious institutions in the cities were the *irmandades* ("brotherhoods"), which were voluntary associations with diverse aims and activities. Church involvement in colonial life, then, was largely at the local level—priests were subservient to the land-owning families in the rural areas and employees of the irmandades were answerable to the brotherhoods in the cities. The church's control over this weak and essentially rural framework was tenuous and largely unconnected.[9] From 1551 until 1676, for instance, there was only one bishopric, in Salvador, and during the following two centuries, until the founding of the Republic in 1889, the number of ecclesiastical divisions had increased to just one archbishopric, six bishoprics, and two prelacies. No serious efforts were made to develop any sort of national institution; indeed, this would have proven impossible given the absence of a national state structure and the church's even greater lack of structure and internal communication.

Considering this background, an explicit antichurch policy could have devastating results, which is exactly what happened in the late eighteenth century. Sebastião de Carvalho e Mello, the marquis of Pombal, who was Portugal's prime minister from 1750 to 1777, was a "modern" statesman in that he created an absolute monarchy in his country along the lines of those of Spain and France. To accomplish this he seized for the state the power held by the nobles, the papacy, the diocesan churches in Portugal and its colonies, and the religious orders. Under Pombal the church at all levels was brought under the complete control of the state and suppressed. Pombal particularly oppressed the Jesuits, forcing them out of Brazil in 1759. This was an important loss since the Jesuits were by far the most organized, dedicated, independent, and disciplined order in Brazil. It was their cohesive organization and high degree of autonomy, in fact, which made them an effective instrument of church influence; they could bring their influence to bear when the rest of the institution could not. They maintained their own lines of control, generated resources beyond those provided by the state, and were less caught up in local society. Undoubtedly, the Jesuits' success proved their undoing, for Pombal correctly perceived them as a primary threat to state control.

The results of their expulsion from Brazil were far reaching. The country lost its largest and most dedicated contingent of clergymen, which was not replaced by any other, and, without an effective force to promote the church and religion, the church vegetated during most of the remainder of the colonial period.

A similar pattern, of state controls and lack of stimulus for the church, continued during the Empire (1822-1889). The church's bases of influence and religious commitment had never really been firmly established, its political power from the time of Pombal was nil, and the clergy were increasingly adopting alien doctrines (such as Liberalism and Jansenism) which actually ran counter to the church's best interests. It is true that many priests had become politically active during this period, but these were primarily revolutionaries seeking Brazil's independence from Portugal. Even after Brazil became independent, in 1822, the church-state relationship did not change. Article 5 of the Constitution declared that "the Roman Catholic, apostolic religion will continue to be the religion of the Empire." The emperor, Pedro II, was constituted as "the first ecclesiastical authority of the country in the sense that to him belonged not only the choice of personnel—the formation of the church hierarchy—but also the supreme judgment of all the laws and decrees of the popes and councils."[10] Unhappily for the church, Pedro II, although not explicitly anticlerical, was indifferent toward the church and found religion tiresome, an attitude which in no way prejudiced the use of his full legal authority regarding the powers of patronage and the accrued powers of recourse and the placet. He turned down the pope's offer of a cardinalate in Brazil—the first offered to Latin America—as he had no wish to become further involved with the Holy See, and he founded only three dioceses during his fifty-year reign.

During this time the church was treated exactly as any other government bureau. The emperor nominated bishops, collected tithes, paid the clergy, and decided what directives from Rome would be implemented. Indeed, many of his controls were designed to be tedious: bishops were forbidden to leave their dioceses without government permission, under penalty of losing their offices; military chaplains were put under state control and authorized to use the bishop's ring; even the number of candles in churches was regulated. Petty regulations and directives of this nature decreased church influence and simply allowed the organization to continue, at the whim of the government.[11] In some cases, legislation seemed intentionally designed to reduce the church's influence, especially if the matter being legislated implied a closer connection with Rome. An example is the suppression of the religious orders, which began in 1827 and culminated in 1855 with José Nabuco's circular specifically prohibiting the acceptance of novices into the orders. Admittedly, the Jesuits were already expelled, but the priests of the remaining orders were generally superior to secular, that is, diocesan priests in terms of commitment, education, and discipline. Their gradual attrition and the almost total collapse of the orders (for example, in 1868 Brazil had only eleven Benedictine monasteries, housing a total of forty-one monks) left about seven hundred secular priests, almost all of whom had been educated in state-controlled seminaries, to minister to fourteen million people spread out in the vast country. In sum, during the empire the church was not specifically persecuted; it was simply tolerated. An astute observer of the Brazilian church reported that "during the monarchical era, Catholicism showed no signs of development, or activity, except for individual acts of Faith and religious ceremonies which, incidentally, were . . . greatly distorted in the life of the parishes."[12]

With the end of the monarchy in 1889, the church was separated from the state for the first time and forced out of the public realm, to develop on its own, and in conjunction with Rome. This separation and the ratification of the Constitution of 1891 were somewhat abrupt and far-reaching: freedom of worship was recognized; only civil marriages were valid; education was secularized, religion omitted from the curriculum, and the government prohibited from subsidizing religious education; the Catholic clergy was to be supported by the state for only one more year; members of religious orders who obeyed a vow of obedience were disenfranchised; and so on.

Several factors explain the separation of church and state, among which were the church's lack of ideological and organizational influence with the new government's leaders, and the patterning of the new constitution after other countries' constitutions (particularly those of France and the United

States) which did not recognize church-state alliances. A further consideration was the so-called Religious Question of 1874, which pointed out that the role of Rome vis à vis the national churches was likely to be greater under the papacy of Pius IX; the statesmen of the republic were even less keen than those of the empire to become further involved with the Holy See.[13]

The church hierarchy immediately responded to this exclusion from the public realm by vociferously demanding to be let back in, and, indeed, until 1930 the church tried through various tactics to gain reinstatement to what it considered its proper public position. Although they paid lip service to the idea of more independence from the government, the bishops still believed in the necessity of state support and in their approach to influence they sought to regain political power. During the so-called First Republic it is unlikely that the lower-level clergy or local groups and associations were greatly affected by the legislation, but at the national level the church was excluded from public life and state support.

Because of the separation of church and state and the elimination of formal and informal means of state control, the Brazilian church entered into a "normal" relationship with Rome for the first time and approached the organizational model of the Roman Catholic church. This organizational model called for institutional development. The Brazilian church had never really evolved as an institution because it had always relied on the state and the state had never been willing to allow the church's development or expansion. After 1891, the Brazilian church started almost from scratch, consisting of only 12 dioceses. By 1900 there were 17; in 1910 there were 30; in 1920, 58; and by 1964 the total reached 178 ecclesiastical divisions, which represented an increase of 1,500 percent in some seventy years. It is worth pointing out that the bishops chosen to head these new dioceses were selected by Rome.

Another indication of organizational growth was the founding of seminaries and the founding or reopening of convents and monasteries which had been closed in the mid-nineteenth century. Because of a shortage of vocations in the country, the Holy See encouraged foreign orders to send in priests, nuns, and brothers to staff the orders and congregations. Indicative of this policy was the large number of priests born outside Brazil (in 1946 there were 2,964 secular priests and 3,519 order priests, two-thirds of the latter from abroad), a situation which persists to the present day. Similar data can be cited for all sectors and levels of the Brazilian church to show the rapid organizational development which occurred between 1891 and 1930. Granted, communication, cohesion, and leadership were slower to develop, but by 1930 the church resembled a relatively efficient, large, bureaucratic organization.[14]

The salient point is that this growing bureaucratic organization was patterned in almost all respects on a European model largely irrelevant to Brazilian life. The mechanisms of influence resembled those of Europe in the period because the Brazilian church was now linked to the universal Church, from which it received orientation and a substantial portion of its personnel. Thus the establishment of parochial schools for the middle classes and of various pious groups and associations, combined with the administration of sacraments, were being directed primarily at an urban, bourgeois society, although Brazil remained predominantly rural and underdeveloped. The original goal of full conversion with state support was set aside for the time being, although never wholly abandoned. The church concentrated instead on promoting a pastoral strategy and providing the organizations called for by an essentially middle-class, European orientation and neglected the reality of Brazil. This process has been termed the "Romanization" of the Brazilian church.[15]

It should not be assumed that no alternate models suggested themselves to the church at this point. Indeed, one of its most forceful speakers and prolific writers around the turn of the century was Pe. Júlio Maria, the first Redemptorist in Brazil and a powerful advocate for social justice. Pe. Júlio Maria was particularly distressed by the clergy's concern for empty rituals, by its separation from the laity, and by its lack of interest in social affairs. As he so forcefully stated the matter:

The Brazilian church still has not accepted in practical terms the teachings of the Pope [Leo XIII]. The clergy live separated from the people; it is as though the people don't know them. The clergy content themselves with a certain aristocracy of the faithful. It is as though their aspirations can be summarized in seeing the churches nicely decorated, the choir well-trained, and, in the midst of lights and flowers, their vestments glowing. All of the activity of the clergy can just about be summarized in this—festivities for the living and ghastly formalities for the dead.[16]

However, the church failed to follow the admonitions in his books and sermons to look to the people (*o povo*) as its main focus and basis of support. Nor was the church concerned with the social issues of the time, except in theory. The church remained aloof, or even hostile, to the vast majority of the population and their patterns of popular religiosity and became increasingly engrossed in internal church matters.

Turning a deaf ear to the exhortations of Pe. Júlio Maria and ignoring the concrete needs of the laity, the church instead adopted the strategy of Sebastião Leme de Silveira Cintra and reentered the public realm by cooperating closely with the government. Dom Leme, first as bishop of

Olinda/Recife and, from 1921, as bishop of Rio de Janeiro, was the predominant national leader of the Brazilian church after the death of Dom Macedo Costa in 1891. As bishop and then cardinal in Rio de Janeiro until his death in 1942, Dom Leme defined and implemented the strategy whereby the church hoped to increase its influence. In his first pastoral letter in 1916, Dom Leme perceived a paradoxical situation: Brazil, traditionally a Catholic country, was characterized by a church with little prestige or influence. Dom Leme's solution was to educate the population in the religion, to involve elites in the church's offensive, and to regain political power in order to promote religious influence. From the beginning of his episcopacy in Rio de Janeiro, Dom Leme mobilized sectors of the church with an eye to regaining political power, and, most extraordinary, he succeeded. Unlike other national churches also forced out of the public realm but obliged to find other bases of support (in Mexico, Chile, and France, for example), the Brazilian church reentered the public domain, and on extremely favorable terms.[17] This was possible because the successful revolution headed by Getúlio Vargas in 1930 offered the opportunity for a change of institutional arrangements—including those regarding the church. Dom Leme took advantage of the opportunity presented by Vargas, cooperated fully with him, and thereby regained substantial privileges for the church and guaranteed support for President Vargas's efforts to maintain order and stability.

One is tempted to say that the church had reverted to its colonial origins. Of course, this was not the case, for it was now a very different institution: by 1930 it was strong, unified, astutely and actively led by Dom Leme, and very aware of the need for political power. It had been forced out of the public realm after 1889 because it lacked political power and a solid structure; this was no longer true, and the church became, therefore, a desirable ally for Getúlio Vargas. Even though Vargas was an agnostic, he and Dom Leme became close friends. What is more, in the Constitution of 1934 the church again attained prominence, and its new position was reiterated in Vargas's imposed Constitution of 1937. The 1934 Constitution invoked God in its preface; the state could now assist the church financially "in the collective interest"; members of religious orders were allowed to vote; spiritual assistance was provided for the military; religious marriage was recognized in civil terms and divorce prohibited; and, probably most important, religious education was allowed within school hours and the state could provide subventions for Catholic schools.[18] The significance of these constitutional measures was that religious influence was guaranteed through political power. From the early 1930s until very recently the church cooperated intimately with the

Brazilian state. Christianity and order prevailed. Yet the church, in ignoring Pe. Júlio Maria's admonitions, passed up an opportunity to develop a real base of support among the people. The goal was, again, formal conversion of all of society, which the church accomplished through its own structures and those of the state. The European orientation carried the day, however, and the preferred sector remained the urban middle-class, which particularly benefited from the establishment of pious groups and associations, parochial schools, and other church-related institutions. The church may be said to have passed from a situation before 1889 in which it and the state divided society and cooperated extensively ("Christendom"), to one of increasing consolidation of the institution until 1930 (as a valuable resource for Vargas's political strategy), to further consolidation and eventual reentry of the church into the political realm ("Neo-Christendom").[19]

2. Religious Beliefs and Practices

Historical Antecedents

Those who have studied religion, culture, and small communities in Brazil have consistently remarked on the tremendous variety of religious beliefs and practices and the ease with which the people adopt new religious patterns. Journalists who have attended Spiritist ceremonies at the public centers have emphasized the exotic in Brazilian religion, and tourists who visit the beaches in Rio de Janeiro and Santos on the night of December 31 also witness the diversity of religiosity in this Catholic country. Indeed, by now it is common to point out that Brazil's claim to being the largest Catholic country hides far more than it suggests. The church is frequently regarded as a social necessity—a comfortable presence rather than a compelling force. As Thales de Azevedo states in his classic *O catolicismo no Brasil*, "It is well accepted, even among ourselves, that in general terms 'our Catholicism is a Catholicism of pretty words and exterior acts' which 'does not live in the conscience' of the people, but is merely transmitted from one generation to the next like a tradition of lessened influence."[1]

Another widely acclaimed observer of Brazilian history and society, Gilberto Freyre, makes the same point as he notes that in Brazil "Catholicism became 'an easy religion, domestic, almost familial'."[2] It should not be surprising that such an accommodating faith has given rise to varied and noticeable patterns of religiosity. Amazing illustrations of this diversity may be found frequently in the pages of the research report of the Institute of Theology of Recife (Instituto de Teologia do Recife—ITER) and its publication *A fé popular do Nordeste*, which quotes some seven hundred phrases concerning the religious beliefs and practices of individuals in that area.[3]

The present variety and flexibility in Brazilian Catholicism is due to its organizational history (covered in Chapter 1), to the particular type of religion originally implanted in Brazil, and to the context in which both the church and religion have always been located. A number of observations are still in order regarding the first point. We must recall once again that adherence to Catholicism was obligatory. Everyone had to belong: there were no options. Colonial society was comprised of not only European immigrants but also Indians and Negro slaves. Both of the latter groups, of course, already had their own religions, and in sheer numbers alone the slaves imported into Brazil were extremely important. According to Taunay, some 3,600,000 slaves were brought to Brazil between the sixteenth and nineteenth centuries. According to official statistics for 1817-1818, there were 1,930,000 slaves and 585,000 free blacks and mulattoes in a total population of 3,817,000 (excluding Indians). In the early part of the nineteenth century then, blacks and mulattoes made up some 65 percent of the population.[4]

As already noted, the ecclesiastical structure in the colony and empire was limited, weak, and under direct control of the crown. "The members of the clergy are considered public functionaries, paid by the Royal Treasury." And these considerations applied not only at the national level but also locally: "In the colonies the ecclesiastical decisions are normally made by the municipal chambers at the local level, by the captain in charge in his respective captaincy or by the general governors in the whole colony."[5] Because the Jesuits had been expelled in 1759, there was no body in Brazil to implement the reforms called for by the Council of Trent, which were intended to unify the institution, purify the faith, and link religion more closely with the sacraments. Moreover, even the Inquisition failed to make much of an impression. Eduardo Hoornaert indicates that about two hundred individuals were sent to Portugal for prosecution, but that implementation of laws was lax and more attention was paid to form than content.[6] Thus, a pattern evolved: until at least the latter part of the nineteenth century the clergy in Brazil were represented in two unflattering ways—as political strongmen delivering votes for their *patrão* ("boss"), or as subservient toadies to women's devotional groups. Frequently the priests could be very bad indeed, as the numerous accounts of their poor discipline and lack of morals attest:

In a country where the ecclesiastical state is embraced more frequently for family convenience or [material] interest than for piety, it is not unusual to find ministers of the altar who dishonor their religious character by bad conduct and even crimes . . . . In general, these rich friars and canons do not obey the vow of chastity;

they have women and children, which does not create much scandal; but, what is surprising: they legitimize them with the intention of having them enter into [holy] orders.[7]

In effect, the religious organization was unable (and probably unwilling), given its integral links with state and society, to make the religion more orthodox by linking it more closely to the sacraments.

For this reason it is important to pay particular attention to the original faith imported from Portugal and the context within which it evolved. The context has already been touched on; particularly important was the extremely decentralized nature of society, characterized by a countryside controlled by large landowning families and a few cities in which the irmandades predominated. The church was part of this decentralized system with "priests . . . living 'on the ranches of the Portuguese who supported them, giving them room and board all year long plus forty or fifty thousand reis allowance as well as other advantages'."[8] Religion was "lived principally in the small localities separated from each other, where the influence of the bishop was not much felt, let alone that of Rome."[9] Thus religion evolved according to a local and decentralized dynamic, rather than one imposed by any kind of central organization.

The religion that came from Portugal was not that of the Tridentine reforms, which emphasized dogma, the sacraments, and orthodoxy of beliefs and practices. Instead it was an earlier model—almost medieval in character—which all observers agree was already very "mixed" and "popular." As José Comblin states, following Thales de Azevedo and Gilberto Freyre, it was even then a very human and understanding religion, "a Catholicism that everyone could accept without being inconvenienced." Indeed,

the Catholicism that came to Brazil was essentially the popular Catholicism of the last centuries of the Middle Ages. The only thing that Brazil received from the Middle Ages was the popular religion of the Portuguese. It received the popular religion without the armor of the medieval church. As the Tridentine reforms had not anticipated limiting the popular use of the liturgy (beyond the rubrics) or the popular liturgy (of the saints, etc.) popular religion continued its development spontaneously and unhindered. It mixed with indigenous, African, and even Oriental contributions imported by the caravelles returning from India or China. Far from Protestant criticism the popular Catholic liturgy did not assume the aggressive form that it always had in Europe. On the contrary, it assumed the aspect of a religion [that was] very familiar, patriarchal, of a paradisiacal simplicity, idyllic. A religion that consoles and causes nostalgia.[10]

The religion which was to be further mixed and diluted in Brazil sprang from a Portuguese Catholicism largely untouched by reform and already well integrated with Moorish and Jewish traditions and practices. It was, as Donald Warren has shown, a folk Catholicism which was not in harmony with salvationist Christianity, much less Tridentine Catholicism. It was, rather, a religion which included a belief in communication with the souls of the dead, a religion where the *almas penadas* ("pining souls") were commonly referred to, and where "the dominant culture permitted witches to perform their works undisturbed."[11] When this religion was transported to Brazil, where the Amerindian *pajés* ("witch doctors" or "shamans") were at work, the Portuguese witches continued to thrive.

Aside from belief in supernatural beings, souls in another world, and witchcraft, René Ribeiro has convincingly shown the role given to the intervention of saints in earthly affairs by means of "promises and other practices...[in which] there is a pluralism and specification of these Catholic saints, each one protecting against certain kinds of misfortunes or acting as patrons and protectors of cities or even entire countries."[12] This original faith evolved into a pattern of what might be termed a household or local religion in which devotions are centered on a cult of saints, promises, communications with the dead, processions, and so forth, largely to the exclusion of doctrinal matters and the sacraments. As Riolando Azzi informs us, the church actually sponsored and promoted this form of religion, which could thrive without any clerical and institutional intervention or mediation and indeed was obliged to do just that, given the shortage of clergy.[13] This process was abetted by a weak clergy, lack of organization, and a folk Catholicism based on a medieval, unreformed, and highly superstitious model which had evolved largely on its own during most of the colonial and empire periods.

One additional element must be included to explain the more recent evolution of folk Catholicism into Spiritism; this is, of course, the contribution of Negro slaves to the religious life of the country. The religions the slaves brought to Brazil included a belief in spirit possession, which was allowed to survive because of church default and only superficial conversion. The church did not prevent the slaves from preserving some of their traditions almost intact by means of dances and celebrations in groups such as irmandades and *confrarias* ("sodalities" or "confraternities"). These elements of religion also penetrated popular Catholicism, for "the Portuguese Catholicism was well-disposed to a policy of assimilating African religions."[14] As the African religions persisted, they adopted the exterior forms or symbols of Catholicism, and rather than being changed by the church, they in fact changed Catholicism. One need not go as far as Francisco Cartaxo Rolim in his theory about the

Africanization of Catholicism nor agree with Hoornaert when he argues that "Spiritism . . . is more than anything else the expression of the religion lived by the majority of Brazilians" to realize that many elements of the African religions have found their way into popular Catholicism in Brazil.[15]

The changes and reforms that took place in the church after separation from the state in 1889 did not so much replace popular Catholicism and Spiritism as overlay a pattern of European Catholicism, which, albeit closely linked to the church, was generally alien to the earlier patterns. Both folk Catholicism and Spiritism were deeply engrained in the culture of the people and could not be rooted out by a centralizing and growing institution which was implementing reforms and practices more appropriate to bourgeois Europe than to rural Brazil. During this period a split developed between the religion practiced by the people and that promoted by the church. Pedro Ribeiro de Oliveira has demonstrated how the church, in becoming institutionalized and adopting European models, failed to integrate changes ("reforms") at the lower levels; rather than reforming the devotional groups, irmandades, and so forth, new models were superimposed on old structures with little consideration as to their appropriateness and value.[16] A gap developed between religiosity and religion, between church law and religiosity. As the cardinal of Salvador stated in 1938, "In order to be fair if we wanted to define the religious spirit of our people we would have to confess: much religiosity, religion, far less than would appear. But religiosity and religion are very different matters."[17] This, of course, is the nature of the difference between the strategy proposed by Pe. Júlio Maria and that implemented by Cardinal Leme. The former wanted to reach the people, internalize their beliefs and unfortunate way of life, and see the institution evolve toward them. He admitted that religion as practiced by the people was weak and varied in nature, but he felt that the clergy still had the responsibility to deal with the people and their religiosity. Cardinal Leme, on the other hand, blamed the people for the weak and mixed nature of their religion. Alberto Antoniazzi points to a basic contradiction in Dom Leme's general argument: he saw all of Brazil and her people as Catholic (and thus certain privileges should accrue to the institution); however, these same people could not be Catholic unless they were orthodox (and he realized that they were not); yet, it was not their fault that they were so "ignorant, superstitious, incongruous, and fanatic" for the state had denied them a Christian education.[18]

Dom Leme's strategy of course triumphed. The church reentered the public domain in a pattern of Neo-Christendom and adopted a pastoral strategy from abroad with the continued importation of foreign personnel, all of which conspired to either ignore or denounce the religion of most of the population, which continued to be practiced much as it had been a century before. But an orthodox Catholicism similar to the European pattern and to the ghetto church of the immigrants in North America did develop in the cities and in those areas most closely tied to the institution. Since this is a common pattern and will be dealt with later in this chapter, there is no need to elaborate on it here; however, Spiritism and popular Catholicism are less well understood phenomena and require some discussion.

It is probably valid to posit a common basis for popular Catholicism since it is part of Brazil's Portuguese heritage and, as one of the most acute observers of religion in Brazil has argued, popular Catholicism almost constitutes a national form.[19] A substantial literature exists to illustrate and elaborate on religion in Brazil. Priests, anthropologists, and sociologists have argued that basic religious beliefs in Brazil are characterized by a heightened awareness of man's lack of control over his life and environment, and of his need to rely on the benevolence of God and spirits. This passive attitude toward concrete reality is contrasted with an active belief (in the form of actions such as devotions and promises) in a world of spirits and the like, whose aid and protection must be solicited. The most important relationship is with saints, and, in fact, "the majority of Brazilian Catholics have as the center of their religious life the cult of the saints, and this applies as much to those following official Catholicism as to others."[20] In order to control his environment, the individual must deal with supernatural beings, and he thereby develops a personal relationship with one or more, depending on the supplicant's particular need and on the saint's specialization. This relationship includes the making of promises, the offering of novenas and benedictions, the staging of processions, and so forth, for the particular saint whose intervention is being sought. The system of making promises to saints in return for the granting of a wish is basically a reciprocity relationship of the client/patron variety.

In light of the foregoing, it is understandable that forms of religion which are not divergent from the basic thrust of popular Catholicism but certainly incompatible with the official church may be pursued. Essential to this religiosity is a direct and unmediated link with the holy, be it saint, soul, or God. It is widely acknowledged that the Pentecostal movement in Brazil is growing rapidly. The evidence suggests that there are some similarities between this movement and popular Catholicism, but that Pentecostalism functions better than other forms of Protestantism in Brazil's changing environment. Pentecostalism, like popular Catholicism, emphasizes a direct relationship with the deities and allows a tremendous amount of flexibility in personal expressions of faith.[21]

The growth of the Pentecostal sects is particularly striking. In 1960 all Brazilian Protestant churches claimed 1,527,200 members, with Pentecostals making up approximately 38.5 percent of the total. By 1970 Protestants totaled 2,623,550, and the Pentecostals accounted for 49.4 percent. The average yearly growth in Brazil for all Protestant faiths was 5.6 percent, broken down to 3.5 percent for traditional denominations and 8.2 percent for the Pentecostals. These are very high rates of growth and show no signs of diminishing.

Brazil 1980: The Protestant Handbook indicates that Pentecostal growth rates are higher in the more rapidly changing or modernizing areas.[22] One need not accept the *Handbook* authors' premise that with modernization people have more liberty and that "many use this new-found liberty to choose Jesus Christ" to realize that rural-urban migration, and economic development, seem to prefigure increased conversion to Pentecostalism.

Many of the same points may be made concerning the various forms of Spiritism which also are proliferating. Notwithstanding the official census, which indicates an unrealistically low number of Spiritists, it is clear that Spiritism is gaining adherents, although membership is harder to define than for Protestantism because no clear-cut decision to convert is involved; that is, Spiritism can easily coexist with local popular Catholicism. Estimates by Frei Boaventura Kloppenburg point out that around 30 percent of the Brazilian population is in some way involved in Spiritism; Frei Raimundo Cintra indicates a 20 percent involvement, with an even higher rate in Rio de Janeiro. There are an estimated one thousand Spiritist cult centers in São Luis do Maranhão, twenty thousand in Rio de Janeiro, and thirty-two thousand in São Paulo.[23] It seems reasonable to estimate, therefore, that 20 percent of the population has some ongoing contact with one or more of the various Spiritist forms, of which there are almost as many as of cult centers.

Essentially, Spiritism is a mixture of African beliefs. In its purest form it is called Candomblé. The most popular form of Brazilian Spiritism is Umbanda, derived from Candomblé and mixed with Kardecist Spiritism. Umbanda goes by different names in different parts of the country: Batuque, Macumba, Xango, Catimbo, Nago, or Pajelança. The basic belief involves spirit possession of the bodies of mediums, who can then consult individually with sect members. The relationship between the spirit and the medium is a direct one. Doctrinally, Spiritism is Christian-Reincarnationist, and views most personal problems as having a spiritual basis.

That communication between cult member and spirit occurs in a particular location, at a given time, via a medium recognized as such, means that Spiritism is institutionalized.[24] In many ways it is an extension of popular Catholicism—it uses prayers and rituals borrowed from Catholicism and has adopted, and renamed, the constellation of saints—but it has without a doubt evolved into a system of beliefs and practices in which the institutional church has no leverage. This is so because Spiritism provides certain distinctive new beliefs, which supersede popular Catholicism, and also because the church simply has lacked influence with the people. As Seth and Ruth Leacock state, "The Catholicism of Batuque members is a folk Catholicism that is largely independent of the official Church . . . . The official clergy are not really necessary for Catholic devotions."[25]

It should be obvious that the institutional church enjoys little influence among converts to other religions, such as Pentecostalism, nor among adherents to Spiritism, who do not regard themselves as separate from Catholicism. Evidence exists, in fact, that the church has little influence on any part of the population other than a very small minority, evidence which includes mass attendance estimated at 10 to 15 percent of the population (in the cities, where there are scheduled masses); an awareness, even among priests, that the sacraments are used by Spiritist adherents in a different sense from their orthodox functions; the realization that many lay people, even those affiliated with the official church, have their own understanding of the meaning of religion, an understanding which in no way compromises their essential "Catholicism."[26] For example, Lais Mourão mentions a catechist of Maranhão who believed in a dual purpose baptism—to remove the stain of original sin and to free the child from the *mae d'agua* ("water spirit").[27]

On the basis of long observation Thales de Azevedo concluded that Catholicism in Brazil "is relatively independent of the formal Church."[28] Pedro Ribeiro de Oliveira carried out a survey in which he formulated three styles of being Catholic, characterized by the use of the sacraments (or orthodox), the petitioning of saints, and the requesting of intervention by holy beings. Survey results from two dioceses indicated that only a minority of the sample could be called orthodox and that the other two styles, termed popular Catholicism in his report, were dominant and did not require the church for mediation. "Popular Catholicism, expressing a direct and personal relationship between man and the sacred, avoids the control of the institutional Church."[29]

In another study, in Rio de Janeiro, the results were essentially identical to Oliveira's: the orthodox Catholics represented only about 21 percent of the sample (the sample itself comprised only two-thirds of the original sample, the other one-third having been cast out, as avowed Spiritists, members of other religions, or as nothing).[30] Paradoxically, or maybe logically, the largest Catholic country in the world seems to be characterized by a religiosity that is extremely diverse and which generally lies outside the influence of the institutional church.

A generalized awareness of the weakness of the institutional church, the exotic nature of many religious activities, and the desire to learn more about actual beliefs and practices have prompted many attempts to describe and analyze the religious phenomenon in Brazil. A number of studies were done, in the style of Gabriel LeBras in Europe and Joseph Fichter in the United States, on mass attendance and parish life, but it was subsequently realized that the indicators used in those studies might not be appropriate to Brazilian culture, with its great diversity of beliefs.[31] Later, a number of studies appeared in which varieties of Brazilian Catholicism or Catholics were defined. Most of these typological studies suffered from an overlap of nondistinctive types, from a focus on externals, and from an absence of data. Even the most ambitious failed to follow through by describing types of Catholicism or Catholics from a conceptual point of view and eventually ended up by focusing on the official church.[32]

The most applicable study for our purposes is Ribeiro de Oliveira's because he formulated a typology of the three styles of being Catholic which comprise the one religion. There is a problem, however, in his separation of type two (saints) and type three (intervention of holy beings), since these types seem inseparable in popular Catholicism. A more serious conceptual point he himself raised in his notes for a seminar on popular Catholicism at the Instituto Nacional de Pastoral, that is, that popular Catholicism should be defined in terms of its divergence from official Catholicism.[33]

I prefer to follow a less-restrictive approach, one suggested by Comblin and Hoornaert, which regards each pattern of religiosity as an autonomous religious system. This approach seems appropriate because most of the relevant literature indicates that these patterns are autonomous religious systems and that, as Hoornaert indicates, the definition of the church and of official Catholicism changes and is not precise. Official Catholicism of the sixteenth century has become the popular faith of today.

In order to test empirically patterns of religiosity it seems more efficient to view each as a separate system, test for links or connections between them, and leave popular Catholicism "open-ended" instead of defining it in comparison to church dogma. From the literature, from other question-naires, from participant observation, from discussions with experts, and from reflections based on a pretest survey, questions were formulated to cover the gamut of religious beliefs and practices. I expected to find at least three types or patterns of religiosity (as did Oliveira), with a maximum of six: an official or orthodox type; one or more popular or folk types; possibly a Spiritist type; and in some cases a type that results from the church's new social, or progressive orientation, a social Catholic type. The general findings from the questionnaire will be described first, then a methodological technique known as factor analysis will be applied to the findings in order to define the Brazilian patterns of religiosity. (See Appendix 2 for a discussion of the data analysis.)

Most of the literature dealing with popular Catholicism notes the passive tendencies of its adherents who, the literature alleges, are disposed toward a fatalistic acceptance of the world, and who look to the saints and other supernatural forces to regulate the earthly environment. As Frei Bernardino Leers puts it:

The form in which the sacred works out in the behavior of the rural people is to function partially as an "opium" which conditions the meek and listless fatalism of "this is the way God wants it," "let God be served" and the solution in many cases, "only God." The omnipotent deity is formed in correspondence to human impotence. "God must work it out" is always a consolation and a hope where man admits defeat.[34]

This passivity toward life on earth helps maintain a particular social structure: "By channelling their efforts into continuous invocations of the supernatural the peasants in effect buttress the existing social, economic, and political relations."[35]

Survey Data

It must be emphasized that this survey, which was designed to capture the religious beliefs and practices of the people, was not carried out as a probability sample of the whole population nor are the findings intended to be readily generalizable to the entire country. Rather, the intention of this survey was to test and analyze the relationship between change in the Brazilian church and patterns of religious behavior and practices found in Brazil. The sample was drawn accordingly and is by intention a good deal more religiously "orthodox" than a representative sample is likely to be. However, it is worth emphasizing that orthodoxy does exist—not all Brazilians are adherents of popular Catholicism. Once the point is made that the phrase "the largest Catholic country in the world" hides as much as it reveals, we can deemphasize the bizarre and exotic in religion and concentrate on what we find, including orthodoxy, without making a special attempt to indicate how far present-day reality is removed from dogmatic Catholicism. Indeed, there are Spiritists in Brazil—but not everyone is a Spiritist, and much of the variety found in religious beliefs and practices is due to the layering that has occurred with the evolution of Catholicism over several hundred years. There have been innovations as the church's approach to religious influence has changed; today's popular Catholicism was the institutional Catholicism promoted in Brazil during the colonial period, but today's orthodox Catholicism is a relatively new form in Brazil and has been promoted by the church only during this century. (We shall see in Chapter 5 that a new pattern of beliefs and practices is increasingly being promoted by the institutional church.)

The orthodox nature of the sample results from two aspects of the survey: the populations of the towns where the questionnaire was administered, and the method of selecting respondents. The questionnaires were administered in towns with populations ranging from 20,000 to 228,000 (1970 census) which had churches offering masses (although in one parish at the center of a northeastern diocese there is no mass one weekend per month). We avoided the huge urban centers, in which links with the church and religion are thought to be particularly weak, as well as the extreme outlying areas with no services at all. Survey design required a minimum church presence, by no means found throughout the country. We had to be certain that our sample had direct contact with the church and, presumably, could be influenced by it, so we selected almost one-half of it from individuals found at mass on a Saturday evening or Sunday. (This group will henceforth be referred to as the "attendance sample.") The attendance sample, in combination with the members of the religious groups (or "group sample"), comprises 55 percent of the total sample of 1,912. In sum, our sample, by design, should be very ecclesiastically orthodox, which is what was needed in order to determine the degree of the institution's influence over religious beliefs and practices. If these people cannot be influenced, then who can be?

In response to a question on perceived closeness to the institutional church, we found that 94 percent of our respondents considered themselves close to the church. This, of course, is a subjective evaluation, but is supported by data on practices the church itself considers orthodox.

We can compare our findings to those of another survey done in Brazil which included questions on religion to better appreciate the orthodox nature of our sample. The Brazilian study was carried out in 1972-73 by Peter McDonough and Amaury de Souza, who applied 1,314 questionnaires to a probability sample located in the six southeastern states of Brazil.[36] Although our categories for frequency were not framed in exactly the same way as McDonough's and de Souza's, they are similar enough to provide a comparison. The mass attendance data from both questionnaires are presented in table 1. Our "once or more a week" response by 62 percent of the sample compares to McDonough's and de Souza's similar combination of "daily" and "weekly" attendance by 41 percent; our minimal "sometimes a year" response by 12 percent compares to their minimal "annually" of 21 percent; and our "never" of 1 percent is much less than the 4 percent of the earlier survey. Judging from other available data from their survey, our sample is orthodox, as it was intended to be. We must keep this in mind in the later analysis of our data, but even so, variety will be apparent. Even though we succeeded in obtaining what can be considered an orthodox sample, it will nonetheless demonstrate the variety of religious beliefs and practices thought to be typical of the Brazilian population.

Table 1
Frequency of Mass Attendance

Frequency	Percentage of Sample
McDonough/de Souza Survey (N=1,117)	
Daily	02.0
Weekly	39.0
Monthly	34.0
Annually	21.0
Never	04.0
Bruneau Survey (N=1,909)	
Once or more a week	62.0
Sometimes a month	25.0
Sometimes a year	12.0
Never	01.0

It might be useful to define the consistency, or orthodoxy of our sample a bit more before discussing its heterogeneity. In the very few studies conducted in Brazil on level of attendance at mass, it was found that attendance increased in the higher social class and among females and decreased among those above age twenty, only to increase again after age fifty.[37] These studies were not done as probability samples, and we might recall that our quota sample sought to stratify by sex and education but not age (see Appendix 1). Of course some 56 percent of the sample was not found at mass, and the definition of class in the analysis is a good deal more complex than is the definition of education level. There is enough

variability to have a basis of comparison with these earlier studies.[38]
There is indeed a moderate relationship between attendance and sex
(Kendall's Tau C of −.18), as can be seen in table 2.

Table 2
Relationship between Sex and Mass Attendance
(Percentages)
(N=1,912)

Sex (% of Total Sample)	Frequency of Mass Attendance			
	Once or More a Week	Sometimes a Month	Sometimes a Year	Never
Male (48.0)	53.0	30.0	15.0	2.0
Female (52.0)	70.0	21.0	8.0	1.0
Total Sample	62.0	25.0	12.0	1.0

There is no overall relationship between age and mass attendance
(Kendall's Tau C of −.02), but some interesting variations for particular
age groups can be seen in table 3.

Table 3
Relationship between Age and Mass Attendance
(Percentages)
(N=1,890)

Age (% of Total Sample)	Frequency of Mass Attendance			
	Once or More a Week	Sometimes a Month	Sometimes a Year	Never
20 and under (18.0)	68.0	23.0	7.0	2.0
21-30 (24.0)	56.0	26.0	17.0	2.0
31-40 (21.0)	59.0	29.0	12.0	1.0
41-50 (17.0)	64.0	24.0	11.0	1.0
51-60 (12.0)	69.0	23.0	7.0	1.0
over 60 (9.0)	63.0	24.0	14.0	0.0
Total Sample	62.0	25.0	12.0	1.0

We see that mass attendance is high for that part of our sample under the age of 20 and over the age of 50 but drops off substantially after age 20 and remains at the marginal level or less for most of middle age. The other studies are thus supported by our data.

When we looked at the relationship between social class and attendance at mass, however, we did not find any variation (Kendall's Tau C of −.02) and only one mildly interesting relationship, as shown in table 4.

Table 4
Relationship between Social Class and Mass Attendance
(Percentages)
(N=1,845)

Social Class (% of Total Sample)	Frequency of Mass Attendance			
	Once or More a Week	Sometimes a Month	Sometimes a Year	Never
Lower (58.0)	60.0	27.0	12.0	1.0
Middle (32.0)	66.0	23.0	10.0	1.0
Higher (10.0)	60.0	23.0	14.0	4.0
Total Sample	62.0	25.0	12.0	1.0

As generally expected, the middle class was likely to attend mass more frequently than the others, but the data from table 4 say little about either the lower or the upper classes. For our sample, at least, class is not important in determining attendance at mass, and it seems safe to assume that our three classes are equally likely to be exposed to the influence of the church, insofar as influence is promoted by mass attendance.

Again, this was our intention, for we wanted a mixture of classes and a balance of the sexes in order to ascertain the institution's level of influence. The existence of variations in mass attendance and their relationship to other studies are interesting but not central to this study.

We can now look to expected variations by class and region, for religious practices other than mass attendance. The only question is whether or not our sample is too orthodox to include a variety of religious practices.

Some 88 percent of our sample made their First Communion. Table 5 shows the relationship between class and First Communion (Kendall's Tau C of .11). It is clear that the lower class was less likely to partake of this sacrament than was the middle, let alone the higher class. What is more, the relationship varied by area. In the Center the relationship was strongest

Table 5
Relationship between Social Class and First Communion
(N=1,616)

Social Class (% of Total Sample)	% Making First Communion
Lower (58.0)	83.0
Middle (32.0)	94.0
Higher (10.0)	97.0

(Kendall's Tau C of .20), in the South it was weakest (Kendall's Tau C of .04), with São Paulo and the Northeast falling in between (Kendall's Tau C of .09).

What we find then is the suggestion of some variation by class and by region, the latter, of course, being in line with the discussion in the earlier part of this chapter and in a great many studies on regional variations in practices and beliefs. The findings also suggest that in our later analysis of church influence we should make intraregional rather than national or interregional comparisons for our sample.

If we question respondents concerning beliefs and practices not necessarily intrinsically linked to the church-as-institution (the way the sacraments are), we find that our sample does demonstrate variety, for all its orthodoxy. In response to a question on the frequency of prayer, we found that 81 percent professed to pray daily, 13 percent sometimes, 4 percent rarely, and 2 percent never (out of 1,912 responses). As in the case of mass attendance, the relationship of prayer to class was weak (Kendall's Tau C of .03); it was also weakly related to age (Kendall's Tau C of .06), and moderately related to sex (Kendall's Tau C of .19).

However, when we proceed from the act of praying to the recipients of prayers, we begin to see some variety. Of the 1,912 respondents, 87 percent prayed to God, 82 percent prayed to Christ, 81 percent to our Lady, 71 percent to souls, and 66 percent to saints. Table 6 indicates that the frequency of prayer to a particular deity varies by class. The lower class prayed to these five deities more than did the other two classes, and when we looked to the particular deities we found that there were significant variations. Our Lady can go under many different guises and names, and for her we found a Kendall's Tau C of .10, as opposed to .04 for God and .05 for Christ, a Tau C of .14 for souls, and a Tau C of .20 for saints.

We know from the historical and ethnological material on Brazil that

Table 6
Relationship between Social Class and Prayer
(Percentages)
(N=1,814)

Social Class (% of Total Sample)	Deity Prayed to				
	God	Christ	Our Lady	Souls	Saints
Lower (58.0)	88.0	84.0	85.0	76.0	74.0
Middle (32.0)	85.0	81.0	79.0	68.0	61.0
Higher (10.0)	82.0	77.0	65.0	49.0	38.0
Total Sample	87.0	82.0	81.0	71.0	66.0

people in need traditionally petition our Lady, souls, and the saints for intervention. Whereas God and Christ are thought to be far away and difficult to implore successfully, our Lady, the saints, and souls are considered more approachable and sympathetic. This is supported by the data in table 7, which shows the relationship of class to what people consider the purpose of prayer. Although there was no significant variation in praying for virtues (strength, peace, justice), there was a clearer trend in the higher class toward offering prayers of thanks than in the lower class.

Table 7
Relationship between Social Class and Purpose of Prayer
(Percentages)
(N=1,803)

Social Class (% of Total Sample)	Purpose of Prayer				
	Virtue	Thanks	Material Problems	Indul- gences	Other
Lower (58.0)	46.0	20.0	31.0	3.0	0.0
Middle (32.0)	48.0	26.0	22.0	3.0	2.0
Higher (10.0)	46.0	38.0	11.0	3.0	2.0
Total Sample	47.0	24.0	26.0	3.0	1.0

Presumably, members of the higher class have more to be thankful for. The opposite held true for the lower class; its members more often requested assistance in concrete matters (work-related problems, health, family difficulties). It is clear that the less advantaged prayed for things they felt they could not otherwise arrange.

The data presented in table 8 reinforce the idea of class distinctions found in stated purposes of intervention requests. We know that in Brazil there is a tradition of local and personal saints, and that in most cases the relationship with them involves a request for some benefit, followed by the requestor's payment. What is more, we would expect this relationship to vary by class, since the lower class generally has more reason to petition.

The same relationship applies to promises. The lower class made more promises to the deities than did the upper class, again, presumably, because its members request things they would otherwise be unable to arrange. In our sample 59 percent of the lower class, 55 percent of the middle class, and only 32 percent of the upper class made promises (Tau C of .11).

Table 8
Relationship between Social Class and
Selection of Most-Important Holy Day
(Percentages)
(N=1,807)

Social Class (% of Total Sample)	Holy Day				
	Easter & Christmas	Local Saint	Special Saint	All Holy Days	Other
Lower (58.0)	65.0	9.0	9.0	14.0	4.0
Middle (32.0)	76.0	5.0	5.0	12.0	2.0
Higher (10.0)	85.0	2.0	3.0	9.0	2.0
Total Sample	71.0	7.0	7.0	13.0	2.0

The relationship between class and the making of promises also varied by region, as it did in regard to the making of First Communion. In the South the Kendall's Tau C is .08, in the Center .15, and .26 in São Paulo. However, in the Northeast there was no relationship at all between class and the making of promises. If we compare the making of promises for all classes we find that in São Paulo 46 percent of the sample made them, whereas in the Northeast 69 percent did, with the upper classes in the Northeast being almost as likely as the lower classes to engage in this religious activity.

A breakdown by deity shows that 81 percent of the sample group made promises to our Lady, 66 percent to the saints, 66 percent to God, 61 percent to Christ, and 55 percent to souls. Our Lady was favored for requests, with little difference among the others.

The relationship of class to promise making varied by region and by deity. For example, with regard to making promises to our Lady there was an overall weak relationship to region and class (Tau C of .07), which disappeared in the Northeast and Center and was slightly stronger (Tau C of .11 and .15) in the other two regions. Making promises to souls was related to class everywhere except in the Northeast, but the making of promises to God and to Christ was not significant when related to class for the sample. In other words, relationships exist between the making of promises and social class, but vary according to the particular deity being invoked and the region involved.

In order to define further popular Catholicism we asked whether the respondent thought God and the saints perform miracles; approximately 90 percent responded affirmatively. However, because the definition of "miracle" is somewhat ambiguous (since some things recounted in the Bible can certainly be considered miraculous), we also asked whether the respondent had ever benefited from a miracle; 62 percent responded positively. Again we found a relationship to class similar to that found in the making of promises. There was a moderate relationship (Tau C of .13) to class, with the lower classes having said they benefited more than the upper classes: 67 percent for the lower, 58 percent for the middle, and 45 percent for the upper. No relationship to class existed in the Northeast, however, where all classes believed they had benefited equally.

In order to see whether religiosity has evolved from popular Catholicism to Spiritism, we asked two questions dealing with Spiritist practices, as well as another two behavioral questions dealing with attitudes. We can see from table 9 that although a majority had never attended a Spiritist session (or had attended just once and therefore probably for touristic reasons or out of sheer curiosity), 13 percent of the total sample had attended frequently enough to be considered involved with Spiritism. There was a weak relationship between class and attendance at Spiritist centers (Tau C of .07).

What must be strongly emphasized, however, is the fact that the greatest part of the discussion thus far has concerned behavior (which can be expected to reflect less variety) rather than attitudes. A brief overview of some responses may serve to illustrate the greater variety found in attitudes. In response to a question on how the respondent would characterize Jesus Christ, we found that out of 1,851 responses, 58 percent characterized Christ as the Son of God, 14 percent as the liberator of the poor, 18 percent as the most powerful saint, 8 percent as a great prophet, and 3 percent as "other." Thus, 58 percent made what might be termed an orthodox response, 26 percent (18 percent plus 8 percent) a popular

Table 9
Relationship between Social Class and
Attendance at Spiritist Centers
(Percentages)
(N=1,851)

Social Class (% of Total Sample)	Frequency of Attendance		
	Sometimes a Year	Only Once	Never
Lower (58.0)	15.0	21.0	63.0
Middle (32.0)	12.0	15.0	72.0
Higher (10.0)	6.0	19.0	75.0
Total Sample	13.0	19.0	67.0

Catholic or a Spiritist response, and 14 percent a social Catholic response (to be discussed in some detail later).

In reply to a question as to whether the souls in purgatory can help people on earth (a major belief in the history of Portuguese and Brazilian Catholicism), 56 percent of the 1,745 respondents at least partially agreed that the souls in purgatory can help on earth, and 30 percent at least partly disagreed.

When asked about whether Spiritist works such as the evil eye and hexes are effective, we found that out of 1,836 responses, more than half (59 percent) adhered to an orthodox line, and one-third (34 percent) followed a more Spiritist or popular Catholic line.

On the question of whether the church should do away with saints' statues (which has been done in some places in order to discourage people from following a certain kind of popular Catholicism), we found that only 18 percent (out of 1,859 responses) agreed with what the orthodox church had done, and an overwhelming 75 percent indicated that they would rather follow the traditional pattern in which the saints serve as intermediaries between the people and God, or as the actual focus of prayer.

This brief review of some aspects of the data indicates that the sample was characterized by a degree of religious variation by class and region, despite a sampling strategy which emphasized orthodox adherence to the faith. The analysis confirms the religious traditions of Brazil. The deities referred to and the conditions under which they are petitioned are well within the traditions of what is commonly called "popular Catholicism."

Further, the presence of a Spiritist component in the sample also suggests that there is more heterogeneity than was anticipated, given the orthodox nature of the sample.

Factor Analysis of Questionnaire Items Dealing with Religion

There are eighty-three items in the questionnaire that relate to individual religious beliefs and practices. A few of these items have been reviewed and a variety of perceptible patterns has emerged. An item-by-item review of the attitudes and behavior of the sample, not to mention analysis by means of cross-tabulation, would require an inordinate amount of space and could become tedious. What is more, the goal of this book is not so much to display the variety and richness of religiosity in Brazil—a fact recognized by most observers—but rather to analyze the extent to which the institutional church can influence this varied religiosity. We needed, therefore, to distill or summarize the vast amount of data from the questionnaire so that we could evaluate the distinct patterns of religious belief and practice that have emerged and the church's impact on these patterns. We required a technique that did not assume religion to be unidimensional because exposure in the field to the richness of beliefs and practices warned me against such a simplistic assumption. After reviewing the array of techniques available in the analysis of quantitative data, the technique known as factor analysis seemed most appropriate for this study's needs.[39]

Factor analysis is a technique that identifies in a small number of hypothetical items (called "factors") the relationships that hold for all. What is more, factor analysis shows the relationship of the actual items to the hypothetical items. Or, as one proponent states, "They [factors] delineate the distinct 'clusters' or relationships, if such exist."[40] The data are reduced into independent clusters. In so doing, the loadings, or weights, indicate the relationship of an actual item to one or more factors. (For a description of the application of factor analysis to this material, see Appendix 2.)

After an item-by-item analysis by both frequency distributions and cross tabulations, twenty-nine items were selected as being most likely to allow for most possible patterns or varieties of religious beliefs and practices. The twenty-nine items did not appear in sequence in the questionnaire and thus their relationships to the factors cannot be attributed to a "carryover effect" from one question to another. Four distinct patterns, or dimensions emerged, and the items generally relate to them as one might anticipate. The results of the factor analysis are found in table 10.

Table 10
Factor Analysis of Religiosity Items

Religiosity Items	Factors				
	Popular Catholicism Pattern (1)	Spiritism Pattern (2)	Orthodox Catholicism Pattern (3)	Social Catholicism Pattern (4)	Communality
Making of promises	88				78
Making of promises to our Lady	86				76
Making of promises for indulgences	76				58
Making of money- or job-related promises	60				36
Benefit from miracle(s)	40		37		32
Prayer to saints	32		28	-37	32
Attendance at Spiritist center		74			55
Offering to Spiritist deity		68			47
Summoning of Spiritist "priest" or faith healer		52			28
Appropriateness of attendance at Spiritist center		48			29
Frequency of mass attendance		-28	67		55
Closeness to church			65		44
Frequency of prayer			56		33
Attendance at mass for patron saint			48		26
Existence of judgment after death			43		19
Reliance on church			42		18
Prayer to our Lady			32	-32	26
Reliance on church for resolution of social problems				57	34
Reliance on church for resolution of individuals' problems				50	27

Note: See Appendix 2 for explanation of "variance accounted for" and "communality."

Table 10 (*continued*)

	Popular Catholicism Pattern (1)	Spiritism Pattern (2)	Orthodox Catholicism Pattern (3)	Social Catholicism Pattern (4)	Commu- nality
Possession of a Bible				50	28
Belief in church as agent of social change				46	21
Propriety of contra- ceptive use				40	25
Belief in social direc- tion of church				39	21
Catholics as the People of God				38	19
Belief in conscience as guide				36	16
Belief in church's role in society and politics				34	37
Belief in salvation for all religions				33	17
Belief in ability of souls in purgatory to help those on earth				29	9
Belief in Christ as the Liberator				28	7
Variance accounted for	285	169	273	237	966
Percentage of variance accounted for	.09	.05	.09	.08	.33

Factor 1 is most appropriately termed "popular Catholicism," in line with the earlier discussion. This pattern is characterized by an emphasis on making promises under both general and specific conditions. Further, belief in personal benefit from miracles also plays a part in this factor, as does praying to saints, although to a lesser degree. (It is interesting to note what is not included in each factor, since we would not expect persons in an orthodox pattern, for example, to engage in Spiritist activities; that is, there are items which define by inclusion and others which define by exclusion.)

Factor 2 is a Spiritism pattern. Included are every behavioral and attitudinal variable in the questionnaire which deals with Spiritism.

Attendance at a Spiritist center is heavily loaded (loading being the degree to which a variable is involved in the factor), as is the utilization of offerings to Spiritist deities (*despachos*). The attitudinal questions (including the seeking out of a holy man when ill and the justifiability of Catholics attending a Spiritist center) are less strongly defined but quite reasonably loaded. It would seem that the attitudinal variables clearly indicate a particular Spiritist type as distinguished from other types. It is worth noting the exclusion of orthodox variables from this factor.

Factor 3 is an orthodox pattern with particularly heavy loadings of attendance at mass and closeness to the institutional church. Attendance at mass on the Feast Day of a patron saint is strong, as is frequency of prayer. There could be some overlap between this pattern and the popular Catholicism items on prayer to saints and benefit from miracles, but there is a clear contrast between the two patterns in the matter of mass attendance and the anticipation of judgment and salvation after death. Again, it is interesting to note exclusions from the factor, such as possession of a Bible. Whereas the orthodox pattern shows certain similarities to the popular Catholicism pattern, as it should, since present-day orthodoxy was grafted on to popular Catholicism, the two patterns are clearly distinguishable.

Factor 4 is a pattern of social Catholicism. All the variables of this factor are attitudinal, with the exception of possession of a Bible; there were no specific activities on which to base questions. The significance of Bible possession lies in the fact that many individuals in the groups to be described in Chapter 8 use Bibles in their religious activities. Even though the items in this factor are attitudinal items, and thus tend to be weak in their loadings, they cohere in a logical sequence and contrast to the other patterns either by weak or negative loading. Thus, possession of a Bible fits only in this factor. Praying to the saints and to our Lady are negative and promise making is excluded. Although there is a reasonably strong loading on belief in salvation for members of all religions, this loading is not supported by participation in or support of Spiritism. Although factor 4 is not as distinct as the other three, which would be expected because of the attitudinal variables in this factor, social Catholicism is a strong pattern in that the particular combination of loadings is clearly contrasted to those of the other three factors.

The fact that we have come up with four separate patterns of religious practices and beliefs supports the arguments in the literature on the multidimensional charcter of religion.[41] Each of these patterns is distinct from the others, and the loadings indicate that people can be Catholic in different ways. Each pattern, of course, may be understood in terms of its particular evolution: the historical church gave rise to popular Catholicism; Spiritism was an offshoot of popular Catholicism, with the added influence of Candomblé and Kardecism; orthodox Catholicism was initiated with the Tridentine reforms and implemented institutionally after the turn of this century; social Catholicism will be understood when the more-recent changes in the church's approach to influence are explained in later chapters and the four patterns are analyzed in relation to changes in the institutional church to see if in fact the church does exert influence over individual religious beliefs and practices. First, however, it might be worth investigating the relationship of class, age, and sex to the four patterns.

Those items loading most heavily in each factor were made into a scale for that particular pattern. Thus, popular Catholicism could range from 0 to 5; Spiritism from 0 to 4; orthodox Catholicism from 0 to 6; and social Catholicism from 0 to 6. These scales were then run against the class, sex, and age variables, with differing results. (See Appendix 2 for a discussion of the data analysis.)

The relationship between popular Catholicism and class was moderately negative, since members of the lower class were more likely to adhere to this pattern (Kendall's Tau C of −.14). However, definite regional variations do exist in the popular Catholicism pattern. The association was strong in São Paulo (Tau C of −.23) but almost disappeared in the Northeast (Tau C of −.06). Women were much more likely to fall in this pattern than were men (Tau C of .23), and there was no appreciable relationship between age and popular Catholicism (Tau C of .07). In short, this pattern is characteristic of the lower classes (except in the Northeast) and of women, and generally comports with our results, based on the item-by-item review.

Because Spiritism, as the review of some of the questions has indicated, has little kinship to class, no relationship appeared when considering the whole sample (Tau C of −.01). There was a moderate relationship in the sample from the Center (Tau C of −.12), however, meaning that the lower classes there were slightly more inclined to follow this pattern than were the other classes. There was no relationship either by sex or by age in the whole sample. These results support the literature, which states that Spiritism effectively cuts across class, sex, and age distinctions.

The results for orthodox Catholicism as a pattern parallel our item-by-item findings. There was little relationship by class in the overall sample (Tau C of −.08), although there were some weak relationships in some of the regions (Tau C of −.10), which indicated a slight inverse relationship between class and this pattern. There was a moderate relationship by sex (Tau C of .16) and by age (Tau C of .12), which indicate that women and older individuals tended slightly more toward this pattern than did men and younger persons.

The social Catholicism pattern was not emphasized in the item-by-item analysis but emerges in the factor analysis and apparently holds together only when seen as an entire pattern. This may be due to the fact that it must be based mainly on attitudinal questions and, given the level of education and the regional variations in our sample, could not be very well-defined. We found that in the overall sample there was a significant, though moderate, relationship with class (Tau C of .14), which weakened in the South (Tau C of .07). There was no overall relationship by either age or sex. Care must be taken to control for class when running this particular scale in order to avoid misleading conclusions.

3. Initiation of a New Approach to Influence

Of the four patterns defining religious beliefs and practices, the first, popular Catholicism, can be viewed as a logical outgrowth of the model of religiosity implanted by the Portuguese church in the colony but largely neglected by the weak institution. Spiritism follows from popular Catholicism but has been influenced by Candomblé and other Spiritist forms, such as Kardecism, and the third pattern, orthodox Catholicism, is a result of attempts to strengthen the institution, purify the religion, and provide groups and organizations to link the people with the church.

The fourth pattern, social Catholicism, is certainly the most difficult to explain in terms of the historical account thus far provided. It is distinct from the other three and in certain important respects even contradictory to them. Social Catholicism does not imply the practices of the other patterns, and the attitudes suggested regarding obligations and the proper role of the church are very different indeed. This pattern is the one presently being promoted by the Brazilian church, in line with the decisions made and commitments assumed in the Second Vatican Council, in subsequent papal encyclicals, in the meeting of the Latin American bishops in Medellín in 1968 and Puebla in 1979, as well as in numerous other international and regional meetings. The significance for Brazil, however, lies in the fact that this pattern was promoted before any of the abovementioned events took place, and while Mons. Montini (Pope Paul VI) did play a role in the inception of this model, it was before he became a bishop. The Catholic church in Brazil began to promote this new approach to influence before the model was adopted elsewhere, and we must understand the structures and processes which made this possible.[1]

The church organization continued to grow during the Vargas era (1930-1945, 1950-1954), with considerable assistance from Europe, and to cooperate with the state in promoting Neo-Christendom. Because of structural and resource support from the state, the church did not have to innovate or rely on the people for support. Limited reform movements based on the philosophy of the Centro dom Vital in the 1930s and around the liturgy movement of the Benedictines in the 1940s took place, but these movements remained at the elite level and did not affect the institutional church's approach to influence. The church during these years closely resembled society in general: stable and conservative. The authoritarian regime of Getúlio Vargas shielded the church from such threats to influence as the Communists, the Fascists, militant labor movements, and committed Liberals—all of which were endemic elsewhere. By preserving his own regime, of which the church was an integral part, Vargas also protected the church, which in turn supported and legitimated his government.[2]

Following the Second World War and particularly after 1955, Brazil changed very rapidly in all respects. The country industrialized by means of a strategy of import substitution, and the economy expanded enormously. Industrialization gave rise to massive urbanization, which was further encouraged by the urban policies of the government and several years of severe drought in the Northeast. In addition, the political system opened up briefly and labor movements emerged in urban and rural areas, and political parties formed to contest elections at all levels. During this period (the so-called Pre-Revolution) Brazil was undergoing change in all aspects and at all levels of the economy, the society, and the political system. The institutional framework elaborated by Getúlio Vargas during his long tenure had been designed to prevent change; therefore, the political opening-up resulted in threats to the regime's very nature and the class structure it protected. After the order and stability of the 1930-1950 period, Brazil became unstable, disorderly, and even chaotic during the next fourteen years. The culmination was the military coup of 1964.[3]

The period from 1950 to 1964 was a time of ferment and change throughout Latin America. In 1961 only one military government remained on the continent (in Paraguay), and the example of Cuba (after 1959) was being felt everywhere as rural guerrilla movements emerged in several countries. It was certain that Brazil would change, but no one could foresee which of the competing societal models would triumph.

The church was in the midst of all this and maintained Europe-oriented pastoral strategies still heavily reliant on the state for support, and with little direct support from the population. The processes and movements prevalent in Brazil during these years threatened the church to its very roots. Processes of change included urbanization, which presaged lower attendance at mass, fewer vocations, and an increased interest in Spiritism and conversion to Protestantism. Movements for change meant that the church lost labor and student support, as well as support in rural areas after peasant leagues borrowed religious terminology and objects to promote structural change. It was unclear to everyone what kind of government would eventually come to power. If the Communists had managed to take over in Cuba, then a similar takeover was also possible in Brazil. The similarities between the Brazilian Northeast and Cuba were obvious and widely publicized,[4] and the church was still painfully aware of its losses in Eastern Europe after World War II.

It is important to understand that the church perceived these threats not only in the abstract but also as very real, immediate dangers to be taken seriously. Articles in the Centro dom Vital's publication *A Ordem* documented an awareness of the weakness of Brazilian Catholicism, and a publication for the church hierarchy and elite laymen, *Revista Eclesiástica Brasileira,* emphasized the threat from the growth of Protestant and Spiritist movements. The *Plano de Emergência* (an emergency plan devised in 1962 in response to the Cuban situation) was formulated by the bishops assembled in the CNBB to point out their increasing realization that Brazil's position as the largest Catholic country in the world was somewhat misleading because most people didn't actually practice the religion. And, they admitted, "the hierarchy became concerned in evaluating the real level of influence of the church in Brazil."[5] The dilemma facing the church was probably most cogently argued by foreign-born priest, Michel Schooyans, in his *O comunismo e o futuro da igreja no Brasil* (*Communism and the Future of the Church in Brazil*), in which he elucidated not only the many threats to the church because of its weaknesses and lack of support, but also its responsibility for assuming the lead in the sociopolitical field before the Communists did: "It is legitimate, then, to hope that the crisis threatening the church in Brazil gives it initiative and vitality."[6]

If the church did not take the lead in the sociopolitical field, it at least participated in the promotion of serious structural change during the Brazilian Pre-Revolution. By means of a series of national, regional, and local statements, bishops voiced support for structural change in society and politics and committed themselves to participation in its implementation. In universities and secondary schools Catholic movements took the lead in stimulating and encouraging students to participate in the changing of society. By means of the Basic Education Movement (Movimento de Educação de Base—MEB) the church at the national level and in more than fifty dioceses promoted literacy and used a method that encouraged a rising political awareness. In the rural areas church-sponsored unions worked with peasants to establish their legal rights and to improve their work situations. In urban areas church-affiliated unions worked to help mobilize workers in ways employed previously only by unions sympathetic to communism. In general, a momentum gathered, promoted by bishops, clergy, and laity, which placed the church on the side of serious structural change and employed parts of the institution, alone or in conjunction with other, nonchurch, groups or movements, to promote such change as quickly as possible.[7]

What occurred during this time was essentially a reorientation of the church's former approach to influence toward what might best be termed "preinfluence." That is, elements in the church came to believe that society must be transformed before it could provide conditions in which people could feel fully human; at such time, and only then, would religious influence make sense. In pursuit of this reinterpretation of influence, the environment was perceived as underdeveloped—unable to provide the conditions for individuals to be fully human, let alone Christian. The church's role in this environment was to use all possible means, from statements to group action, to improve the miserable social situation. Since the urban middle class, traditionally favored by the church, was not suffering, this reinterpretation of influence had to include a change of preferred sectors, which would turn the church's attention to peasants and, to a lesser extent, the urban poor. By pursuing this new approach to influence, the traditional pastoral and institutions were neglected and new ones, such as radio schools, unions, and lay movements, were promoted.

During the redefinition of the approach to influence, all innovations, with one exception, were in the sociopolitical field and could not strictly be termed religious. Certainly the legitimacy of the church was used in the change process and the statements and justifications were couched in religious symbolism, but the intention was not to purify or strengthen religion, but rather, to change society. The only significant religious innovation was the Christian Family Movement (Movimento Familiar Cristão—MFC), which caught on in the 1950s in Brazil but was, after all, promoted from abroad and directed mainly at the urban middle or upper-middle classes. Compared to the church's shift to the sociopolitical field, the Christian Family Movement was, at that time, not very significant.

It should also be emphasized that this new approach to influence was not supported by everyone who might be considered to be in the church. Conservative bishops and laymen reacted violently, and large marches took place to protest the church's involvement in political and social structural change. What is more, the church's historical commitment to education and social welfare, which had been supported by the state since Vargas's time, continued largely unchanged and, paradoxically, was further strengthened just as the new approach to influence was being defined.[8]

Probably because there was little time to finalize the new approach to influence, it remained largely an elite movement; although it was intended to reorient the church toward the people (much as Pe. Júlio Maria had advocated fifty years earlier), it touched very few of them directly and certainly not in religious terms. The priests and laity who were promoting this new approach had little appreciation for popular religiousity, which they tended to ignore, if not to denounce outright as an opiate. Innovation was important for all that because it reoriented the church's approach to influence and aligned it with other forces for change in Brazil at the time, an alignment very different from the church's traditional position.

The organizational base of the Brazilian church's new approach to influence was the CNBB. The CNBB grew out of the Brazilian Catholic Action (Ação Católica Brasileira—ACB) experience in terms of both personnel and strategy. Catholic Action and the CNBB evolved concurrently until approximately 1962, when the lay organization progressed beyond the bishops' group and lost ecclesiastical support.

The CNBB was founded by Dom Helder Câmara in 1952, with support from the Holy See, most particularly from Mons. Montini of the Secretariat of State of Pope Pius XII. The CNBB was to coordinate and unify the Brazilian church, which by this time (1952) had more than 110 ecclesiastical units and, since Cardinal Leme's death in 1942, no single leader.[9] The CNBB was able to do far more than coordinate and unify however. Because in the crisis-ridden period from 1950 to 1964 the organization occupied a central position in the church and in its relationship to society, the CNBB reoriented, at least in the public's view, the church's approach to influence. Thus it was not the entire institutional church that adopted a different approach to influence, but rather a new organization within the church, one with very little formal jurisdiction.

During this period the CNBB consisted of Dom Helder Câmara, its secretary general, a group of progressive bishops predominantly from the Northeast, and a small group of committed clergy and laity. The CNBB spoke, however, in the name of *the* church, held meetings and conferences, provided support for church-related groups and movements, and generally gave the impression that the whole church was part of the Brazilian Pre-Revolution. What is more, it attempted to bring the whole church around to its progressive sociopolitical position by means of various plans and programs.

The CNBB was able to function, to represent the church, and to reorient the approach to influence because of the juxtaposition of conditions which existed nowhere else in Latin America except Chile and which allowed the national churches of Brazil and Chile to adopt certain orientations well before other churches on the continent. The most important condition was the openness of a state that, finding itself in question, had begun to promote structural change in society. SUDENE (Superintendência do Desenvolvimento do Nordeste—Superintendency for the Development of the Northeast) and many rural unions were formed during this period, and the government assisted the church in supporting basic education. In an open regime where the state itself was promoting change and everything was up for grabs, various parties and movements were experimenting with the generation of support for their societal models.

There have been other historical periods when governments have promoted change but the church has remained unaltered. This had certainly been the case after the Renaissance and particularly after the First Vatican Council in the late-nineteenth century. The situation changed, however, after the Second Vatican Council (1962-1965), as the church took stock of the world and its position in it and decided to promote internal as well as external change. By forming the CNBB the Brazilian church was able to take early advantage of the move toward social change which came out of Vatican II. In Brazil, the experiences of Pe. Joseph Lebret, the impact of progressive European theology, the wide dissemination and promotion of the social encyclicals of Pope John XXIII (even before the Council), and the very positive and active role of the papal nuncio prior to the Second Vatican Council not only allowed that Council to initiate change in Brazil, but also allowed it to consolidate processes already under way. The Brazilian church can be considered a precursor of the church of the Second Vatican Council and a promoter of Vatican II's ideology at least five years before such an orientation was actively discussed and implemented anywhere else in Latin America except Chile. The CNBB acted as a platform for the promotion of the Vatican II ideology, was not constrained by the legacy of the institutional church, and was dynamic and flexible enough to act quickly.

Yet, this dynamism and lack of constraint indicated that the CNBB was not really representative of the entire institutional church. The Conference's legal stature was very weak, its head and most active members from somewhat marginal dioceses, and its approach to influence counter to the actual historical role of the church.

The CNBB could survive, and indeed act, because of a third condition operative at that time. The church, in the persons of the bishops, felt threatened by the tremendous changes, both occurring and anticipated, in Brazil after the Second World War. The CNBB appeared to be in tune with the times and responding to these changes for the church, so that those bishops who sensed a need for change accepted its actions (except for a very few who spoke out in opposition). Most of the Brazilian church hierarchy, though, was probably only hazily aware of what the CNBB was doing and saying in the name of the church. In sum, the CNBB was able to reorient the Brazilian church because the bishops and Rome gave it leeway to do so in this prerevolutionary situation and because the Holy See and the Brazilian state were supportive of its efforts. By no means did all of the church adopt this orientation, nor did all of the state.

The full extent of the CNBB's anomalous character became clear after the 1964 coup. The ambiguities of the Brazilian Pre-Revolution were resolved when the armed forces took power and guaranteed the continuation of the class structure and external relations policy. In so doing, they eliminated such threats to the military regime as rural and urban labor unions, student movements, and political parties. They eliminated the very pressures that had allowed the CNBB to grow and respond on behalf of the church.

This situation was quickly reflected in the CNBB when Dom Helder Câmara was replaced as secretary general, and the structure redefined to represent the whole episcopacy. What part divine intervention played in this reorganization is unknown, for in a one-year period (1964) the supportive papal nuncio, Dom Armando Lombardi, and two key archbishops, Dom Carlos Coelho and Dom Mousinho, passed away.

The CNBB changed fundamentally after 1964, and its structure and orientation approached that of the institutional church at the very time the Second Vatican Council was committing the universal Church to almost precisely the position formerly promoted by the CNBB. In the short run, then, the position of the Holy See (in the Council and then in Pope Paul VI's encyclical *Populorum Progressio*) is not the principal determinant for a national church. The political situation has more of an effect, at least in cases where the traditional approach to influence includes integration with the state and reliance on power for influence.[10]

Even though the CNBB could not play the role it once had, a process began a few years after the coup which has returned most of the institutional church to a position occupied some ten years earlier by the CNBB. This process was possible because the military regime was dictatorial and apparently determined to reinforce and expand a socioeconomic system detrimental to the interests of the majority of the population. It was, in addition, an arbitrary regime, given to torture and other uncivilized means to ensure its supremacy. In the face of this regime, elements in the church began to speak out, legitimated by the CNBB's legacy (which had never been negated, but simply ignored) and by the church of Vatican II and of the Medellín conference of 1968. When some elements, mainly associated with the pre-1964 CNBB, spoke out, the larger institution was obliged to come to their defense.[11] The CNBB has again become a spokesman, but of a generally more progressive church than before. The conflict process has been combined with some internal efforts at reform (in line with the orientation of Vatican II), and the whole institution is now promoting a new approach to influence. The nature of the regime to which the church is reacting is described in the next chapter, and the consolidation of the church's new approach to influence is described and analyzed in Chapter 5.

4. The Brazilian Regime: 1964-1980

The nature of the Brazilian regime must be examined to substantiate the argument that the church has changed in relation to it. In my first book, *The Political Transformation of the Brazilian Catholic Church,* I analyzed seven years of conflict (1966-1973) between church and state, conflict which continues to the present. As the years passed, the tentative aspects of that period became more definitive and obvious: the government continued to evolve toward centralization and authoritarianism and frequently relied on torture and repression. Now it is clear that the economic model is failing and that the government is more divided and unstable than at any time since 1968. Still, it is this authoritarian and arbitrary regime which has been instrumental in shaping the church's present stretegy of influence. In *The Political Transformation of the Brazilian Catholic Church* I argued that the determinant issues, or sources of conflict between church and state, centered around the social mission of the church, the defense of the church-as-institution, the government's approach to development, and the political situation. The nature of this conflict has changed, but all of these issues remain operative and have, if anything, expanded as the church has broadened its areas of concern to include defense of the Indians, the Amazon in general, land tenure, and human rights.

The church's strategies and their effectiveness can be determined only in relation to the government, and at least a synthesis of observations and analysis of the regime must be formulated. Until very recently most of the middle-range political analyses of Brazil were written by foreigners. The Brazilians themselves (with some notable exceptions, such as Fernando Henrique Cardoso and Hélio Jaguaribe) tended to write about specifics in a journalistic style or about abstracts in the tradition of the grand approaches to political sociology. The reason for this can be found in the nature of the regime. It has been in power uninterruptedly since 1964, has remained under the control of the military, has limited decision making to a small group at the top, and generally has been closed to inquiry. There has been intermittent censorship, so that no general fund of information has existed which could be relied on for description and analysis. Now, however, with greater development of the social sciences in Brazil, and the more or less controlled opening of the political system under way, there is more middle-range political analysis available. It has become possible for disenchanted members of the elite, as well as journalists, to publish detailed materials on the inner workings of the political system.[1]

Reference is often made to the "Brazilian model," and there may be some reason to think of Brazil in terms of a model, or precursor, if only because of its size and potential power. Ray S. Cline, who rates the international perceived power of nations, ranked Brazil in sixth place in 1975, just after China and ahead of Iran, the United Kingdom, Canada, and Japan.[2] And, as Ronald Schneider states, "In terms of foreign-policy capacity, it is an upper-middle power with the potential to move into the ranks of the five great powers that presently occupy a place in the international stratification system below that of the two superpowers, the United States and the U.S.S.R."[3]

Brazil has the geographic (fifth-largest), population (120 million—sixth-largest), and natural resource bases to become a major power, and even though it is still viewed as an underdeveloped country, its economy is now the world's tenth-largest. Other countries have recognized Brazil's potential as a major power. Tremendous foreign investments have come from North America, Japan, and Europe, and the United States (in February 1976) and Germany (in June 1978) signed protocol agreements with Brazil which explicitly recognize the country as an emerging world power. Brazil is, therefore, in the same league as Nigeria and India, which aspire to become major powers and already wield commensurate influence in their respective geographic spheres.

These observations are significant partly because Brazil's potential for eminence has been evident for a long time; but the fulfillment of that potential has constantly been frustrated. The saying, "Brazil is the land of the future and always will be," is indicative of this thwarted desire for greatness. This unfulfilled potential provided justification for the military takeover, as the military argued, not unreasonably, that the government of João Goulart was leading the country to ruin. The theme has been embellished since 1964, and the generals claim a certain political legitimacy, since the country has industrialized and the economy has grown to the extent that Brazil can now claim to be an international power. Sufficient material exists on pre-1964 Brazil, so little will be repeated here. However, a few observations are required to set the stage for the post-1964 regime. The democratic experience of 1945-1964 was, from the time of Brazil's independence in 1822, somewhat unusual. No long tradition of democratic participation had to be rolled back, since the country was accustomed to authoritarian regimes of one sort or another. Further, there is little history in Brazil of autonomous formation of groups and movements to challenge the power structure; the civil society was weak and largely unstructured, so few strong groups or associations had to be disbanded in 1964.[4]

Reasons for Brazil's lack of social mobilization include its geography and the fact that, before 1964, its political parties only slowly broadened their bases of support. However, in the period from the late 1950s until 1964—Brazil's so-called Pre-Revolution—there was a growing awareness among some politicians, including President Goulart and many in the opposition, that institutional impediments to mobilization and democratization had to be eliminated. They strove to encourage political participation by mobilizing the working classes in the rural and urban areas to change the institutional structure. They hoped that this mobilization would result in a broader power base for Goulart and strengthen the powers of the presidency. As noted earlier, the church also participated in this mobilization by means of the CNBB, the universities, rural unions, and the Basic Education Movement. However, mobilization and agitation within the established institutional order failed to supersede it. The military, with a great deal of civilian support, moved in to rule provisionally until it could be sure that populism, demagoguery, and general agitation had been laid to rest and that Brazil was safely on the road to economic stability and a continuation of the existing socioeconomic structure.

When the generals took power, they, as well as many national and international observers, were surprised at just how easy it was for the military to eliminate potential opposition to its rule. While consolidating the government, however, the military discovered that it could not both have power and not have it. Thus began a process in which the civil political realm became increasingly circumscribed, evidenced by the Second Institutional Act of 1965 and the Fifth Institutional Act of 1968. The military was legislating by decree even though its Constitution of 1967 (revised extensively in 1969) remained operative when convenient. In effect, the military came to occupy the state apparatus and consolidated its powers throughout that apparatus and the whole of society.

Yet, not all civil aspects have been usurped. While the military does occupy instrumental positions in the government and industry, it also employs a capable—and civilian—technocratic apparatus and now allows political party activities. The technocratic apparatus is important, but political party activities had not been, except as an internal escape valve and as a means of promoting international legitimacy by serving as symbols in support of the contention that the country is returning to democracy.

The primary legitimating factor—indeed, ideology—of the military has been what is known as the Doctrine of National Security. Athough the economic growth of the country has been an important and concrete factor in legitimating military rule during certain periods, the Doctrine of National Security has remained a constant. This is not generally stressed by those following structural approaches such as dependency analysis, because they are not prone to recognize (much less emphasize) the role of ideology in determining anything. Nor is ideology emphasized by economists writing about the country, since they depend less on ideas than on proceses which can be quantified and on institutions which seem to play some role in politics. However, I and other observers feel that ideology (in the form of the Doctrine of National Security) is clearly important to the military.[5] What other reason for the extensive security apparatus, the torture, the repression—all in the name of national security—if no underlying ideology justifies such an approach? If economic growth were the only legitimating factor for the regime's tenacious hold, it would follow that the decrease in growth after 1974 would have caused political instability. This has not happened, despite pressures from outside the military, and I feel that the continued stability of the regime is largely due to the self-justifying role of the Doctrine of National Security, which gives the military internal justification even if external legitimacy is lacking. Furthermore, unless some emphasis is placed on this doctrine, it seems impossible to understand the reasons behind the implementation of operations like "moral" and "civic" education in the schools, the political, social, and economic integration of the Amazon area, and the minute control over concerns such as river transport. Unless the role of the doctrine is admitted, the dynamics of the conflict between church and state become incomprehensible. Considerations such as economic growth or personal careerism are important, but we must understand this doctrine in order to grasp the unique component of the Brazilian model, which has since been generalized elsewhere. The doctrine figures in most of the speeches of the military members of the regime, and, as José Comblin puts it, "The National Security Doctrine . . . has been the official ideology in

Brazil since 1964."[6]

The doctrine was based on those elements of American military thinking concerned with internal aggression and revolutionary war and was initially elaborated at the National War College (Escola Superior da Guerra) in the years following the college's founding in 1949. The doctrine was further sophisticated by means of studies and practice and contact with local reality. The idea of total war is integral to the doctrine, as succinctly stated by General Umberto Peregrino:

> We are in a situation of total war, this war that becomes an incredibly complicated game, where the facts include political economy, social psychology, general geography, and the most recent discoveries in nuclear physics . . . . In this framework the military institutions will be organs of planning and direction of operations, for total war asks of the whole nation the full exercise of all its facilities coordinated for a single higher goal. From this arises the intransigent subordination of the basic activities of the nation to its security. And it becomes a duty, alongside this rigid central principle of the modern fundamental problems of the nation and to prepare superbly prepared groups of men to deal with them. This is the function, in Brazil, of the National War College.[7]

Specifically, the justification is one of security and development (the latter to ensure the former). The doctrine assumes the presence of internal enemies working in conjunction with international communism to subvert the state; considers economic development vital in order to create national power; emphasizes the nation and therefore is intolerant of "unreliable" elements within it; sees power as indivisible; and firmly believes in Brazil as a future world power. Since the "total war" ideology can justify practically any action in response to practically any situation of internal unrest, the military's reliance on severe repressive measures can be defended. As Comblin shows, starting in about 1967, the military came to stress economic growth above all other national security considerations as it perceived the enormous power diffference between countries and the role economic growth played in such disparities. Economic development thus provided the elements for national power and came to be included in the concept of total war.[8]

In the current regime's conception of the state and nation, the term "people" has no meaning; the concept of the population en masse, let alone as individuals, never appears in the national security literature. The power of the state is absolute and indivisible; society is subject to that power, and the individual is rewarded only indirectly by the country's increased economic power and international prestige. The Doctrine of National Security is presented as total nationalism: it is an end in itself, and, as

Comblin points out, all policy is derived in a totally deductive fashion from the postulate of total war. "The Doctrine derives its principles and corollaries in an inflexible form, without attending to the complexities of history, without considering the delicate analyses of situations and complex processes in the various areas of human activity."[9] With such a doctrine to rely on, the military can justify its role in the state, the state's superiority over the society, and the growth of the economy to attain that grandeur which is Brazil's destiny—irrespective of the social costs or human suffering involved.

Obviously, in the implementation of this doctrine the structures and procedures of democracy have little function. This was evident in the constitutional amendments of 1969, which altered the military's Constitution of 1967. In that constitution, as Dom Cândido Padin shows, the most significant changes concerned national security and the armed forces. Thus the Council of National Security (Conselho de Segurança Nacional) was defined in article 87, section I, as "the highest organ in the direct advising of the president," and as having as its function "the formulation and execution of the policy of national security." The Council's primary purpose is "to establish the permanent national objectives and the bases for national policy."[10]

The legislative and judicial branches of government function under the direct supervision and control of the executive; they, in fact, are controlled by the president in conjunction with the Council of National Security, the National Information Service (Serviço Nacional de Informações), and the Civil Household of the President (Casa Civil). It may be worth noting that both Presidents Garrastazu Médici and João Baptista Figueiredo were chiefs of the National Information Service. A façade of liberal democratic institutions is visible in Brazil, but the real power is centralized in a security apparatus from which emerge the leaders and the justification for authority based on the Doctrine of National Security. The military regime has overlaid the whole society with its ideology and organization and has thus far tolerated no opposition.

In economic terms the military has succeeded spectacularly in attaining for the country status as a power.[11] The years from 1968 to 1974 saw a remarkable economic boom, with an average growth in Gross Domestic Product of 10.1 percent. In 1975 GDP was $90 billion, double that of 1968. Moreover, industry was the leading sector and expanded at a yearly rate of 12.2 percent. Within industry the highest rates were achieved by such sectors as transport equipment, machinery, and electrical equipment. Table 11 gives some idea of growth rates between 1956 and 1975.

There was also a dramatic increase in exports: from a relatively stable

Table 11
Yearly Growth Rates of Real GDP, Per Capita GDP,
Industry, Agriculture
(Percentages)

Year	Real GDP	Per Capita GDP	Industry	Agriculture
1956-1962[a]	7.8	4.0	10.3	5.7
1962-1967[a]	3.7	1.3	3.9	4.0
1968	9.3	6.3	15.0	1.5
1969	9.0	5.9	11.0	6.0
1970	9.5	6.4	11.1	5.6
1971	11.3	8.2	11.2	12.2
1972	10.4	7.3	13.8	4.1
1973	11.4	8.3	15.0	3.5
1974	9.6	6.5	8.2	8.5
1975	4.0	1.3	4.2	3.4

Source: Adapted from Werner Baer in Riordan Roett, *Brazil in the Seventies,* Washington, D. C.: American Enterprise Institute, 1976. Calculated from data of Centro de Contas Nacionais, Fundação Getúlio Vargas. Published in *Conjuntura Econômica* (various issues).
[a] Yearly average.

$1.3 billion average during the 1947-1964 period, exports rose to $7.9 billion by 1975, all the more important because of the growth of manufactured exports. These totaled $229 million in 1964 and had grown to $2,599 million in 1974, or 37 percent of total 1974 export earnings.

The economic planners who shaped Brazil's policies after 1964 attributed the decline of the economy during the 1962-1966 period to "the imbalanced way in which it had grown during the import substitution industrialization years, and to the distortions in the allocation of resources that had resulted from the combination of inflation and price controls."[12] Their immediate concerns centered around controlling inflation, eliminating distortions in price structures, and allocating resources more effectively. Classic stabilization policies were employed to these ends: government expenditures were curtailed; taxes were raised; credit was tightened; and the wage sector was squeezed. Measures were adopted to eliminate such price distortions by increasing utility rates, and the capital market was modernized and strengthened by means of new credit mechanisms, special funds for financing, and the indexing of financial instruments. Tax incentives were instituted to influence resource allocation among various regions and sectors (such as the Amazon and the Northeast) and in the areas of tourism and exports. The government pursued an essentially capitalist socioeconomic approach in which it fortified markets, improved the functioning of the price system, and increased the state's role in the economy to the point where "the present system can be considered one of state capitalism."[13] The state at present plays an enormous role in the economy as a manager by means of fiscal measures or outright regulations, as an economic agent through ownership of banks and other financial institutions, and as a producer in the steel and petroleum industries. In the manufacturing sector alone, government firms in 1971 were estimated to account for 18.5 percent of total manufacturing assets. Moreover, these firms were concentrated among the high forward-linkage industries of steel and chemicals. In terms of relation of government expenditure to GNP, the figure in 1947 was 17.1 percent and by 1969 had risen to 32 percent. As further proof of the state's involvement in the economy, of the top 5,256 firms in the country (rated by assets) the state now owns 46 percent, Brazilian nationals own 38 percent, and foreigners 16 percent.[14]

Werner Baer has forcefully argued that much of the economic growth since 1968 is due to the impact of government programs, and, given the elaborate and comprehensive control mechanisms of the state, the allocation of resources is more the result of government policies than of market forces.[15] Schneider may overstate the case, but not by much:

Brazil is engaged in a game of forced-draft "catch up" industrialization in which the state plays a leading role, and which bids fair to transform the country, in one generation, nearly as completely as Germany was transformed during the Bismarckian era. Certainly this transformation has been a triumph more for the military-technocrat alliance than for free enterprise, more for the state than for the private sector.[16]

There is some debate about whether the post-1968 growth was really attributable to government policies or was merely a continuation of the boom-and-bust quality of Brazilian economic history. There is no debate at all, however, concerning the huge role of the state in the economy, and in a certain sense the penetration of the society by the Doctrine of National Security is replicated in the relationship of the state and the economy. An apparent contradiction exists, however, for, although the Doctrine of National Security posits as a goal the independence of the economy from foreign domination, the pattern of economic growth is one which has opened the economy totally to the outside by means of imports and exports, loans and investments, and facilitating legislation on the free movement of goods and resources.[17]

There is some question of whether this strategy of economic growth has made the country more or less dependent, but none at all as to which sector of the population has benefited most from the growth. The multinational corporations which have been encouraged to set up in Brazil generally utilize the most modern technology and, consequently, require skilled labor. And, since they sell products produced elsewhere, they aim primarily at a market composed of the middle and upper classes. Both factors have resulted in an increasing marginalization of most of the population, which can neither afford these foreign-manufactured products nor develop the requisite employment skills. This situation is aggravated by a labor surplus in the rural areas, which is easily transferred as unskilled labor to the urban areas, and thereby wages are kept down.[18] Data from the 1970 census confirmed what observers had already predicted, that is, that there is a growing maldistribution of income. Table 12 indicates changes in income distribution, and although everybody agrees to the validity of the data, a tremendous debate has raged as to the causes and long-range implications of the maldistribution.[19]

Table 12
Changes in Brazil's Income Distribution

% of Population	% of Income		Per Capita Income in U.S. Dollars	
	1960	1970	1960	1970
Lower 40	11.2	9.0	84	90
Next 40	34.3	27.8	257	278
Next 15	27.0	27.0	540	720
Top 5	27.4	36.3	1,645	2,940
Average			300	400

Source: Adapted from Werner Baer in Riordan Roett, *Brazil in the Seventies,* Washington, D.C.: American Enterprise Institute, 1976. Calculated from IBGE, *Censo Demográfico,* 1970.

It is, however, undeniable that the government's policies have encouraged and abetted these definite tendencies toward the continuing concentration of income. Government industrialization policies continue to subsidize capital, which keeps employment and pay scales down. No agrarian reform whatsoever has been promoted, so the population is not fixed on the land; the people remain available and mobile, thus there is no pressure to raise wages. Indeed, government policy in the rural areas has concentrated holdings, changed crops, and forced people off the land. A series of tax incentive schemes for encouraging investment in exports, in certain regions, and in tourism have been promoted, all of which schemes favor the higher-income groups. The unions are government controlled and strikes officially prohibited, so that workers are in a weak position from which to demand higher wages. One wonders, with William G. Tyler, what would have happened if the government had subsidized labor instead of capital, but it has not, and the indications are that the maldistribution of income is as bad today as it was at the time of the 1970 census.[20]

Two of the masterminds of this economic strategy, Roberto Campos and Mário Simonsen, have, as have other proponents of the regime, recognized the maldistribution and justified it in terms of the necessity for sufficient economic growth before redistribution. This is part of what they term the "cruel premises" of unpopular measures necessary in Brazil today so that the country will be greater and richer tomorrow. There seems to be substantial evidence, however, that a progressive redistribution of income at the present time would have little effect on aggregate growth.[21] Be that as it may, the social implications of the economic model pursued with such vigor since the late 1960s are fairly obvious and increasingly better perceived by large sectors of the population.[22] These implications are all the more serious today in the face of a very severe economic crisis, evidenced by tremendous foreign indebtedness (more than $50 billion at the end of 1979), continuing trade deficits ($2.7 billion in 1979), and an inflation rate which is likely to exceed 100 percent in 1980.

It is precisely the social implications of the Brazilian model of economic development which compromise the current process of *abertura* ("opening") in the political system. In this process of controlled liberalization directed toward a conservative democratic system, there have been tremendous vacillations and ambiguities as the military seeks to remove itself from direct power (and thus from blame), while maintaining its prestige.

The causes of the opening are varied and interact with one another in very complex ways indeed. Legitimacy, and its loss, is at the forefront, since it is a problem for any military regime which cannot base its right to rule on the interests of the people as reflected in elections. The legitimacy derived from the Doctrine of National Security has diminished as the threats of communism and subversion have faded in Brazil as a result of successful political repression, changes in key aspects of the international situation, and the pragmatism of the military regime in trading with countries regardless of ideological coloration and in being the first to recognize the MPLA (Movimento Popular para Libertação de Angola—

Popular Movement for the Liberation of Angola) government. Legitimacy based on economic performance has disappeared as the economy has gone from bad to worse, a situation which is particularly serious if one considers that there was in fact a period of tremendous growth until the mid-1970s, during which expectations increased to match the rapidly expanding economy. In addition, the church has provided alternative criteria and models for severely questioning the legitimacy of the regime.

Besides questions directly dealing with legitimacy, there are those related to it tangentially. The military as an institution has found it increasingly difficult to maintain unity after sixteen years in power, as reflected in the extreme centralization of power in President Geisel's hands (caused in part by his awareness of a lack of unity in the country). This centralization of power has created even more problems to the extent that Geisel's military candidate for a successor—General João Baptista Figueiredo—was opposed from within the military and even opposed in the election by a retired army general.

The lack of unity (and also the problem of legitimacy) is related in turn to the tremendous changes which have taken place in Brazilian society during the almost two decades of military rule. There is now a large middle class, a very highly qualified industrial working class, even a large entrepreneurial group worried about the huge state role in the economy and in society. The modernization of society has resulted in illegal strikes by workers, protests in the media and through whatever political channels they can find by entrepreneurs, and the formation of groups. Again, as we shall see in subsequent chapters, the church has been active in the formation of groups and in the exertion of pressure on sectors of the government whenever possible.

These domestic factors must also be related to changes in the international situation. President Carter's human rights campaign may not have been decisive in any single context but it was a policy which complicated the matter of stability for a military regime closely aligned with the United States. At the very least, the campaign gave moral support and a certain amount of legitimacy to groups within Brazil—particularly church-related groups—which have been fighting for human rights. Then too, the international situation has changed somewhat in that dictatorships collapsed in southern Europe in the early 1970s, the conservative, modernizing regime in Iran was overthrown in late 1978 because it lacked flexibility and did not innovate politically rapidly enough in the face of rapid modernization, and European political parties and unions have taken the initiative in promoting liberalization in most of Latin America. This is not the place to provide an integrated analysis of the process currently under way in Brazil but rather to suggest that indeed there exists such a process, its path unclear even to those involved, and that the church has played and continues to play a very important part at all levels of this process.[23]

At the present time the opening, or controlled liberalization, means that there are more possibilities for individual participation in the political system because of the greater number of political parties allowed by the party reform of late 1979. It is also likely that municipal and gubernatorial elections will be direct in 1982. The repeal of Institutional Act V in 1978 eliminated the most pernicious aspects of the dictatorship, aided by the abolition of most media censorship during the same year, and by the establishment of habeas corpus. A general amnesty has also been granted, which allows most political exiles to return.

All of this adds up to a very substantial change from the heyday of the dictatorship (from 1970 to 1973) and even from the situation in 1975 and 1976. However, we must bear in mind that the central bureaucracy is huge and remains powerful, that the president may employ "constitutional safeguards" for corrective intervention, and that the goal is a restricted democracy built on conservative political bases. So far the regime has been successful, in its negotiations with the opposition(s), in establishing the bases for this slightly different system. The opposition is willing to engage in negotiation because the regime still specifies the terms of the political opening up and because, if anything, the likelihood of a right-wing coup would be even greater if they did not negotiate. Still, strikes are illegal and generally repressed (as was the case in São Paulo in spring 1980), and the peasantry has very few rights. The system is indeed evolving but has yet to be transformed, and the general social and economic situation remains as bad as ever for the vast majority of the population.

The church's most recent interpretation of a pattern of influence has been determined in relation to a regime that was formed in the early 1970s and continues in power, even though in question and evolving. The political, economic, and social context of Brazil has had important implications for the church. First, with modernization, and more particularly under the Doctrine of National Security, there is less need for religious justification, since the regime already provides its own legitimacy. Second, state expansion has brought under direct state control many structures which had been the church's particular preserve, especially in education and social welfare. And third, given the generally oppressive economic and social conditions of the regime, the church—if it continues to claim a social mission—must involve itself in thorny situations and strenuously criticize the government, a most unrecommended practice.

Thus an interesting, not to say paradoxical, situation has resulted: the church is being forced, ideologically and structurally, out of much of society at the same time that it is defining a new role for itself as spokesman of the ignored and repressed majority of the population. And, because few other groups or organizations have been allowed to exist, the church, with its elaborate structure, finds itself sought out by and obliged to become involved with elements such as protest groups, students, and political parties, which seek protection and legitimacy. The Brazilian regime limits the church's options and in a sense compels it to adopt an orientation which is in opposition to the regime.

5. Current Church Responses and Strategies

In the early 1970s I argued, possibly somewhat peremptorily, that the church and state in Brazil had entered into a process of conflict, and, as the church defined its goals increasingly in terms of a prophetic mission, the conflict process was bound to escalate. Fourteen conflicts were analyzed in *The Political Transformation of the Brazilian Catholic Church*, and increased autonomy seemed inevitable, given the church's developing awareness of its role in the political, economic, and social systems. It was argued that because, as an institution, the church had adopted a prophetic mission of denouncing injustice and defending the poor as the state became increasingly authoritarian and estranged from the population, the two had embarked on a course of polarization, with dialectically opposite positions.

On returning to Brazil in October 1974, it seemed that my earlier analysis and subsequent prognosis of the situation might have been somewhat optimistic, not to say misfounded, since there was little obvious evidence of continuing conflict between church and state. The regime had not changed intrinsically (although the government was going out of its way to avoid conflict and improve its image), and apparently the church had either been duped as to the nature of the regime or had simply buckled under. In general and national terms, relations between church and state were pacific. Three incidents occurred which might belie this observation, but none gave rise to a conflict situation, as would have been the case a year or two earlier.

The three events occurred in 1973, around the time of the tenth anniversary of the papal encyclical *Pacem in Terris* and th twenty-fifth anniversary of the Universal Declaration of Human Rights. One incident was national (under the auspices of the CNBB), and consisted of a campaign to inform people about and stimulate discussion of human rights.

Thousands of pamphlets were distributed and dozens of conferences promoted to discuss this theme in the Brazilian context. The campaign carried little weight at the time; President Geisel had promised to bring torture and repression under control, and it was apparently felt by some church people that the church was being overly pessimistic.

The other two incidents were regional: the publication by bishops and religious order superiors of the Northeast of *Eu ouvi os clamores do meu povo (I Have Heard the Cry of My People)*, and the publication by bishops of the Centerwest of *Marginalização de um povo: Grito das igrejas (Marginalization of a People: Shout of the Churches).*[1] Both documents were in effect monographs in which the implications of the regime's economic model were analyzed in structural terms and then severely criticized. It was clear in both documents that the signatories opted for evangelization of the poor in their areas. However, these two regional statements had little apparent national impact, and it is worth noting that, with one or two exceptions, the signatories had been involved with the CNBB earlier and were well-known critics of the regime.

During this time the national church ostensibly directed most of its attention to pastoral duties, meaning religious activities with minimal sociopolitical implications. The CNBB continued to promote change nationally, in the dioceses and in institutions such as schools, but the overwhelming sense was one of religious renewal with emphasis on *cursilhos* (short, intensive courses for the rejuvenation of faith), Christian charismatics, and other exclusively religious activities. Politically, church relations with newly elected President Geisel were extremely good, as highlighted by the visit of Cardinal Agnello Rossi, president of the Vatican's Sacred Congregation for the Evangelization of People and former archbishop of São Paulo, to Brasília in July 1974. Dom Agnello projected a very positive view of Brazil and its government and indicated that relations between church and state were totally harmonious.[2] Admittedly, the cardinal had always emphasized the positive side of this relationship, and the government had always sought to deny the gravity of the conflicts, but at the time it appeared that Dom Agnello and President Geisel were on the level. Had relations indeed been as harmonious as Dom Agnello testified, it would have meant that the church had returned to purely religious concerns, thereby denying the process of evolution—nationally and internationally—of at least a decade.

This apparent church-state concord was taken seriously for at least two reasons. The first was censorship, which made it very difficult to determine what was going on in the country as a whole, to say nothing of what was happening in the progressive sectors of the church. Neither of the regional episcopal statements of 1973 received attention in the press, Dom Helder Câmara could not be mentioned, and incidents that might be considered evidence of conflict were not publicized. Censorship applied not only to the national media (which engaged in a good deal of self-censorship on church issues anyway) but to the church media as well (including *O São Paulo* of the Archdiocese of São Paulo and church radio stations in many dioceses).[3] Since it had become almost impossible to learn about protests (most of which were taking place in the more-isolated areas of Amazônia) and the reaction of various church elements to them, no momentum could build up.

A second reason for the apparent goodwill between church and state was that fewer incidents were occurring than in the past because of President Geisel's promises to end repression and torture and to open up the regime generally. He, more than any of the three previous general-presidents, emphasized, at his inauguration, that a serious liberalization was in the offing and took steps to decrease censorship and improve relations with all potential critics of the regime—particularly the church. The president and the chief of the civil household, General Golbery do Couto e Silva, established contacts with the church and repeatedly reassured the bishops that, given time and support on the bishops' part, the security apparatus would be diminished and all tensions between church and state eliminated. Unlike in the past, when contacts were between individuals such as Dom Leme and Getúlio Vargas, they were now between the CNBB, acting as spokesman for the bishops and thus the entire Brazilian church, and the president and his civil household. Contacts between government and church tended to become institutionalized, particularly CNBB contacts, who sought to channel and mediate all possible arguments. It is true that the initial contacts were facilitated by a long friendship between General Golbery and an important layman close to the CNBB, but once established, contact continued between the CNBB and the president and his civil household. Presumably the papal nuncio could have acted as intermediary between the church and the state, but recent experience had indicated that the nuncio leaned more to Rome's than to Brazil's interests; the bishops did not feel that he understood their problems and, consequently, had little confidence in him.

The CNBB, on the other hand, with Dom Aloísio Lorscheider as president and Dom Ivo Lorscheider as general secretary, enjoyed the confidence of the overwhelming majority of the bishops—irrespective of their sociopolitical views. Both men had served in the CNBB since approximately 1971 and were reelected in 1974. After 1974 they organized the CNBB very effectively and established a series of commissions, institutes, and seminars by means of which the conference could maintain contact with all levels of the church. The CNBB has become an efficient organization and has been regarded since the beginning of the Geisel presidency as the spokesman for the bishops and the church in national matters.[4] It undoubtedly became the main means of avoiding misunderstandings and subsequent conflict between the church and the state. This does not imply that Dom Ivo and Dom Aloísio gave in to the government positions, because the two were extremely effective in dealing with the regime; rather, a means existed via the CNBB to presumably avoid church-state conflicts. The CNBB served, then, to institutionalize conflict and keep it within bounds, and, as a not-unimportant corollary, to keep the public largely unaware of that conflict.

By 1976, however, my earlier prognosis was largely justified when conflict became obvious once again as large and significant sectors of the church opted for a pattern of influence in line with the earlier CNBB orientation toward progressive theology. By 1978 a momentum had developed which consolidated all the progressive elements of the previous two decades. Briefly, this influence model is one in which the church has chosen to work primarily with the lower classes in assisting them to seek liberation in an environment characterized by repression and injustice. The other classes are not ignored but are regarded as being less in need of the few resources the church has available. The instruments of change range from statements, the creation of groups and organizations, and eventually, of grass-roots communities. In fact, the mechanisms consist of all possible structures and ideological elements that the church can bring to bear, the main task being to reorganize and redirect past commitments and resources to the new goal of assisting in the liberation of the lower classes.

The change in church goals has initially been facilitated by the growing awareness that the church can neither influence the people nor rely on political power. It is, so to speak, free—in terms of both the historical legacy of Christendom and Neo-Christendom and of freedom to change. Research on popular Catholicism has been carried out at CERIS and in a series of studies and seminars supported mainly by the National Pastoral Institute (Instituto Nacional de Pastoral—INP). Independent research on the church's lack of influence and power had existed for several years and finally was brought together and synthesized.

Official public documents of the CNBB, speaking for all the bishops, make observations such as the following on the position of the church vis à vis society and the state:

An analysis of Catholicism itself reveals the existence—alongside an important practicing minority whose religious life is inspired in the Gospel and particularly in sacramental practice—of a majority of the faithful whose devotions and religious practices are not well integrated into the ecclesiastical community and [who] follow predominantly an individual relationship with the sacred.[5]

The church cannot rely on a prepared and committed body of the laity, nor is it regarded with any particular deference or respect. "Great decisions concerning political, social, and economic life, with profound repercussions on the cultural profile of the nation, are made without taking into consideration the forms of influence or the option of the church [which were] considered in the recent past."[6] Thus the church is increasingly ignored in decision making, a not unexpected outcome considering the "fact that the important political decisions are being made by a restricted elite, without participation of the people."[7] Furthermore, with increased secularization and modernization, "the presence and direct action of the institutional church in worldly realities, in general terms, seems to have diminished . . . . The recent evolution of Brazilian society , . . . and the more effective assumption on the part of the state of its proper role frees the ecclesiastical institution from many suppletive tasks."[8]

Church structures in the areas of education, charity, and related fields are also decreasing in size and importance, and in light of these societal and political changes the church is losing power (or the illusion of power) and is freed to assume other roles:

If this situation makes the church less powerful, poorer, and at times, more threatened in its pastoral structures, it also assists her to rediscover the primacy of her prophetic mission, to liberate her from complications not always favorable to the Gospel, and to restore to her more fully her own and essential vocation of announcing the Good News of Christ, sign of hope, unity, and peace for all men.[9]

Although all the bishops and clergy may not fully appreciate the implications of this loss of influence and power, at least the CNBB has brought to light a situation long recognized by many clergy and most scholars.

A second more short-term trend is the growing appreciation of the implications of the Brazilian economic model. By 1975 discussion of burgeoning income inequality had penetrated the church hierarchy, and in that year the Justice and Peace Commission of São Paulo published the telling study *São Paulo 1975: Crescimento e pobreza (Growth and Poverty).*[10] The significance of the model for rural areas was becoming obvious to everyone, and bishops from regions normally noted for their conservatism (Bahia and Sergipe, for example) began questioning and criticizing the socioeconomic system. The analyses and conclusions from the two regional statements of 1973 became commonplace as the implications of income inequality were correctly perceived as being long-range and irrefutable. Once it was concluded that something was amiss with the "Brazilian miracle" of income concentration, inflation, foreign indebtedness and inhumanity toward the poor, increasing evidence reaffirmed those implications.[11]

The economic model and finally President Geisel himself lost all credibility among the bishops. Their initial good will toward the president evaporated as torture and repression continued, as Indians and settlers were forced from their lands, as the rights of workers were ignored. The last straw was undoubtedly the "Package of April" of 1977, when the president closed the recalcitrant Congress and decreed measures intended to keep the oposition out of power indefinitely. It then became evident that this regime was not liberalizing or opening up, but rather the reverse, and that the self-styled democrat was a complete autocrat. This package was a watershed not only because it gave evidence to the progressives that a tight regime was closing up still further (thereby belying the president's positive gestures of three years earlier), but also because it showed that the CNBB's analysis of the church's lack of political power was accurate and because it allowed a divorce law to be passed (Amendment No. 9, 226/159). The divorce law infuriated the conservative bishops, many of whom had tended to ignore the implications of the regime's economic model but who could not ignore the passage of a divorce law.[12]

The cardinal of Rio de Janeiro, Dom Eugênio Sales, long a defender of the government and particularly of Geisel, would no longer meet with the president for "mutual understandings." Even the most cynical and calculating elements of the church hierarchy realized they had little to gain, and much to lose, by remaining close to a regime over which they had no influence. Further, far too many conflicts had occurred to allow any self-respecting organization, let alone the church, to be identified with the regime.

A third factor which allowed for change can be seen as a kind of motive force involving a series of incidents which can be termed a dynamic of conflict. These incidents mostly resulted from some social involvement on the part of the laity, clergy, and bishops in order to promote the interests of the rural and urban poor. As the situation of the lower classes became increasingly serious as a consequence of the regime's economic model, elements within the church felt compelled to act and speak out in line with past CNBB ideological commitments. As these elements acted, there was a corresponding reaction on the part of some sectors of the government, and a new level of polarization and self-definition was reached. Incidents of particular gravity included the torture and death of the journalist Vladimir Herzog in São Paulo in October 1975 by elements in the military, even though guarantees had been given to the cardinal that Herzog would not be harmed; the murder of Pe. Rodolfo Lunkenbein by ranchers in Amazônia in July 1976 for defending the rights of Indians; the murder, also in Amazônia, of Pe. João Bosco Penido Burnier in October 1976 by the police for defending women tortured by these same police; the kidnapping, beating, and general abuse of the bishop of Nova Iguaçu (a poor suburb of Rio de Janeiro) in September 1976 by right-wing elements who subsequently blew up his car in front of CNBB headquarters.[13] Church-state conflict in the late 1970s took essentially the same format as conflict in the early part of the decade. The situation is more serious now, however, as positions on both sides have become more clearly defined and the regime's economic model has become better understood. As the bishops' statement of November 1976 attests, a choice is involved, "but her [the church's] option and her preferred ones are the weak and the oppressed."[14] From this choice come certain responsibilities to work for the weak and oppressed: "Our word is directed as well to the great and powerful to point out to them their responsibilities for the suffering of the people."[15] The "great and powerful," however, are not very receptive to such instruction from a church they would prefer stick to themes of anticommunism for the public and morality for their wives and children.

The combination of these three facts—realization of internal weakness, awareness of an intolerable regime, and stimulation from conflictory events—has had, in my view, a profound effect on how the church defines its role in Brazilian society, a role which is in fact a consolidation of the model of influence originally promoted by the core group of the CNBB, prior to 1964. Accordingly, the poor and oppressed are the church's preferred target in an environment characterized by injustice and repression, and the tasks at hand are the reorientation and mobilization of the remaining resources of the church to assist in the liberation of the people. This new model of influence, and some aspects of the process which has helped shape it, will be discussed in the next section, and though it will be made clear that the church is not a monolith, the illustrations will show that a very substantial part of it—including at the national level—is committed to this new approach to influence.[16]

CNBB Statements

The first indication of a unified stance by the bishops after General Geisel assumed the presidency appeared during the last week of November 1975, when the forty-member Representative Commission (of the CNBB) met and issued a national statement. The political context at the time included the death of Vladimir Herzog, a veritable reign of terror unleashed by the military in São Paulo, plus the threatened expulsion of Dom Pedro Casaldáliga, bishop of São Felix in the Amazon area, for his outspoken defense of the settlers who were being forced from their land. At this time, some twenty months into President Geisel's term, the bishops simply reaffirmed their right and obligation to assist in changing society and to denounce injustice as they saw it:

In one word, it is by the light of the Gospel that the church is endowed with her inalienable prophetic mission. She would undoubtedly fail in the historical exercise of this mission if she did not point to the sin, the social inequity of our time, involved in the exploitation of man, which divides humanity into oppressed and oppressors, from the level of businesses and groups even to the level of nation and of peoples; if she did not denounce the abuses of a nation that considers itself above good and evil when pursuing its objectives; if she was not alert to the egoism of peoples and groups of people who sacrifice their fellow men to their own interests. To criticize means to seek out evil to denounce it and good to announce it. When the church recognizes good it is accused of conformity; when it denounces evil it is accused of subversion.[17]

Regional statements were published at the same time, the most notable being the one from the State of São Paulo, entitled *Do Not Oppress Thy Brother (Não oprimas teu irmão),* but the next national statement was again made by the Representative Commission of the CNBB. The text had been prepared in October 1976 but released only in late November, after the municipal elections, so that the bishops could not be accused of playing politics.[18] The political context at that time included the murders of two priests in the Amazon area, the attack on Dom Adriano Hipólito in Nova Iguaçu, the continuing censorship relating to Dom Helder Câmara and *O São Paulo,* violent attacks on groups such as the Order of Brazilian Lawyers and the research center CEBRAP (Centro Brasileiro de Planejamento—Center of Brazilian Planning), and a general state of lawlessness and violence, which was tacitly, if not overtly, being tolerated by elements in the government. The bishops denied that they were issuing another denunciation, but indicated that the facts in themselves were a denunciation. They asserted that the Gospel required a clarification of their position and pointed out that elements in the church were attacked and slandered when they came to the defense of the poor, the oppressed, prisoners, and the victims of torture. The series of conflicts obliged the church to look at society to discover the underlying causes of violence which had led to this predicament. Stated another way, the violence directly affecting the church forced it to reflect more critically on the government and its socioeconomic system.

The document went on to indict a legal system which favored the rich and abused the defenseless poor, a police force which was literally getting away with murder, an invidious system of land tenure which stressed concentration of holdings and which resulted in the forced expulsion of small settlers and Indians, the generalized exploitation of the Indians in a development model which had no use for them, and a centralized state legitimated by the Doctrine of National Security, which denied any individual personal security. In such a situation,

the church must follow the example of Christ. She cannot exclude anyone and must offer to all, great and small, the means of salvation received from Christ. But her option and her preferences are the weak and oppressed. She cannot remain indifferent to the plight of the Indian forced from his land and the destruction of his culture. She cannot close her eyes in the face of the grave situation of insecurity in which the defenseless live, before the starvation of the poor, and the malnutrition of the children. She cannot ignore the uprooted, the migrants looking for new opportunities, who only find shelter under bridges or lose themselves in the outskirts of the large cities.[19]

The position taken in this forceful statement was reinforced by a more general statement approved by the episcopacy at the Fifteenth General Assembly in February 1977. This particular document is important in that it was approved by an overwhelming majority of the bishops (210 to 3), and the very title—*Christian Requirements of a Political Order (Exigências cristãs de uma ordem política)*—made it clear that basic principles were provided by which a government could be judged.[20] This is significant because the Brazilian regime has steadfastly emphasized its Christian orientation and firmly identified itself with the West. Although the statement is less specific and emphatic than *Não oprimas teu irmão*, it nonetheless points out the failure of the Brazilian regime to meet the requirements of a truly Christian political order.

Christian Requirements of a Political Order declared that the bishops are obliged to apply Christian doctrine and ethical principles to assist in resolving the country's problems, since salvation must begin on earth and that the political order is subject to a moral order, and thus the church, with the light of Faith, "proclaims the requirements and demands that Christians assume their specific function in constructing a society in accord with these principles." The document further averred that the church must accept responsibility for all men, "especially the poor whose situation of misery is eloquent testimony of the sin that is found in the heart of man, contaminating all his personal, family, and social life." Furthermore, the state does not grant rights to individuals, but rather vice versa, and it is the state's function to respect, defend, and promote individual rights—"All force that is exercised at the margin of and beyond the law is violence." Not only must the church promote the common good, the statement continued, but it also must assist pressure groups which represent the people's interests. The extent of marginalization is proof that the common good is not being achieved and that "important decisions are made on the basis of class or group interests and not on the basis of the interests of all the people." In fact, the bishops asserted, the state must encourage political participation so that the people can develop fully as human beings. Although a government can hold some concept of security, this must not collide with the common good. "Security, as a good of a nation, is incompatible with the permanent insecurity of the people." And the state must promote human development, but not just economic growth, which frequently impedes integral or complete development:

People develop when they grow in freedom and through participation; when their rights are respected and they possess at least primary resources for defense, for example, habeus corpus; when they have systems that discipline and assure mechanisms of control on the ascendency of the executive; when they can count on respect for the representation of subsidiary communities and the right to organize social institutions such as political parties, labor unions, and universities; when their right to information and the circulation of ideas is not limited by arbitrary forms of censorship; when they can freely choose those delegated with authority.[21]

Although not specific in its denunciation, this document elucidated the requisites for a Christian society, and the Brazilian regime and its model of socioeconomic development was found lacking in all respects. Further comments on the Brazilian model by bishops and other clergy left no doubt that the church was not itself proposing a model, but rather suggesting certain underlying principles by which any model can be judged.[22]

Another important statement which emanated from the CNBB was a position paper written for the Third General Assembly of the Latin American Episcopal Conference, originally scheduled for Puebla, Mexico, in October 1978. This document, prepared in April 1978, was a straightforward account of the Brazilian church's position vis à vis society and politics. This national statement took into account dozens of regional documents which were written with a tremendous amount of popular participation. The Puebla meeting galvanized grass-roots church sectors throughout the country, and the CNBB statement represented this high level of concern and participation.[23] The document pertained to all of Latin America, but was firmly based on the Brazilian situation.

The paper noted the weakness of the church, as evidenced by a devalorization of the sacraments and a lack of influence among the people, and called attention to positive aspects such as "a church that, more concerned with the people and more interested in the simple, knows how to assume prophetic positions." The bishops extensively described the sociopolitico-economic situation and observed "an exacerbation of conflict between oppressors and oppressed due to a situation of clamorous social injustice." They called special attention to the rural situation, to the elimination of the Indians, to the increasing marginalization of the population, to the concentration of wealth, and to the absolutization of the state by virtue of the Doctrine of National Security. They noted that "the situation of injustice is maintained by mechanisms of institutionalized violence, by forces of repression functioning beyond the law and enjoying the neglect, complacency, or complicity of the powers and generating desperate means which offer the pretext for more violent repressions."

In such a context the bishops offered suggestions for the evangelizing action of the church in Latin America and agreed that the pastoral action of the church should be based on the proclamation of the Good News and on the denunciation of injustice, all the while helping the faithful assume the responsibilities inherent in being the People of God. Liberating evangelization must exist side by side with the formation of grass-roots communities: "The presence of the church in the world must be presented as the presence of evangelic ferment which seeks to transform society in fraternal harmony, but in such a way that this fraternity is concretized in economic and political structures which permit the participation of all the people in the definition of the objectives to be achieved and which encourages a just distribution of income without privileges." Further, "The church assumes its prophetic mission with concrete actions, confronting the conflicts dividing Latin America in regard to human rights, the Doctrine of National Security, rightist and revolutionary radicalizations, and trilateralism."

Subsídios para uma política social (Aids for a Social Policy), published in August 1979, is evidence that this commitment continues even as the political system is opened up somewhat.[24] This document, prepared by the CNBB with the assistance of the church's research and training institution, IBRADES, was extremely important for it recognized that the political opening up was intended to defuse opposition and to coopt a broad range of political elements while continuing to consolidate the socioeconomic model. The main characteristics of the model were analyzed and it was argued that the only basis for a redistributive model should be the population's needs. Indeed, the whole approach to development as pursued in Brazil was questioned and it was suggested that other approaches from which the people would benefit were both necessary and possible.

The episcopal statements since 1974 have taken specific note of the weak position of the church, of the nature of the regime and its economic model, and of the persecution of those opposing this regime from within and without the church. By means of these statements the bishops have consolidated a new approach to influence which defines itself in opposition to the regime and opts for the lower classes. The bishops and clergy have reviewed the church's structures and processes in order to align themselves in accordance with this commitment to the oppressed. In order to illustrate their option in favor of those suffering as a result of the system, it may be useful to review briefly the church's activities in the areas of human rights, land holdings, and the plight of the Indians.

Defense of Human Rights

The CNBB-sponsored campaign to stimulate discussion and provide material on human rights got off to a slow start, largely because most people in the church took President Geisel at his word when he spoke of bringing the security apparatus under control. When it became obvious, by late 1975, that there were still flagrant violations of human rights, the campaign accelerated. At the national level, the Justice and Peace Commission assisted in the formation of regional and diocesan commissions, which, by 1978, were found in four regions and included some forty-two student groups.

There were a number of dimensions to this campaign: the publication and promotion of human-rights literature directed at all classes; research on specific instances of violations of human rights; legal assistance for those in need of it; provision of diocesan support and defense for those being persecuted and their families; and an informal communication network throughout the country.[25] It is hard to generalize from one region to another, but, essentially, a network and a procedure came to exist whereby violations of human rights could be made public, those being harmed could be assisted, and pressure could be brought to bear on the government to stop violations. Since repression has been haphazard and random, although an active policy, the network has had to be extremely flexible and only vaguely defined. It is worth noting that the larger, structural causes of human rights violations, the "causes of violence," were amply denounced in the various documents discussed previously.

As much of what happens in Brazil can only take place because of international power and trade relations, and because the Brazilian model, including the Doctrine of National Security, has become generalized else-where in Latin America, elements within the Brazilian church realized that human rights could not be defended within an exclusively national context. At the 1973 meeting of the General Assembly of the CNBB, the bishops agreed to promote an international project to more effectively defend human rights. It was decided that the CNBB would establish contact with other churches and institutions throughout the world in order to promote discussion of human rights prior to an international meeting called "International Study Days 'For a Society Overcoming Domination'." In the words of one of the documents they produced,

This project is aimed at deepening the concern and activity of churches and cultural and educational institutions throughout the world regarding the various types of domination to which peole today are subjected, to the violations of human rights consequent on those systems of oppression, and to the possibilities of educating people to understand, overcome and transform the structures of domination and the mechanisms of oppression.[26]

The project was promoted jointly by Dom Cândido Padin, bishop of Bauru, in Brazil, and by a Brazilian in Paris. In preparation for the International Study Days they commissioned extensive studies on the structural nature of the various types of systems of oppression and explored alternatives for achieving a more just social order, as well as denounced violations of human rights and the structures that allow those violations.

Over a period of two years a great many religious, intellectual, youth, and assistance organizations from several continents became involved and circulated documents and studies to all parts of the world. By spring 1978, there were fifteen hundred members in ninety countries, but the main coordinating offices remained in Paris and Brazil.

The International Study Days, originally scheduled for May 1977, were postponed to May 1978. Early in 1978, however, the Vatican ordered the CNBB to cease coordination activities. Nevertheless, at the CNBB General Assembly in April the bishops voted overwhelmingly to complete the final phase, publication of all the documents distributed during the project and of the conclusions from the meeting.

The International Study Days were held in João Pessoa in northeastern Brazil in July 1979, with the participation of 120 people from twenty-one countries. The project continues and the Brazilians also continue to promote it, although not officially through the CNBB.[27]

The Church and Land Tenure Conflicts

Even though a number of agrarian reform laws have been on the books, including one passed by the military government in November 1964 (Estatuto da Terra—Land Statute—law no. 4,504), it is correct to state that agrarian reform has never actually occurred in Brazil.[28] Rather, an unequal distribution of land persists, with the majority of the rural population passively struggling on their small holdings and a few owners controlling an overwhelming quantity of the land, as table 13 demonstrates.

Because the military government consolidated its regime by the agency of the Doctrine of National Security, extended its control over all of society, and further elaborated its economic model, the backward and unjust system of land holding worsened. For both political and economic reasons the government forcefully extended the capitalist system throughout the country, and changed thereby the traditional forms of subsistence agriculture: politically, to ensure control and avoid potential revolt by a disgruntled peasantry; economically, to encourage growth by expanding areas of cultivation and intensifying production. To increase the amount of land under cultivation and to intensify production, the government has relied on regional incentive schemes which allow individuals and corporations to write off a portion of their taxes if they invest in certain areas of the country, such as the Northeast and the Amazon, and in tourism and export-oriented industries. Moreover, the government will also aid investors in targeted areas by providing services such as electricity and communications.

All available studies show that these regional development schemes have resulted in some investment of foreign and domestic capital—heavily subsidized, of course—which has concentrated land into fewer units and created very few new jobs. Indeed, highly capital-intensive patterns are being followed in the industrialization of the Northeast and Belém and Manaus in the Amazon.

In the case of agriculture the prevailing pattern has been to clear the land in preparation for cattle raising. A very capital-intensive technology is employed in agricultural development as well, and again, capital is subsidized.[29] Subsistence farmers and their families have been forced off the land and have become virtual nomads in their own country, even though as settlers (*posseiros*) they presumably have legal rights. This type of regional development uproots local populations and there is no strong evidence that anything is being produced on this land. Much of the land concentration is the result of speculation by those seeking a hedge against inflation, and although such land acquisition is subsidized, it is not

Table 13
Landholdings by Category, 1972
(Percentage of total)

Category[a]	North		Northeast		Center-South		Brazil	
	Number	Area	Number	Area	Number	Area	Number	Area
Minifúndio	69.8	5.3	79.5	20.0	68.8	11.0	71.9	12.5
Rural enterprise	1.8	5.2	1.4	5.2	6.3	12.0	4.8	9.7
Latifúndio (A)	28.4	78.2	19.1	71.0	24.9	72.8	23.3	72.9
Latifúndio (B)	0.0	11.3	0.0	3.8	0.0	4.2	0.0	4.9
Total	100.0	100.0	100.0	100.0	100.0	100.0	100.0	100.0
Absolute number[b]	72,596.0	39,427.6	998,948.0	86,030.3	2,315,629.0	244,817.4	3,387,173.0	370,275.3

Source: Adapted from Dennis J. Mahar, *Desenvolvimento econômico da Amazônia: Uma análise das políticas governamentais*, Rio de Janeiro: IPEA, 1978, p. 211. Data are from Instituto de Colonização e Reforma Agrária (INCRA), *Estatísticas Cadastrais/1*, Brasília, 1974, pp. 311-312.
[a] Established by *Estatuto de Terra* (Law no. 4-504, 30 November 1964).
[b] in thousands of hectares.

necessarily promoting the growth of the economy.[30]
In the midst of this turbulence and these tensions the church first became involved in the area most dramatically affected—the Amazon. Land was rapidly becoming concentrated, and since the social infrastructure is so slight in the area, the people being evicted had no means of defense and no one to raise issue except the church. In 1971 Dom Pedro Casaldáliga, bishop of São Félix, issued *Uma igreja da Amazônia em conflito com o latifúndio e a marginalização social (A Church in the Amazon in Conflict with the Latifundia and Social Marginalization)*, a 125-page document describing and analyzing the situation in his diocese, with particular emphasis on the problem of land.[31] Casaldáliga's statement was similar to the statement issued by the bishops of the Centerwest in 1973 *(Marginalização de um povo)* in that both dealt with the agrarian situation and showed that the predicament of the rural population was worsening and both outlined the church's responsibilities to that population.

Once attention was called to the land tenure issue by those in the areas most seriously affected, it became clear that the same type of problem was epidemic in Brazil. Throughout the Northeast, in Bahia, and even in São Paulo, people in the church became aware of the significance and severity of the land tenure situation. Moreover, they correctly predicted that this would shortly cease to be a uniquely rural problem, since people forced off their land would inevitably end up in the cities and thus swell the *subúrbios* (slums) on the periphery.

As the problem became evident, it was decided that the national Justice and Peace Commission, in conjunction with the CNBB, would hold a national conference in Goiânia in June 1975 to discuss the issue and propose a strategy for dealing with it. The conference participants took steps to promote agrarian reform through all possible agencies, to found a Comissão de Terras (Land Commission) linked to the CNBB for the purposes of assessing reform programs and publicizing and denouncing cases of injustice, and to encourage diocesan groups to organize juridical assistance and undertake information campaigns aimed at peasants and pastoral agents. All of these steps have been carried out as a national team travels around the country to promote studies and organize various local teams.

In November 1977, the commission, now called the Pastoral Land Commission (Comissão Pastoral de Terra), convoked the First National Assembly on the Land Pastoral in order to take stock of the operation and develop further strategy. Some of the commission's activities included a monthly bulletin, studies on the law, documentation of land-acquisition cases, and case studies of conflicts which had led to people being forced from their land.[32] In dioceses throughout the country minicommissions were set up to function along the same lines as the Pastoral Land Commission as well as to specifically assist people in defending themselves against unscrupulous individuals and groups who were attempting to take their land —frequently with the support of the authorities. At the national level attention was drawn to this increasingly touchy topic by a Parliamentary Commission of Inquiry called in 1977 by the opposition in Congress to look into the situation in the rural areas. The several bishops invited to testify at the Parliamentary Commission made extremely forceful statements and have continued to call national attention to the problem.[33]

The land situation has become worse, with increased violence on the part of large landowners answered by those being forced from the land. The bishops, assembled for the eighteenth General Assembly of the CNBB in February 1980, overwhelmingly approved (172 to 4) a scathing critique of Brazil's land situation and government policies which, in their view, aggravate this situation.[34] The bishops linked the socioeconomic implications of the development model to the land situation and argued for serious agrarian reform. Their position, as reported in this document and as supported by their institutes and publications, brought them into direct conflict with the regime, which was seeking to "rationalize" or "capitalize" the land situation in order to bring in more foreign exchange.

Land tenure is a vital area of concern and the church's involvement in it is crucial. The agrarian situation in Brazil has never been particularly favorable to either the lower classes or productivity, and the effects of the regime and its economic growth model have caused the situation to deteriorate that much farther. In the face of serious economic problems and the human suffering involved, elements in the church have become involved and have the support of the CNBB and other national organizations linked to the church. By means of a number of national meetings and a commission dedicated specifically to this problem, the church has drawn national and international attention to the land tenure issue and has frequently encouraged active resistance on the part of those being forced off their land. This issue, more than all the other problems facing Brazil today, is focal, for it links rural unrest to urban conflicts, national economic policy to international investment, and radicalizes those involved at the lower levels. Land tenure is the stuff that the classic French, Mexican, and Chinese revolutions were made of, and the authorities seem intent on creating just such a situation in Brazil through policies of what can be termed "conservative modernization."

The Church and Defense of the Indians

Another ecclesiastical organization which in many ways parallels and overlaps the Land Pastoral is the Native Missionary Council (Conselho Indigenista Missionário—CIMI), established in 1972 in an attempt to defend the few remaining indigenous Brazilians. The history of the Indian in Brazil is unfortunately similar to that of the North American Indian and is essentially an account of the elimination of a people—an unintentional (or otherwise) genocide. At present there are only 150,000 to 200,000 unassimilated Indians remaining, and their very existence is increasingly tenuous because the government's planned development of the Amazon and Centerwest effectively guarantees their total extinction within the next ten years.[35] As SUDAM (Superintendência de Desenvolvimento de Amazônia—Superintendency for the Development of Amazonia) projects, other development projects, national integration schemes, and so forth, concentrate land and open roads, the Indians lose their territory, are moved from one reserve to another, are infected, forced to work, abused, considered a romantic holdover that a developing Brazil can ill afford, and are generally encouraged to disappear from the face of the earth. Their precarious situation is documented in a score of books and receives attention in the world media and, interestingly enough, in *O Estado de São Paulo*. There is no evidence, however, that the government pays much attention, but rather the inverse.

The original Indian Protection Service (Serviço de Proteção dos Indios—SPI) was so corrupt that it was replaced in 1968 by the Fundação Nacional do Indio (National Indian Foundation—FUNAI). The then-head of FUNAI, General Bandeira de Melo, gave an indication, in July 1970, of the organization's effectiveness in defending the Indians when he stated that "we will pay attention to the Indian, but without impeding progress."[36] Since the regime's view of progress is well documented, little elaboration is needed to show that the Indians are not being defended against loss of land, invasions, and general ill treatment. Benign neglect in such a situation is undoubtedly disastrous.

The church has always been involved with the Indians, often to the Indians' detriment. With the general development of a new approach to influence in the late 1960s—which coincided with increased pressure on the Indians as the economic model became consolidated—elements in the church began to take stock of the situation and realized that they were at least partly to blame for the plight of these people and that if the church were not to defend them nobody would. However, responsibility in the abstract was one thing and action another, and the church was obliged to admit that it was unprepared to deal with the problem in a concrete manner. For centuries the isolated areas of the country had been served by missionaries and even in the late 1960s most ecclesiastical jurisdictions (normally prelacies) in Indian territories were staffed by foreign priests who were geographically isolated, out of touch with linguistics and modern anthropology, Europe-oriented, and more at ease with their few white parishioners than with the Indians. From approximately 1967 on, several bishops and missionaries acted to remedy this situation; the founding of CIMI in 1972 with the support of the CNBB was the eventual result. By 1974 CIMI had assumed its present form and had evolved considerably in a number of ways, all aimed at coordination and improvement of church involvement with the Indians. CIMI holds conferences for missionaries, teachers, and lay volunteers at local, regional, and national meetings (such as the National Assembly in Goiânia in June 1975) to exchange information and map out strategies; arranges meetings of Indian chiefs from various tribes to coordinate defense strategies, particularly with regard to the government; offers courses for missionaries and others involved with the Indians; publishes a bulletin (*Boletim do CIMI*) and other documents which support the Indians and denounce their loss of rights and land; and intervenes with the government to amend legislation (for example, the Estatuto do Indio, [Indian Statute] 1972) or ensure the implementation of existing laws.[37] As stated by CIMI in 1977, "the native pastoral today is a liberating process inspired in the Gospel of Jesus Christ."[38]

It is important to note that CIMI has been linked to the CNBB since its inception and that the General Assembly of the CNBB acted in 1977 to make this connection even stronger. A director of CIMI sits on the Pastoral Commission of the CNBB, activities of CIMI are coordinated regionally in conjunction with regional and diocesan plans, and CIMI is integrated into the Joint Pastoral and has a voice in the Justice and Peace Commission as well as in the Pastoral Land Commission. A close connection between the two organizations not only increases efficiency in coordination of plans and programs, but also supports and legitimates CIMI when it is attacked by opposing factions. Attacks are common at the local level, where CIMI personnel are frequently denied access to the Indian reserves, at the regional level, where CIMI people, because of harassment or blocked communication, are not permitted in meetings of Indians hosted by FUNAI, and at the national level, where the organization is directly denounced. Since the government controls the reserves, CIMI can only protest these incidents of bad faith. For instance, in early 1977 the Minister of the Interior, Rangel Reis, referred to the

position of the church as "unreal, feudal and backward-looking with regard
to the Indians . . . . Further, I do not believe in the good faith of a certain
religious minority calling itself defender of the humble and casting the
government as the persecutor of the less favored population." He indicated
that he had never seen a constructive proposal from CIMI and cast doubts
on its jurisdiction. He stated that the government would tighten up on
contacts with the Indians, and anyone involved would have to follow the
government's program of "progressive emancipation."[39]

CIMI has maintained its momentum as its orientation has come to be
more clearly defined. The conflicts it has been involved in have further
served to justify defense of the Indians, even while eliminating the
possibility of reliance on state structures and resources. Conflicts have
included personal attacks on and intimidation of such bishops as Dom
Pedro Casaldáliga and Dom Tomás Balduíno (president of CIMI), frontal
attacks on CIMI by FUNAI elements, and the murders of Pe. Rodolfo
Lunkenbein and Pe. João Bosco Penido Burnier in 1976. More recently,
Dom Estevão Cardoso Avelar of Conceição do Araguaia and Dom Alano
Pena of Marabá (both in the Amazon area) were interrogated and accused,
under the Law of National Security, of a connection with an armed
confrontation between settlers and the military. Although found innocent
by the military court, they and other church personnel have endured the
constant slander of General Euclydes Figueiredo, former commander of
the Eighth Military Region in Pará and now subchief of the Army Chief of
Staff's office. It is interesting that this General Figueiredo is the brother of
General João Baptista Figueiredo, former head of SNI (Serviço Nacional
de Informação—National Information Service) and now president of the
country.

Because harassment and arrest are manifestly unsuccessful, the
government is attempting another ploy, based on the large number of
foreign church-personnel in the Amazon. During recent years the
government has refused to grant permanent visas to church people going to
this area, in an attempt to dry up the pool of potentially radical elements.
Furthermore, at least in the case of grants from the United States, such as
Inter-American Foundation fellowships, prior approval of the Brazilian
government is required before these funds can be released. Such
indications seem to presage a general attack on the international linkages of
the church in order to isolate and suppress those elements the government
considers inimical. In my view, this strategy not only will fail but will
backfire as more Brazilian laity are drawn into the fray, with even greater
likelihood of radicalization of the populace. The current trends and the
church's response to these trends are well expressed in the following

statements from the November 1976 *Boletim do CIMI*:

Why aren't things going well? Why is it that all these things are happening [death and persecution of settlers, Indians, and religious]? We remember, the people remember, and the church remembers that it was in recent years that things got worse—for the people, naturally: peons, settlers, Indians, small farmers, workers . . . . Amazônia has been taken by force by the large agri-industrial firms, by large estates, by cattle, sytematically forcing people from the land they cultivate. The people who have come here from far away, who have already migrated several times, who have traveled all over the country, who have watered this land with their sweat, again being forced from the land they clear and till . . . for the large estates, for the cattle. The present is critical as there is nowhere else to go, everyplace is full, some places two or three times over. And the large estates keep coming, growing, strangling, expulsing and massacring the small, the people who want to live honestly from their own work and for this reason need land.

This is the conflict that confronts the Indian and the settler with the land shark or the new owner, men with cattle; the weakness of the small producer with the abundant incentives for the large enterprise; the abandonment of the worker with the legal (and police) protection of the large owner.

For the people's church the option is clear: either silence in the face of the facts and omission before so many injustices, or by assuming a position in defense of those persecuted by this iniquitous system, living the same lives and running the same risks. Consistency to the Gospel demands commitment to the oppressed, with the man who suffers and is persecuted.

The Archdiocese of São Paulo

At first, it may seem inappropriate to include a discussion of São Paulo in a chapter which presumably deals with national illustrations. However, there are a number of compelling reasons to illustrate the main characteristics of pastoral action in the Archdiocese of São Paulo. By size the largest Catholic archdiocese in the world (eight million people, of whom at least seven million are baptized), it is as large as many countries in Latin America. Although only one archdiocese—albeit divided into seven regions, each with its own bishop—it carries a great deal of weight within the State of São Paulo, which ultimately reverberates to all parts of the country. This is due not only to sheer size, but also to the fact that São Paulo is the financial and industrial center of Brazil; it is, to use the analogy popular in São Paulo, the locomotive pulling the other twenty cars. São Paulo's significance is important in real and symbolic terms for the rest of the country, and, as the showcase of the Brazilian miracle, it represents, in many ways, the direction the rest of the country would like to take. Those people being forced off the land in the Amazon are generally ousted by São Paulo-based corporations and will probably try to come to São Paulo to live and work.

The previous cardinal-archbishop of São Paulo, Dom Agnello Rossi, has been tagged as a conservative, cooperative with the government and disapproving of CNBB-prompted change in the church. However, Cardinal Rossi was removed to Rome in 1971 and replaced by his most able auxiliary bishop, Dom Paulo Evaristo Arns.

Dom Paulo has achieved prominence in defending those oppressed by the regime and has confronted the government, and particularly its security apparatus, on a number of occasions. This caused enmity between him and members of the government, including the secretary of security in the State-General's office, Erasmo Dias, and President Geisel. The cardinal opposed the president's request to refrain from participation in an ecumenical eulogy to commemorate the murdered Vladimir Herzog. In retaliation, the police invaded the Pontifical Catholic University not long after, while Dom Paulo was in Rome, and arrested over 700 students on the grounds of "subversive demonstration." The archdiocesan radio station was shut down and the archdiocesan newspaper, *O São Paulo*, was censored long after other papers had been freed. The positions assumed by the cardinal, however, have won attention and praise from opposition elements (who are actively seeking his political support) and from large numbers of people who view him as their defender. For example, on the Feast of Corpus Christi in 1978, some 120,000 people gathered before the cathedral in the Praça da Sé (Cathedral Square) to hear him speak on unity. This was not a general middle-class audience from the urban areas, but rather grass-roots groups of people specifically organized in the periphery communities. It is hard to imagine any state, or even national politician being able to attract this many people.

Although the personal prominence of the cardinal is important, and although as an individual he lends a certain set of priorities to the archdiocese, it is also important to indicate what is going on in the archdiocese apart from the cardinal's activities.

As will be seen in Chapter 6, change in any diocese involves the relationship between the person heading it (bishop or archbishop), the group around him, and the larger religious and sociopolitical environment. In São Paulo, as in the other dioceses undergoing change, the archbishop and his group are committed to redirecting the church's approach to influence, so their perception of the environment is important. Studies (particularly *São Paulo 1975: Growth and Poverty*) have shown that development has benefited the few to the detriment of many, so the archdiocese has involved large segments of the church in a program of study and planning whereby the people have a say in determining church priorities. To prepare the archdiocese's first two-year plan, in 1976-1977, a church group spent eight months analyzing the situation in the city and the specific needs of the people. They then narrowed the priorities down to twenty-five and selected four of these as the most important. Through this process the orientation moved from internal church concerns, or the pastoral narrowly construed, to what the people themselves valued. It was, in the words of one of those involved, seeking out the key problem-areas for the people, and led to what the study group termed "politically liberating evangelization" as the focus of the church's role in society.[40] This means that the resources and main interest of the church in São Paulo were directed primarily and with the highest priority to four areas in 1976-1977 and again in 1978-1979.

The first priority area was the Basic Christian Community (CEB). These grass-roots communities, mainly on the periphery of São Paulo, were the home of three million people struggling to survive. The CEBs sought to relate concrete societal and political problems to religious themes, or, in the words of those involved, to link Faith and Life.

The second priority area was that of human rights. Support for the marginal components of society was expressed in books, pamphlets, newspapers, and by means of legal assistance and denunciations of human rights violations. The movement was sponsored at the archdiocesan level by the Justice and Peace Commission of São Paulo, as well as by some of the periphery parishes.

The third area concerned the Workers' Pastoral, by means of which workers, particularly those in industry, were assisted in organizing to defend their rights. Many of the participants in the successful, if illegal, strikes in early 1978 and April and May 1980 were involved in this Workers' Pastoral.

The final priority area for 1976-1979 dealt with the Pastoral of the Periphery. This pastoral involved the building of community centers, assistance in the training of indigenous community leaders, and the encouragement of joint action between the periphery communities and the archdiocese of São Paulo to generally improve personal security and transportation and other basic services. In the fourth plan (1980-1981) the areas have been expanded somewhat to include the land situation, the formation of intermediary groups, and emphasis on the need for new social, economic, and political models.

These priorities, which are actively and concretely being implemented, indicate a certain redirection of the São Paulo, and national, church away from past approaches to influence. These areas all involve elemental issues with tremendous and polemic sociopolitical implications, and the priorities indicate, of course, an alternative approach to influence which favors the lower classes. This option has alienated some people in the other classes, who have referred to Dom Paulo's archdiocese as "his church which is not the church of all the people." On the other hand, the new approach to influence enjoys tremendous support among the lower classes, and it is impressive to see intellectuals—Catholic and non-Catholic—working with these various components to provide legal advice, to help organize community centers and human rights organizations, as well as to provide expertise for other church programs, such as CIMI and the Land Pastoral.

During the very important and harsh metal workers' strike in São Paulo in early 1980, the archdiocese, as well as the CNBB, provided a tremendous amount of moral and material support for the strikers. The aid provided by the church included supportive statements at all levels, allowing the strikers to meet in the churches, and the provision of various types of assistance for strikers and their families. Again, the commitment to work with the poor, and thereby incur the wrath of the wealthy, was confirmed by actions as well as words.

In conclusion, a newly solidified approach to influence for a predominant archdiocese of the Brazilian church is evident. As will be made clear in the next chapter, this does not mean that all Brazilian bishops (let alone all clergy and religious) are committed to this approach; in fact, a few are actively opposed. However, the combination of the CNBB, now speaking for all the bishops nationally, and the reorientation of the Archdiocese of São Paulo makes for a strong movement. The CNBB statements from 1975 on and the formation of organizations concerned with human rights, land tenure, and Indians, and intrinsically linked to the church, are indications of substantial change in the Brazilian church's overall orientation. The new approach clearly favors the lower classes and other oppressed sectors and seeks to assist them by means of a variety of instruments and processes. Although some middle and upper class support is undoubtedly lost because of this reorientation, it is made up elsewhere. It is worth recalling the tremendous crowd listening to the cardinal of São Paulo on the Feast of Corpus Christi, as well as the popular support for the church's land pastoral. My interviews in June 1978 indicated that politicians— old hacks as well as the young and more radical—are turning to the church for support. And, it may be worth noting, books dealing with the church appear frequently on the best-seller lists: the *Veja* list for 3 May 1978 included three and that of 24 May 1978 included four.[41] Who would have expected such interest in the church ten, or even five, years ago? But in the context of the regime and its economic model, the church's actions seem appropriate and even demanded. It may well be that this decade will witness a resurgent church.

6. Innovations in the Dioceses

Although an examination of the national church can usually provide insight into the process of change in that church, it is the diocese that is the critical level for action in the Catholic church. The church is composed of an agglomeration of dioceses within any country, each headed by a bishop. In Brazil there are 217 ecclesiastical divisions: 32 archdioceses, 138 dioceses, 41 prelacies, and 6 miscellaneous divisions. These divisions are led by bishops who may choose to form a national conference to take public positions representing a majority of them. Although this conference does supposedly represent the bishops, they are by no means bound to its principles or suggestions in the conduct of church business in their own dioceses.

The bishop has always been central to the functioning of the local church or diocese, is answerable only to the Pope, and remains a key figure in spite of the role granted national episcopal conferences; indeed, the Second Vatican Council reaffirmed the importance of the bishop's role. Thus, although the CNBB may develop a national commitment for a new approach to influence as a result of its position in the church hierarchy and may form organizations such as CIMI to represent it in certain problem areas, what actually takes place in any diocese depends, finally, on the bishop.

Certainly any bishop can agree during a national conclave to very advanced social statements, but implementation is another matter. The CNBB is in a tricky situation in this regard. On the one hand, national positions are often assumed and implemented by the CNBB regional subdivisions—in many cases regardless of the local dioceses' orientation in these matters. On the other hand, particularly since 1964, the CNBB has become very much aware of its charge to represent all the bishops, so it cannot extend too far beyond what its members as a whole would want. This ambivalent state continues, and even as the national organization effectively works at maximum efficiency to define positions, it must constantly reaffirm the primacy of the bishop in his diocese. For example, in the same document which recognizes the church's lack of power and influence, and its consequent freedom to change, we find the following: "The 'central' level, as the point of reference for pastoral planning, is the diocesan level. In fact, the local church is the fundamental decision making unit in that which concerns orientation, conditioning, and implementation of church action."[1]

It is up to the diocese, and primarily the bishop as its head, to decide how to act or not to act on any given issue. However, one function of the CNBB is to provide models and services to the dioceses in helping them act to bring about change. This role had been understated and thus it took several years to show results. Since 1971, though, the CNBB has been very active, organized, and obvious in promoting change in the dioceses. It sponsors studies, provides documentation, arranges courses, and supports a very energetic system of communication. Although it upholds the somewhat abstract theses of the Joint Pastoral Plan of 1966-1970, the CNBB also adopts concrete themes. For 1977-1979 CEBs, family pastoral, urban pastoral, and the responsibility of the church in the world were the foci.[2] The Conference provides an impetus, a climate, and some instruments (groups and research, for example) for encouraging change at all levels, but particularly in the dioceses. Since the model promoted by the CNBB is frequently far more advanced than the diocesan orientation toward social change, its orientation can be used as a sort of standard or yardstick for comparison between dioceses. We shall see that there is a continuum of change, with some dioceses having passed far beyond anything the CNBB could promote, while others have merely created formal titles and empty organizations to demonstrate their conformity with the national church. That the latter felt obliged at all to imitate the forms does, of course, indicate that the CNBB serves a model-providing function—models which may or may not be implemented by clergy or the laity.

The information to be presented in this chapter is primarily drawn from eight dioceses, of which two each are located in the South, Northeast, Center, and State of São Paulo. (These dioceses will hereafter be referred to as South 1, South 2, Northeast 1, Northeast 2, Center 1, Center 2, S.P. 1, and S.P. 2.) Our research team spent approximately one week in each diocese interviewing most of those closely connected with the local church, including the bishop, some clergy, and some of the laity. The team reviewed all available documentation (including CERIS data) and generally observed the dynamic of the local church. I personally conducted 80 interviews in these dioceses, primarily with bishops and clergy, and my assistant another 210, mainly with members of both traditional and modern religious groups and associations. I also reviewed the studies carried out by other researchers in the other dioceses, including São Paulo, Rio de Janeiro, Salvador, Recife, Fortaleza, and in the Amazon area. Having consulted as well with students of religion and politics at CEAS (Centro de Estudos e Ação Social—Center of Studies and Social Action), CERIS, IBRADES, and the INP, and with national and regional coordinators of the CNBB, I feel that the patterns and explanations which pertain to these eight dioceses can be generalized to most of the other dioceses in the country.

It must be briefly recalled that the Brazilian church is historically burdened by weak religious influence and regional and derivative variations in structures and approaches to the pastoral. Its reorganization in the twentieth century served to direct it toward Rome rather than toward the people, made it highly structured and largely closed, and left all decision making in the hands of the clergy. At the same time its strategy of influence called for particular attention to the upper and middle classes, evidenced by the establishment of elite institutions such as schools and in the general orientation of religious associations.

The church was generally conservative, strongly antiliberal and anti-Communist, and closely linked to the state from at least Dom Leme's time. This conservatism was somewhat mitigated, as pointed out in previous chapters, by an innovative approach to the sociopolitical situation, demonstrated by the founding of the CNBB and the subsequent activities of the ACB, MEB, and rural and urban unions.

To understand change in the church (which is really a collection of local churches or dioceses), many aspects or facets must be studied in light of the institution's historical vicissitudes, both national and international. Any discussion of change in the church is necessarily multidimensional, but a discussion of three dimensions will serve as an overall outline of the eight dioceses rather than as a comprehensive look at any one diocese. These dimensions will be viewed as a continuum, from the traditional model to an example proposed by the CNBB for the future.

The first of the three dimensions is the normative, or the church's ideological or programmatic approach to its role or mission of influence. This dimension is derived from categories of the CNBB as seen in documents and statements in support of a national orientation, and may be broken down into three aspects: the corporate, or institutional, the religious, and the political. The first deals with the church's institutional role in the Christian world. Is the church a monopoly which plays a dominant role, or is it a service which must prove its worth to the individual and society? The religious aspect of the normative dimension has to do with the church's religious purpose. Is the church's primary role that of dispenser of the sacraments to an already-committed flock? Or is the church to actively evangelize on the assumption that the flock has yet to be won (or, that it was won on the wrong terms)? The third aspect treats the church's political role in society. Is the church to stay out of politics and rely on past understandings with the elites? Or is it to admit its past role as supporter of the status quo and accept for the future the role of liberator (as suggested by the Medellín documents and elaborated in CNBB statements)?

The second dimension deals with structures and processes within the church, which is to say, decision making structures and processes and the type of involvement the church is willing to undertake. Ultimately this boils down to who is and who is not "the church." The first point necessarily deals with the individuals or organizations involved in making decisions of any importance. Is all decision making centered in the bishop, and possibly the clergy, despite the fact that most dioceses have adopted at least the rudiments of pastoral planning as promoted by the CNBB? Or is decision making decentralized to include the laity, even down to groups at the grass-roots level? The second point involves the style of the approach to questions and issues of importance in the matter of change. Is the style closed, definitive, technical, *ex cathedra*, and thereby limits or constrains the process of change? Or is the style open, questioning, reactive, and inclusive so that change can be a continuing process?

The third dimension concerns the structures, programs, and groups whereby religious influence may be exerted and contact established with individuals and society. One aspect of this dimension involves sheer institutional presence. Is the church involved in all aspects of society, with large institutions such as schools, hospitals, and so forth? Does it have many personnel and resources? Or is the church limited to a few priests, nuns, and laymen without sizable institutional infrastructure? This point cannot be viewed on the continuum of traditional to modern, since some dioceses never had many resources, but it is an important feature for understanding limits on change.

A second aspect of this dimension is the orientation and clientele of diocesan institutions and programs (assistance, radio, newspapers). Are they mainly for the upper classes (elite schools run by the orders)? Are they for everyone, but of probable greater benefit to the upper classes (hospitals)? Are they for the lower classes but with a strong emphasis on charity and social welfare (orphanages and dispensaries)? Or are they primarily for the lower classes but with emphasis on self-help and equality (cooperatives, unions, community gardens, basic education)? To what degree do these institutions and programs rely on state support to carry out their functions, and does this support compromise the diocese with local and national government?

A third point concerns diocesan groups which involve the laity, and the key links mediating between diocese and individual. Traditionally, most parishes contained various religious groups and associations dating from the sixteenth through the early twentieth centuries. Many of these groups still exist and even predominate in some dioceses. However, newer associations and movements were formed during the 1940-1960 period which seek to deepen the faith of the individual, such as the cursilhos and the Christian Family Movement (MFC). Since the mid-1960s there has been a trend toward the formation of groups which ostensibly function to involve the individual more deeply in religious and administrative activities, that is, to prepare the laity for the sacraments, the reading of the liturgy in the Mass, administration of parish facilities and finances, and so on.

In addition, there is currently a trend in Brazil and other parts of Latin America to form Basic Christian Communities (Comunidade Eclesial de Base—CEB), which tend to replace not only the other groups, but also, in large part, the parish structure itself. These communities are vigorously promoted by the CNBB and carry great social and religious implications.

The Normative Dimension

The normative approach to the church's role or mission is often difficult to ascertain, as all of the eight dioceses have at least formally adopted the CNBB's statements and positions—sometimes slavishly so. However, the purpose of the interviews and observation in the dioceses was to distinguish between word and action and evaluate formal statements in light of other information, with the various structures and activities of the diocese kept in mind. We must also consider the extent to which diocesan personnel and structures (such as parishes, programs, and groups) follow a particular approach.

The eight dioceses fell along a broad continuum of the corporate, or institutional aspect of the church in society (see table 14, p. 110).[3] In two of them (South 2 and S.P. 2) the bishops and clergy simply assumed that the church represented the religion of the entire population, although in South

2 the bishop was somewhat upset by the inroads made by Protestantism and Spiritism. Neither South 2 nor S.P. 2 had adopted CNBB programs and plans with any degree of commitment. S.P. 2 was just beginning to discuss a CNBB program, nine years after its initiation at the national level, and South 2 (whose bishop held an important position in the CNBB) had instituted a program in only the most formalistic manner; both dioceses still assumed that the church was predominant and remained as a spokesman for all the society. As South 2 stated in its plan for 1974, "We are not presenting here a pastoral plan for the Archdiocese. This follows the plan for all the region [of the CNBB]."[4] The auxiliary bishop, in charge of implementing the plan, could not explain the plan's details nor how it was to be carried out.

In another diocese (Center 2) the clergy were questioning the predominance of the church and gradually concluding that it could not maintain such a façade and must change. The process of change had just begun, however, and as of 1975 only three priests in two parishes were involved.

In a fourth diocese (Northeast 2) the bishop and priests were more aware of the need for change, since it was obvious that the church lacked influence there. These clergy had formally accepted the progressive CNBB regional orientation, and the preface to their 1975 pastoral statement gave some idea of their tentative commitment to this line: "We hope that the present outline of a pastoral plan will be but one more incentive in the apostolic work of our priests, of our religious, of people working in the pastoral and of the good people of God in this blessed diocese . . . ." Northeast 2 was on the verge of a commitment to a service role, but by 1975 the commitment had been taken to heart by only three or four nuns and two priests.

In two other dioceses (S.P. 1 and South 1) the bishops were strongly committed to the adoption of a new, service function which denied the view of the church as a power structure and saw it in terms of serving the people. In the words of one of the bishops, "The church is the People of God, in which the priest and the bishop must serve. We intend to assist the layman in terms of providing a service with the intention, among other things, of helping him discover his role." The bulletin of South 1 stated that "the general objective of the diocese can be summarized as follows: liberation of the People of God by means of their involvement in vital communities." Although the hierarchical levels in these two dioceses defined this service role and assumed a positive commitment, not all the clergy were in complete agreement.

In the last two dioceses (Northeast 1 and Center 1) the option clearly saw the church as a service institution, an attitude which was assumed by the overwhelming majority of clergy, nuns, and laity involved in the pastoral. In Center 1, an assembly in 1972 was attended by the thirty-five religious personnel in the diocese (bishop, priests, and nuns) plus thirty-eight lay people from a predominantly rural lower-class background, nearly all of whom opted for a pastoral aimed at the lower classes, that is, "preferential attention to those marginalized by the society and by the church." As a consequence, the one dissenting priest in the diocese and most of the upper-class laity all but withdrew their support from the church. Northeast 1 also opted for service in the sense of helping people help themselves. The church emphasized participation, autonomy, and independence, but not without disturbing some of the more conservative members of the clergy and the upper classes. In this diocese, church relations with the military (an army base is located within the diocese) and with local government were somewhat tense, and the bishop was declared *persona non grata* by the municipal government. All remaining priests and nuns were service oriented, and a great many lay people were also involved in the movement.

It is obvious that the positions of the dioceses cover a broad range in terms of this dimension (the approximate positions of the dioceses vis à vis each other are indicated in table 14). Some dioceses were not changed at all by the stance adopted and promoted by the CNBB, whereas others surpassed suggested norms and made a point of giving preferential treatment to the lower classes. In so doing, they alienated some elements within the local church (who then either left the church or moved geographically to find a more congenial diocese) and they are most certainly at odds with the local civil and military powers.

The pattern of the dioceses, views of the religious role of the church in society was almost identical to the pattern of their views of its corporate aspect. South 2 and S.P. 2, however, were joined by Center 2. In all three, the sole religious activity was the administration of the sacraments. In South 2 the bishop and clergy seemed concerned only with filling the churches on Sundays and with the number of people receiving communion, In Center 2 the only frame of reference seemed to be the sacraments, and S.P. 2 prided itself on having the highest mass attendance and communion percentage in Brazil and the greatest number of novenas offered.

In Northeast 2 the primary activity was the administration of the sacraments, but there was beginning a desire to change the nature of this administration. Instead of simply administering and assuming that the task was done, the clergy wanted to use the sacraments as a means to evangelize—that is, to deepen the faith by encouraging awareness. Their

1975 plan indicated this desire "to take advantage of the preparation for Baptism, First Communion, and Marriage as excellent opportunities to evangelize families . . . . To take advantage of important events in the liturgical calendar (Advent, Christmas, Holy Week, Easter) and of the parish (feasts of patron saints in May) and of the pastoral (Campaign for Fraternity, Bible Week) to promote unity for a task in global and systematic evangelization." Northeast 2 was prepared to take advantage of traditional holidays and other religious events to begin evangelization. At that time the use of the sacraments as an evangelization tool was promoted by only a minority of the diocese's clergy, but the process seemed to have begun.

In two other dioceses, S.P. 1 and South 1, the administration of the sacraments remained the principal goal, but somewhat self-consciously so, in line with their evangelizing activities. The clergy were aware that administration carried many social and even political implications. The administration of the sacraments had not yet been cut back, since many of the priests in the dioceses intended to use them for evangelization.

In Center 1 and Northeast 1 the primary approach was to deemphasize the sacraments and actively evangelize. In Northeast 1 it was difficult to find masses, even on Sundays (as we learned to our chagrin, since one part of the survey required application after mass), and the overwhelming trend was to promote social involvement by means of a process of evangelization. Center 1 was even more committed to this line: "[Our] option—less time for the sacraments and more for evangelization and the organization of groups which are the basis of communities and dedicated people." They in effect exchanged masses for evangelizing groups. For example, in one Center 1 parish, which had three priests (an unusually large number), in 1967 there were three masses a day and four on Sundays, with many baptisms and weddings. In 1975 there were two masses on Sunday, one on Thursday, and joint or multiple marriage ceremonies and baptisms at which all social classes were present. Many of the upper-class parishioners reacted negatively to this class mixture and began to go elsewhere for their weddings and baptisms—which, in all objectivity, had been almost purely social events under the previous arrangement.

In this category (the religious aspect) the dioceses were faced with an option which followed from the corporate view of the church in society— either to continue as before and administer the sacraments without too much consideration as to the implications or to choose a strategy which emphasized evangelization.

The pattern in regard to the church's principal political role or purpose in society was almost identical to that of the other two aspects. In two of the dioceses, S.P. 2 and South 2, politics was a "nonissue." S.P. 2 prided itself on contacts with the local government and the resources this amicable relationship provided. The three local newspapers were favorably disposed toward the church and published all religious announcements. Despite the fact that the 1974-1975 plan of this diocese referred to the prophetic role of the church, I heard no critical word uttered by religious personnel concerning any level of government or the local business elites. In South 2, good civil relations were taken as a given, and the official volume issued by the city on its fortieth anniversary bore a cover picture of the city with the cathedral and chancery offices in prominence.

In one diocese, Center 2, there was some discussion of political issues and a tentative acceptance of the liberating role. However, because of the presence of the military, the conservative orientation of the older clergy and the local society, such acceptance was tentative indeed. Our research in this diocese was jeopardized when one of the older priests warned his congregation to be very careful when answering our questionnaire—advice which was given despite prior approval for the survey from the local bishop.

In S.P. 1 and South 1 there was an awareness of politics and a critical attitude toward links with the government. However, the church's orientation was still overwhelmingly religious there. Political matters were dealt with in personal terms, people were advised to resolve their own problems in a responsible manner, and no emphasis was placed on the progressive political role of the church-as-institution. This limited political role may have been due in part to the comparative economic abundance of these dioceses: both were located in prosperous areas with one of the highest per capita income levels in Brazil.

The opposite was true in Northeast 2, which lacked almost all resources yet felt a commitment of some kind was required. It had adopted, and in part was implementing, a liberating role. The general objectives of the diocese, as stated in its plan for 1975, was "to attempt to implement the goal of the church of Vatican II in the diocese, especially by announcing the liberating word giving the people consciousness of their value, dignity, and mission in the world and thereby making them co-responsible in an intense, unified, and realistic pastoral action."

In Northeast 1 and Center 1 a clear and conscious plan was directed toward liberation. In Northeast 1 this plan was recognized and promoted by all the clergy, a situation which led to any number of tensions and conflicts with the local and regional governments. Priests were imprisoned and the bishop defamed. As the clergy stated in an evaluation of its experience, "It is important to stress the methodology adopted: it is a process of consciousness [raising] based on reality and on the Gospel so that reality is illuminated by the Word of God and the Word of God is interpreted and elaborated by reality." The priests were keenly aware of the importance of methodology and were constantly refining and elaborating it, all for the ultimate goal, liberation.

These three aspects of the normative dimension, or the approach to influence of the church, point in much the same direction. If the church still perceives itself as possessing power and influence, administration of the sacraments is its chief function and politics a nonissue. If it exists to serve its members, evangelization becomes the main means of achieving its goal. Where the society is obviously oppressed and impoverished, the political function of the church becomes apparent in assisting in liberation. Most dioceses in Brazil lie somewhere in the middle of this continuum, but the farther they are along the line toward evangelization and liberation, the more problems they encounter with local elites and government.

The Structure and Process Dimension

Presumably all dioceses in Brazil have adopted pastoral structures in line with the decisions of the Second Vatican Council and the Roman Synods, which provide for a redefinition of responsibility within the church, allow a greater role for the clergy (over the bishop) and, most importantly, allow a voice for the laity. Francisco Cartaxo Rolim, however, showed in an early study that even where these structures had been adopted they were not necessarily changing the actual processes of decision making.[5] There is great variety in Brazilian pastoral structures. Furthermore, beyond the process of decision making per se is an orientation termed the style, or approach, to questions, which seems crucial in initiating and continuing a process of change on international— and, by extension, external—matters.

Traditional decision making in the church is represented by S.P. 2 and South 2, where the bishops unilaterally decided all matters of importance and where the few structures that existed for deciding issues of lesser importance included only the clergy. In S.P. 2 the plan of 1974-1975 pointedly cited documents, such as *Cristus Dominus no. 11,* which emphasize the primacy of the bishop. A pastoral plan existed, but the priest in charge lived far from the center of the diocese and was sick and inactive. South 2's plan for 1974 stated somewhat illogically that "the sole legislator in the diocese being the bishop, all lines of pastoral action have been drafted in meetings of the clergy and almost always after reflection by the deaconate." From my observations, this bishop was in control of everything and only the clergy were allowed to attend the meetings. In both these dioceses decision making was completely centralized, and the formalistic pastoral plans barely involved the clergy, let alone any of the laity.

In Center 2 the bishop was unwilling to make decisions on his own, yet apparently lacked the confidence in his priests to give them a greater role. An anomalous situation occurred in this diocese in which structures for decentralization were present (a lay assembly and a group for pastoral promotion), yet were somewhat isolated and powerless in the face of opposition from older priests and the bishop's indecision. Thus, these groups feared action, and there was no real function for the decentralization structures, because the bishop was unwilling to relinquish any authority.

In Northeast 2 the bishop was slow to decentralize on his own initiative but was being pushed along by a group within his diocese which acted in conjunction with a group in the regional body of the CNBB. This diocese had a Diocesan Secretariat of the Pastoral, which included the bishop, all of the clergy and religious, and even the laity. However, not all of the priests were wholeheartedly involved in this pastoral; in fact, it was headed by a nun, which indicated a certain lack of authority. The process here was not really blocked, but neither was it actively promoted.

In S.P. 1 and South 1, there were extremely elaborate and well-mounted schemes and structural systems for decentralization, participation, and continued promotion of lay initiatives. Both published extensive plans and organization-charts, and maintained active participation and involvement. The two bishops amply assisted in decentralizing decision making and encouraged participation at all levels. In both dioceses, however, the bishops and their immediate *equipes* ("teams") were more advanced than most of the clergy and certainly the laity so they were obliged to maintain a certain degree of control. As a consequence, decision making was not totally decentralized.

The last two, Northeast 1 and Center 1, were characterized by their almost total lack of resources in terms of structures, personnel, and finances. This situation made decentralization of authority a necessity. The annual assemblies of laity and clergy of both dioceses had full power to make all pastoral decisions, and both included a majority of laity who acted as coparticipants. Plans and promotions were less elaborate than in S.P. 1 and South 1 and changed frequently, but from my observations of decision-making structures it seemed that all important decisions, even those relating to finances, were made by all involved—at times in opposition to the bishops' priorities. In both of these dioceses decision making was decentralized and occurred at the lowest level, below parish personnel, with structures which allowed unrestricted participation. As decisions were made below they filtered upward.

Obviously there was a great difference between dioceses in decision-making structures. In some dioceses the bishops ruled unilaterally and the pastoral-planning structures existed only on paper. In others the process of decentralization was beginning, but the bishops were either unwilling or too constrained by society or conservative clergy to implement that process. In still others the bishops were willing to relinquish much of their authority, but, given the conservative views of their clergy and laity, had to retain control, since a premature process of decentralization would result in the loss of their progressive orientation. And in Northeast 1 and Center 1 the process of decentralized decision making had gone so far that any prepared and committed lay person could have a say in important matters.

Beyond the actual process of decision making, however, lay the dioceses' style or approach to it, which seemed to have implications for continuous change. In S.P. 2 and South 2 the prevailing attitude was that the bishops should conserve all of their authority. It was assumed that this was the way the church should be run, and decision making was quite literally *ex-cathedra*.

In Center 2 and Northeast 2 there was a vague awareness that change and openness were necessary on the part of the church, but no methodology had been developed to encourage this. Both bishops were ambivalent about relinquishing authority and although they agreed that the church should be more dynamic, they were hesitant to move on their own. Moreover, neither was anxious to throw the topic open to discussion, because of a lack of unity, not to say opposition, among the lower-level clergy. At the time of the study they were following formal CNBB plans, with little initiative of their own.

In South 1 and Northeast 1 an open and dynamic process of questioning, involvement, and change was manifest. An interesting situation existed in Northeast 1, however, as the bishop—albeit completely willing to give up most of his authority and allow full participation—was extremely charismatic, which seemed to inhibit popular involvement. Thus, the process could have been restricted or reversed had he been transferred or had he changed his orientation. In South 1 a real spirit of openness existed, but because the pastoral planning apparatus was complex, the approach to decentralization appeared highly technocratic. Participation and involvement did occur at the lowest levels; however, the institutional presence was so great in this diocese that the decentralization process had to be controlled so that conservative elements in the clergy and society would not impede it. The approach was thus somewhat restricted and limited, in my view, the overall dynamic.

In the last two dioceses, S.P. 1 and Center 1, the change process seemed to be open, reactive, and all-involving. In S.P. 1 there was constant questioning, reflection, and working with structures on the part of the clergy to allow further opening. In Center 1 the bishop and priests began with the recommended CNBB pastoral planning, felt the need to move beyond that, and developed on their own a research project to ascertain the specific needs of their diocese. The clergy were learning about people's needs while becoming increasingly committed and developed a methodology summarized in the phrase *educação se faz na ação* ("education through action" or "learning through doing").

This approach to a methodology for decision making and subsequent change is difficult to express but extremely important. Where the bishop rules unilaterally and pastoral planning structures are only formally endorsed, there is obviously no process to be anticipated. Even where pastoral plans have been adopted and some change has already occurred, it is likely that without the proper approach subsequent development will be limited, as was the case in Northeast 1 and South 1. However, given an open, horizontal, all-embracing approach, change is likely in these two dioceses. Such an atmosphere does not seem to depend on the environment, as one diocese is located in a poverty-stricken area and the other in a very affluent part of the country. What distinguishes the results seems to be the degree of sociopolitical involvement; the poor diocese saw this type of action as necessary, while the richer one did not—at least at this stage of evolution.

The Structures, Programs, and Groups Dimension

The church has many means of making contact with society and exercising influence. This is particularly true when it has been historically prominent. Thus, although the church may once have been totally in charge of education, health, and charity, these structures today carry on with state and private support. However, whereas at one time (even under the patronage system) the church may have had some degree of autonomy and control over its various programs or works, today it must rely on the state for support.[6]

Apart from the structures or institutions mentioned above, the church has also sponsored groups or associations to consolidate the laity for community and religious purposes. These associations, too, have accumulated. The late nineteenth and early twentieth centuries saw the addition of pietistic groups imported from Europe, and more recently, groups which have sought to deepen religious commitment, such as cursilhos and the Christian Family Movement. Most recently, Basic Christian Communities have been promoted in Brazil as well as in other parts of the Third World to facilitate both religious and sociopolitical involvement.

The diocese traditionally has been divided into parishes. This division may be reasonable in Europe, with its small geographic divisions, a homogeneous population, and many priests. However, in Brazil, the parish is increasingly considered inappropriate because of size (5,957 parishes, with an average of 18,103 parishioners each), the shortage of priests (12,624, with an average of 8,528 people per priest), and the great class differences found within one proximate area. The CEBs have been promoted for many reasons, one of which is to replace the impractical parish structure.

Institutional presence can be indicated by the number of personnel (priests and religious), schools, and institutions such as hospitals and orphanages. Generally, the number alone is a reasonable indicator of institutional presence: if there are many religious personnel, there are undoubtedly many institutions; if few personnel, correspondingly few institutions, since the church is obliged to give up or rent out what it cannot staff.

One diocese, South 1, was without exception the most heavily endowed. It had over two hundred religious priests, one hundred secular priests, one thousand nuns, thirty-one religious congregations, and twelve minor seminaries. South 2, S.P. 1, and S.P. 2 were roughly similar to each other, with around eighty priests and two hundred to three hundred nuns, and several minor seminaries. Northeast 2 and Center 2 were also roughly alike, with some twenty priests and two dozen nuns each. Northeast 1 and Center 1 were at the bottom, with fewer than a dozen priests, the same number of nuns, and little else. The ratio of personnel to population within each group was roughly similar, so there were, in effect, four broad categories.[7]

A significant aspect of structures and groups within the church is the "clientele" of these units, that is, the levels of society the church is trying to reach and influence. In South 2 and S.P. 2 programs consisted primarily of schools for the upper and middle classes and assistance in the form of orphanages and medical dispensaries (largely supported by government funds) for the poor. Education for the elites and charity for the needy had been the traditional orientation of the church in these dioceses. No one seemed to question the efficacy of such a program nor see the implications of dependence on the state for support.

In South 1, Northeast 2, and Center 2, this traditional orientation was changing slightly. South 1 had such a huge institutional presence that there was something for everyone, including some training centers for the lower classes which were not simply charitable institutions, but directed toward developing awareness. In the other two, the middle-class schools persisted but there were also training centers and programs oriented toward self-help for the lower classes. The state supported many of these programs, but the church in these areas was aware of the implications of such aid and tried to limit the inherent compromises.

In S.P. 1 the schools, hospitals, and dispensaries were still evident and functioning, but there was a heavier component of aid for the poor and consciousness-raising groups on the periphery of the diocese. This diocese publicly favored the lower classes, and many of the schools had adopted a progressive sociopolitical orientation.

In Northeast 1 and Center 1 church activities were directed exclusively toward the lower classes—and not in terms of charity. Both dioceses promoted block organizations, cooperatives, unions, consciousness-raising movements, and other programs of this sort. From all indications, neither diocese was supported by the state (in fact, both encountered a certain amount of state opposition), but rather, particular programs received support from various foundations in Europe and the United States.

The spectrum of these groups was quite broad, with the more traditional dioceses at the one end still involved in education for the upper classes and charity for the poor, while the most progressive dioceses were almost exclusively working with the lower classes to promote awareness and organization—normally with a great deal of resistance from the state and conservative societal elements. Of course, the majority of Brazilian dioceses fall somewhere between these two extremes, but it is evident that most programs for the lower classes are assuming a content which stresses self-help and awareness rather than simply the dispensation of charity.

The final aspect of the structures, programs, and groups dimension concerns the types of groups and microstructures within each diocese which seek to relate the individual to the institution. In South 2 and S.P. 2 the parish remained untouched as the main division of the diocese. There was little, if any, coordination of pastoral action within these dioceses; it was up to each priest (or religious congregation) to determine the orientation to be followed within his parish. For instance, in South 2, sixteen of the nineteen parishes were staffed by religious (as opposed to secular) priests, and since most of these were imported from elsewhere in the country or from Europe or North America, they estabished—in this era of priest shortages—their own pastoral philosophies.[8] As one told me in regard to the orientation in his diocese, "*Faz o que quiser*" (Do as you wish"). This is one of the liabilities of "head-hunting" expeditions abroad: the bishops may end up with clergy, but at the expense of a coherent or consistent diocesan orientation. Both South 2 and S.P. 2 had a tremendous variety of largely traditional groups. This was not unexpected: since the dioceses lacked a single direction, many different groups proliferated over the years and the importation of personel from abroad increased and diversified this accumulation. Both dioceses maintained the traditional groups, such as the Apostolado de Oração (Apostolate of Prayer), Congregação de Maria (Congregation of Mary), Legião de Maria (Legion of Mary), and the charitable Vicentinos (St. Vincent de Paul Society). In addition there was a large variety of cursilhos, such as the Pilgrimage of Christian Leaders (Peregrinação de Líderes Cristãos—PLC), Christian Leadership Training (Treinamento de Liderança Cristã—TLC), and the MFC, and innovative groups for preparation of the liturgy, catechism, and the sacraments. Certainly a wide variety existed, but all the groups had a traditional religious orientation closely linked to the institution and little given to social concerns.

In Center 2 and Northeast 2 the parish remained the main unit, but tentative steps had been taken by two or three parishes in each diocese to form CEBs (in spite of considerable resistance from older clergy). Both had a variety of religious groups and associations, traditional and modern, and both had adopted the plans recommended by the CNBB.

In S.P. 1 the central level of pastoral planning was very well organized and functioned efficiently. The parish, however, was still the predominant division and efforts to form CEBs had failed. In South 1 the program to form CEBs had gone much farther; the diocese actively sought to promote this orientation, and there were at least five or six parishes with expanding CEB groups at the time of the study. In S.P. 1 and South 1 the priests were also involved in a strategy using chapels throughout the diocese to build on local religious traditions, although both the CEBs and the chapels were coordinated at the parish level. Both dioceses maintained a wide variety of groups. There remained the traditional ones (Apostolado, Legião, Vicentinos), the cursilhos and the MFC, all kinds of preparation groups, such as for the liturgy, catechism, and sacraments, as well as associations for young people and those for charity and social work. What distinguished these two dioceses from Center 2 and Northeast 2 was the fact that S.P. 1 and South 1 groups seemed more oriented toward human promotion and involved far more people.

In Northeast 1 and Center 1 the parish structure had largely been replaced. Northeast 1 decided at the sixth diocesan assembly to supersede the parishes and work mainly with CEBs. Thus communication existed between the CEB groups, at the grass-roots level, with various levels of coordination up to the diocesan level. In Center 1 there was also a decision to bypass the parish and to emphasize the CEB, but more recently the CEB had also been supplanted by more explicitly political evangelization groups. Both of these dioceses maintained a few traditional groups, such as the Apostolado, but they carried on with little encouragement. Neither supported the primarily middle class cursilhos or MFC. Associations for the preparation of the liturgy and so forth existed, but these were linked to promotional groups seeking to increase social awareness through Bible studies and reflection. These two dioceses (in which there was a large and active sociopolitical component) were oriented almost exclusively toward either the basic communities or evangelization groups and had allowed the laity to take over most pastoral action.

Table 14 locates the eight dioceses' positions in regard to the dimensions just discussed on a continuum ranging from "traditional" to "innovative." Clearly, this is not a precise scale but is intended to indicate the spread of perspectives, programs, and processes involved in the change of pastoral strategies. The institutional presence is of a rather different nature, as it does not concern a decision (at least not for the recent past), but rather effects of decisions regarding change in the dioceses, as we shall see. The dioceses are spread along a broad continuum of change. What combination of factors explains the differences between diocese, especially in view of the fact that all eight initially adopted in principle similar commitments to pastoral renovation? In S.P. 1 this process began some three decades ago, and the experience there has at least partially contributed to national pastoral planning. By 1966 the CNBB had assumed its formal position regarding change and pastoral planning, and this common position and its allied plans and processes have been promoted (or not) by the eight dioceses since that time. So it is quite reasonable to review and analyze the variables which contributed to the different positions of the dioceses along the continuum.

The process of change and pastoral planning certainly involves a number of variables, is complex, and seems to occur in stages. The process will continue along some lines, terminate along others, and the most advanced dioceses at the present time are not to be taken as the ultimate models.[9] Furthermore, we cannot assume that all other Brazilian dioceses will follow the same path as the ones studied here, or even, for that matter, that the largely traditional dioceses will enter into the process in the foreseeable future.

In the case of S.P. 2 and South 2, they were so unchanged from their past, traditional situation that there was really nothing to explain. Both remained faithful to the traditional model, in which change and innovation were viewed as alien and irrelevant. In terms of change, they could be viewed as representing the minimum of change in the country. They probably represent about one-third of all Brazilian dioceses, with a preponderance located in the southern part of the country.

In looking at the eight dioceses, the following variables are suggested. First, the key requirement for change is that the local bishop, or an influential core group surrounding him, be committed to changing the local church. A committed bishop will be able to exert his authority and initiate

Table 14
Dioceses in Regard to Aspects of the
Dimensions of Institutional Change
(Location on Continuum)

	Traditional			Innovative
Approach to role/misson				
Corporate view/place in society	South 2 S.P. 2	Center 2 Northeast 2	S.P. 1 South 1	Northeast 1 Center 1
Religious role	South 2 S.P. 2 Center 2	Northeast 2	South 1 S.P. 1	Northeast 1 Center 1
Political role	South 2 S.P. 2	South 1 S.P. 1 Center 2	Northeast 2	Northeast 1 Center 1
Structures and processes within the church[a]				
Decision making	South 2 S.P. 2	Center 2 Northeast 2	S.P. 1	Northeast 1 South 1 Center 1
Approach or orientation to change	South 2 S.P. 2	Northeast 2 Center 2	South 1 Northeast 1 S.P. 1	Center 1
Structures, programs, groups for influence				
Institutions, programs	South 2 S.P. 2	Northeast 2 South 1 Center 2	S.P. 1	Northeast 1 Center 1
Groups, microstructure	South 2 S.P. 2	Northeast 2 Center 2 S.P. 1	South 1	Northeast 1 Center 1
Institutional presence[b]				
Personnel, structures	South 1	South 2 S.P. 2 S.P. 1	Northeast 2 Center 2	Center 1 Northeast 1

[a] Centralized in bishop is traditional; decentralized in laity is innovative.
[b] Abundant is traditional; lacking is innovative.

changes in the most unfavorable conditions; conversely, the most likely diocese in terms of societal context will not be able to adopt or implement reforms if the bishop does not favor them. Thus we found that Center 2 and Northeast 2 lacked a committed bishop. There were a few priests and nuns in each diocese who worked for change, but neither bishop had been "converted." In Center 2 he did not allow any of his priests to take the lead in promoting change and thus stifled innovation; in Northeast 2 the bishop allowed his clergy more liberty, but there were few progressive elements and their impact was limited. In South 1 the bishop himself was not particularly advanced (except for his region), but he was surrounded by an extremely competent group of priests and nuns with a strong commitment to change whom he allowed considerable flexibility. Thus church leaders there, for all intents and purposes, were committed to change. In the other three dioceses (S.P. 1, Center 1, and Northeast 1) the bishops themselves were committed and surrounded themselves with like-thinking clergy and nuns. The commitment has varying explanations having to do with the per-sonalities and backgrounds of the individuals, but a common thread seemed to be experience with Catholic Action and MEB, training abroad (especially in France between 1945 and 1960), and work under other progressive bishops. This last point applied particularly to S.P. 1, where there was a very long tradition of enlightened and active bishops. It is by now commonplace to expect progressive clergy there as well (those clergy who share this orientation are said to belong to the School of Diocese X). At the time of the study probably one-half of the Brazilian bishops were committed to the idea of change in their individual dioceses. They took the initiative, assumed responsibility, and promoted change according to the CNBB guidelines, which, not incidentally, they helped formulate and helped persuade the national organization to accept.

Assuming that the bishop, or a group around him, is committed to changing the local church, the second condition or step necessary for change is the adoption of a plan or process of pastoral planning which initiates reflection on the concrete situation of the diocese and allows a momentum for change to build. The fact that Northeast 2 was slightly farther along than Center 2 seemed due to the very active and well-organized CNBB regional group in the Northeast. This group helped and encouraged dioceses in its region, whereas Center 2 lacked such a dynamic organization. The four more-progressive dioceses (the "1s") adopted the CNBB plan, or a variation thereof.

When a diocese adopts and seriously attempts to implement plans for change it develops certain tendencies or pressures to set up structures for increased decentralization, to assume further normative positions, and to change its programs and groups and opt for the formation of CEBs. It is worth noting that the three most advanced dioceses (Northeast 1, Center 1, and S.P. 1) all surpassed the CNBB's pastoral planning program. All three of them used it for a period of three or four years, eventually decided it was restricting the process of change it had helped initiate, and abandoned the program in favor of an even more decentralized and somewhat spontaneous process which relied on the CEB at one stage and then on evangelization groups at least in one case. A commitment made (or not made) at the review stage to go beyond these plans seemed to determine how open-ended this process ultimately became. If the clergy and laity involved had worked with CNBB projects and had become part of a particular milieu, they tended to relate to that milieu and its more-immediate demands, rather than to the overall history of the institution and its attendant compromises.

An appreciation of this environment is vital, and in the four most-progressive dioceses, research projects of one sort or another were employed to analyze the environment more effectively. In the four dioceses, as in the Archdiocese of São Paulo study carried out in 1975, awareness of the environment assisted a certain process of radicalization.[10] The sense of this process might best be conveyed by citing a statement from Center 1 on its evolution:

There have been frequent comments on the changes taking place in the personnel [of the diocese] beginning with the bishop. It is not hard to see that the demands of the work and the calls of reality as it unrolls constitute the determining factor of these changes. It is a movement of total conversion that makes these demands. As the options become clearer and stronger—thanks mainly to the rectitude of the people who do not get caught up in rationalization but demand consistency with what is stated—then all feel obliged to adopt more consistent attitudes.

Awareness at this stage in conjunction with a close involvement with the environment determined how far this diocese intended to go in the change process.

A third point, intricately related to the awareness and the chosen option of the diocese, is the situation it encounters when it opens up to its environment, a factor which accounts for the location of Northeast 1 and Center 1 on the innovative end of the scale (see table 14). It would have been difficult, if not impossible, to find dioceses in areas of the Northeast and Center as closed as South 2 and S.P. 2. This was at least partially due to the relative abundance in the South and São Paulo and the grinding poverty of the Northeast and Center. In Northeast 1 and Center 1 it was almost impossible to remain blind to the lack of resources, and the unjust division of what little there was became all the more apparent. This matter of relative poverty and affluence was equally valid in all the dioceses that were attempting to change. If the surroundings they encountered were poor, unjust, and miserable, the options seemed increasingly obvious and radical. This has been the pattern throughout the country: once a diocese opens up and realizes in concrete terms what life is like for the majority of the population, it must either shut up and retreat (which is extremely difficult once normative positions are assumed and decentralization begun) or move ahead. However, in much of the South—and certainly in the dioceses we studied there—the environment was not so obviously insupportable, except for the Archdiocese of São Paulo, where a high level of industrialization and urbanization existed concurrently with great contrasts of poverty and wealth and where an obvious process of marginalization was at work. But in the other, more rural, southern dioceses, the contrasts were not so obvious. The church elite in these dioceses may have been committed to a program of pastoral planning and decentralization, but if the environment was reasonably pleasant and affluent, they may have found it impossible to push ahead, since older clergy and conservative elements in society would see no reason to change the existing structures of society or the church.

Apropos of this matter of resources are the assets the environment makes available to the church. Presumably, where there are few societal resources, the church will also lack resources, and where the milieu is relatively affluent the church will also be comfortable. This is generally the case, and it has been easier for the dioceses in the more impoverished areas to change than for those in the relatively affluent South. For example, South 1 was so well endowed that it was only with difficulty overcoming the structural impediments presented by so many clergy, nuns, and institutional resources. This was not the only determinant, however, as Center 1 also had a certain amount of institutional weight, largely for historical reasons. The diocese was able to overcome this handicap because its commitment developed in conjunction with an impoverished and disrupted (by road building) external environment.

Requirements for a process of change seem to be a committed bishop, or other personnel in influential positions, the adoption of a pastoral planning program, reflection on how best to adapt this program to the existing environment, and a move ahead if the environment is clearly impoverished and the institutional weight not oppressive. Even with an entrenched institution and a milieu which is not completely hopeless, it is possible that progressive clergy can force a redefinition of "miserable" and move the local institution to action. In any event, the process remains open-ended and with a great many variables, since change in the church, including local churches, takes place in interaction with an environment in which the political factor is crucial.

An obvious question suggests itself here: since change seems more likely to occur where the environment seems hopeless, where there is little institutional basis, and where a momentum develops which casts off even more institutional weight as schools and other works are left behind, will the church be left with no structures for its mission of promoting change in society? The commitment may remain, but if the church is bereft of personnel and money and has no middle-level structures or other institutional aspects, how is it to implement this commitment? Poverty seems to facilitate change in these dioceses, but does it also restrict or even eliminate any potential impact this change might have had if backed by more institutional weight? With greatly diminished institutions what kind of impact, or influence, can these changing local churches be expected to have?

7. Patterns of Religiosity, Sociopolitical Attitudes, and Change in the Dioceses

In Chapter 2 a great deal of data from the questionnaire was reduced by factor analysis to four distinct patterns of religiosity. Chapters 3 through 6 dealt with the dynamics of change in the institutional church from historical, political, and structural perspectives. Now we return to the analysis of the data and the evaluation of the impact of change in the church (here understood to mean parishes and dioceses) on the beliefs and practices of the population sampled in the survey. In all cases we shall use the scales formulated from the factor analysis, since they would appear to define well enough different patterns, or ways, of being religious. First, however, we shall look to the critical question of the relationship between different patterns of religiosity and attitudes concerning sociopolitical issues. The general question in this chapter has to do with the impact of a changing church on religiosity and the subsequent impact on attitudes reaching beyond the strictly religious. (For details on the questionnaire and data analysis, see Appendices 2 and 3.)

Patterns of Religiosity and Sociopolitical Attitudes

In order to obtain information on the respondents' sociopolitical attitudes the questionnaire included a section with thirty questions, three of which were open-ended. The scope and extent of this section was based on my discontent with the brief and, in my view, inappropriate questions frequently used in surveys in many parts of the Third World. In a sociopolitical system such as Brazil's, it is inappropriate to only ask questions about voting and membership in grass-roots organizations because there is little history in the country of this type of activity, and, of course, the regime strictly limits this type of participation. I collected many questionnaires used in Brazil and elsewhere, reviewed books with possible questions, looked at the general literature on Brazil, elaborated questions jointly with knowledgeable Brazilians, and pretested the survey.[1]

The scales that will be employed to measure sociopolitical awareness and criticism cover as widely as possible the areas of information, interest, and attitudes. The first scale concerns information on political and administrative facts at the local and national levels and is composed of seven items. This scale deals with the respondent's *awareness* of events, personalities, and organizations and seeks to tap respondent information concerning administration and politics. It will be termed a "scale of awareness."[2] The second scale is composed of eleven items which seek to ascertain the respondent's attitude concerning the world in general, society, and processes of government. It concerns how the respondent views the possibilities of *change, control, demands,* and *criticism.* It will be termed a "scale of control and criticism."[3] The third and final scale is the most elaborate. It is composed of three open-ended questions dealing with the respondent's perception of local and national *problems,* their *impact* on society, and the degree of *criticism* elicited in their being reported. Two separate scales were constructed, for local and for national problems, and they contain further information within each category; for simplicity's sake they are combined here. This elaborate scale is termed a "scale of problem impact."[4] What follows is the briefest-possible statement of the results from a long series of questions and combinations. This has been done to simplify the analysis of the relationship between the patterns of religiosity and the patterns of sociopolitical attitudes. As the statistical analysis involved in arriving at the results was cumbersome (with up to six pages of printout per relationship), only final summary statistics (Kendall's Tau C) will be presented. Other techniques could have been employed as well, but the use of Kendall's Tau C is the simplest and captures enough of what is intended.

The four patterns of being a Catholic, measured on scales ranging from 0 to 6, will be cross-tabulated against the three scales of sociopolitical attitudes, and the same four patterns will then be related to the various levels of the institutional church. The relationships between the four patterns of being a Catholic and the three scales of sociopolitical attitudes are shown in table 15.

The first set of relationships shows that greater identification with the popular Catholicism pattern means lower awareness of national and local political and administrative facts; conversely, greater identification with the social Catholicism pattern means greater awareness of these same facts. There are no relationships with the other two patterns.

In the second set of relationships we see exactly the same results: those

Table 15
Relationship between Patterns of Religiosity and
Scales of Sociopolitical Attitudes
(Kendall's Tau C)
(N=1,912)

Scale of Socio- political Attitude	Pattern of Religiosity			
	Popular Catholicism	Orthodox Catholicism	Social Catholicism	Spiritism
Awareness	-.15	.02	.20	.01
Control and criticism	-.16	-.06	.19	-.02
Problem impact	-.08	-.04	.10	.02

in the popular Catholicism pattern are less likely to be aware of the possibilities of change by means of exerting control, making demands, and criticizing; social Catholics are much more likely to recognize this possibility.

In the third set of relationships the general trend continues, but the associations are weaker and all that one can venture is that the relationships of the social Catholicism configuration persist, which suggests that those more definitely in this type are also more likely than those in the other patterns to be aware of problems and their impact and to speak critically.

Since it is my view that the three indices measure a general tendency or propensity to be aware, critical, and demanding—something I would term "sociopolitical progressivism" in the Brazilian context—there is some justification for combining them into one composite scale. The relationships can be seen in table 16.

Table 16
Relationship between Patterns of Religiosity and
Composite Scale of Sociopolitical Attitudes
(Kendall's Tau C)
(N=1,340)

	Pattern of Religiosity			
	Popular Catholicism	Orthodox Catholicism	Social Catholicism	Spiritism
Composite scale	-.17	-.06	.19	-.01

This series of relationships indicates that the different patterns, or configurations, of religiosity have varied associations with the sociopolitical scales, both singly and jointly. Again, the relationships are not strong, but they are consistent and generally come out as might be expected. Popular Catholicism relates moderately and negatively, and social Catholicism moderately and positively to all these scales, and thereby demonstrate that there is indeed an association between types of religiosity and these other attitudes. The relationships for the two other patterns are too weak to suggest conclusions.

If the discussion in Chapter 2 regarding religious beliefs and practices is recalled, together with the four patterns of religiosity defined by means of the factor analysis, we might be tempted to think that these relationships will disappear when the analysis is controlled for class. And, since we controlled for age and sex in that earlier discussion and found some variations, it behooves us again to control for these same variables. If we look at table 17, where the scale of awareness is related to popular and social Catholicism and controlled by class, we find some support for this consideration.

Table 17
Relationship between Popular and Social Catholicism and
Scale of Awareness, Controlling for Class
(Kendall's Tau C)
(N=1,848)

Pattern of Religiosity	Scale of Awareness			
	Social Class			Overall Relationship
	Lower	Middle	Higher	
Popular Catholicism	-.13	-.06	-.04	-.15
Social Catholicism	.18	.11	.07	.20

Not surprisingly, this scale is very largely determined by class, since it deals with the possession of information, and the higher (and thus more educated) class should naturally have an advantage over the lower. For both patterns of religiosity the scale is strongest for the lower class and disappears almost completely for the higher class.

If the other scales are reviewed, however, the relationships do not disappear when class is used as a control. This is probably best summarized by using the composite scale used in table 16 to approximate the relationships for the three other indices.

Table 18
Relationship between Popular and Social Catholicism and
Composite Scale, Controlling for Class
(Kendall's Tau C)
(N=1,291)

Pattern of Religiosity	Composite Scale			
	Social Class			Overall Relationship
	Lower	Middle	Higher	
Popular Catholicism	-.10	-.14	-.16	-.17
Social Catholicism	.11	.23	.14	.19

We find that the relationships for the popular Catholicism pattern vary slightly, with an increase in the negative relationship as the class pyramid is ascended. With the social Catholicism pattern, on the other hand, class is less important, although it is clearly in the middle class that religious and sociopolitical progressivism are most strongly associated.

Tables 19 and 20 indicate that the relationships between these same two patterns of religiosity and the composite scale, when controlling for sex and age, generally remain the same. Here no variations by sex exist and general stability for age is evident across the age categories. It might be worth noting, however, that social Catholicism manifests the strongest relationships among the middle class and young middle age (31 to 40 years).

Table 19
Relationship between Popular and Social Catholicism and
Composite Scale, Controlling for Sex
(Kendall's Tau C)
(N=1,340)

Pattern of Religiosity	Composite Scale		
	Male	Female	Overall Relationship
Popular Catholicism	-.16	-.18	-.17
Social Catholicism	.19	.20	.19

Table 20
Relationship between Popular and Social Catholicism and
Composite Scale, Controlling for Age
(Kendall's Tau C)
(N=1,330)

Pattern of Religiosity	Composite Scale						
	Age (in years)						Overall Relation-ship
	0-19	20-29	30-39	40-49	50-59	60-above	
Popular Catholicism	-.12	-.17	-.20	-.20	-.17	-.03	-.17
Social Catholicism	.17	.19	.29	.19	.13	.17	.19

This analysis demonstrates that the relationships established from a large quantity of data are consistent. There is little to be said about the relationships between the orthodox or cult pattern of religiosity and the Spiritist in regard to these various indices; the associations are too weak for any statement. However, it is clear that those adhering to the popular Catholicism pattern tend to be relatively unaware and uncritical. Those in the social Catholicism pattern are not only more progressive in religious terms but also in sociopolitical matters; they are consistently more aware, critical, and active. However, inasmuch as the social Catholicism pattern was derived from primarily attitudinal questions, it would be somewhat optimistic, to say the least, to argue that these religious beliefs gave rise to sociopolitical attitudes. Rather, I would only state that religious and sociopolitical progressivism are reasonably related to each other.[5] For present purposes this statement suffices, since the fundamental question behind the study deals with the changing church's role in bringing about this progressivism. If we recall that one diocese in each region is characterized by a generally progressive orientation, which the other diocese lacks, then the analysis indicates to what degree these more-innovative dioceses are successful in this endeavor. Whether the pattern of religiosity leads to sociopolitical attitudes is not central to this work; more important is whether the church-as-institution can affect one or the other.

Change in the Dioceses As Related to Patterns of Religiosity

This section analyzes the relationships between the four patterns of religiosity and the institutional church. This analysis will enable us to ascertain whether there is a greater likelihood of the social Catholicism pattern being found in the more-innovative dioceses and whether change in the church leads to the social Catholicism pattern associated with sociopolitical progressivism. Our main interest is the social Catholicism pattern, but the relationships between the church and concerning the other patterns will also be included for possible insights. On the basis of earlier discussion, it would be anticipated that there is no difference between the innovative and the more-traditional dioceses in either the popular Catholicism or Spiritist patterns. The strategies of the innovative dioceses do not, by and large, address themselves to these two patterns. Since the innovative dioceses promote the social Catholicism pattern, however, and de-emphasize more traditional or orthodox Catholicism (see Chapter 6), we should expect to find less of the orthodox pattern in these dioceses. In the following the relationships between the patterns and the eight dioceses are examined with these dioceses divided into innovative and traditional. The relationships within each region are looked at by comparing the innovative (the "1" diocese) with the more-traditional diocese (the "2" diocese) and then dividing each diocese into two parishes. We control by class to see whether the innovative dioceses' strategy of directing their attention mainly to the lower classes is working.

Table 21 indicates that for the entire sample there are no differences at all between the innovative and more-traditional dioceses as regards the social and popular Catholicism patterns. In all instances there is a comparison: four dioceses to four dioceses, two parishes to two parishes, one parish to one parish. A positive number, such as .05, means that there is more popular Catholicism in the more-traditional than in the innovative diocese. The same holds for .15; there is much more likelihood of finding the orthodox Catholicism pattern in the more-traditional dioceses than in the innovative. The −.02 is too weak to discuss, but the −.14 is reasonably important. It means that in the innovative dioceses there is more likelihood of finding people who adhere to the Spiritist pattern of religiosity than there is in the more-traditional dioceses. A positive number always favors the more-traditional diocese. The negative, then, favors the more-innovative diocese.

The innovative dioceses as a block, compared to the traditional dioceses, are not succeeding in promoting the social Catholicism pattern. There are, as expected, differences regarding orthodox Catholicism, with the traditional dioceses more likely to contain individuals who adhere to this

Table 21
Innovative and More-Traditional Dioceses Related
to Patterns of Religiosity
(N=1,912)

Dioceses	Pattern			
	Popular Catholicism	Orthodox Catholicism	Social Catholicism	Spiritism
Traditional	.05	.15		
Innovative			-.02	-.14

pattern. And, somewhat surprisingly, the innovative dioceses are more likely to have individuals adhering to the Spiritism pattern.

We must remember that, because of regional variations in religiosity and abundance of resources, the study was designed to compare two dioceses within one region. Table 22 displays the results of these intraregional comparisons.

Table 22
Innovative and More-Traditional Dioceses in Each of the Four Regions
Related to Patterns of Religiosity
(N=1,912)

Region	Pattern of Religiosity			
	Popular Catholicism	Orthodox Catholicism	Social Catholicism	Spiritism
Northeast	.16	.23	.00	.12
South	-.08	.15	.06	-.21
Center	.10	.16	-.03	-.19
São Paulo	.09	.17	-.14	-.22

It is clear that while the general relationships remain, a number of variations are now evident. The popular Catholicism pattern does not interest us here and it is by and large consistent. The orthodox Catholicism pattern in all four regions is more likely to occur in the more-traditional dioceses. The Spiritist pattern in all four regions is more likely in the innovative dioceses. And, where no relationship with innovative and traditional dioceses existed before concerning the social Catholicism pattern, we now find that there is some relationship in São Paulo. That is, unlike in the other three regions, in São Paulo there is a greater likelihood that the social Catholicism pattern will be found in the innovative diocese

(S.P. 1) than in the more traditional (S.P. 2).

Still, the general level of data analysis may be concealing something, so it is necessary to divide the sample further, into parishes. In table 23 the relationships are compared for one parish in the innovative diocese with one in the more-traditional diocese.

Table 23
Innovative and More-Traditional Parishes in the Dioceses in
Each of the Four Regions, Related to Patterns of Religiosity
(Kendall's Tau C)
(N=1,912)

Region/Parish	Pattern of Religiosity			
	Popular Catholicism	Orthodox Catholicism	Social Catholicism	Spiritism
Northeast				
Innovative	.25	.14	.07	-.18
Traditional	.02	.36	-.08	-.09
South				
Innovative	-.11	.19	.13	-.09
Traditional	-.06	.12	.00	-.33
Center				
Innovative	.02	.18	-.06	-.21
Traditional	.20	.13	.00	-.15
São Paulo				
Innovative	.04	.22	-.17	-.31
Traditional	.14	.12	-.10	-.12

There are some slight variations that need not concern us here in three of the patterns. Of more interest are the variations in the social Catholicism pattern. The relationships, while varying in São Paulo, nevertheless maintain the same general pattern. We now see, however, that there are differences between the two parishes in both the Northeast and the Center. That is, very weak evidence indicates that the strategies in one parish in each diocese were working out better than in the other. Generally, however, the evidence is clear that the strategies in these innovative dioceses were not influencing the population—or at least not the population we sampled.

Since the strategy in the innovative dioceses was to direct their attention increasingly to the lower class, it is necessary to control by class when analyzing the relationship between the social Catholicism pattern of religiosity and the dioceses. Differences in the relationship for the entire sample are too slight to merit discussion.

If the sample is divided into the four regions, some variations in the social Catholicism pattern can again be observed (table 24).

Table 24
Innovative and More-Traditional Dioceses in Each of the Four Regions Related to Social Catholicism, Controlling for Class
(Kendall's Tau C)
(N=1,848)

Region	Social Class			Overall Relationship
	Lower	Middle	Higher	
Northeast	.02	.05	-.05	.00
South	.13	.04	-.27	.06
Center	-.13	.08	.37	-.03
São Paulo	-.17	-.18	-.06	-.14

Although the general trend in relationships holds for the Northeast and the South in that the innovative strategy was not effective for anyone, much less the lower class, in São Paulo the relationship is consistent. The main finding in this regional division by class, however, is in the Center where it is shown that the innovative diocese had made some impact at the lower-class level, a situation which was reversed, and very strongly so, at the higher-class level.

Some preliminary conclusions can be drawn from the foregoing analysis. In the relationships between the patterns of religiosity and the sociopolitical scales, we found that those adhering to the popular Catholicism pattern were less socially and politically aware and less critical. Precisely the opposite can be said for those in the social Catholicism pattern, but in this case causation would be difficult to argue. Nothing can be gleaned about the other two patterns of religiosity from this analysis. However, when these religious patterns were related to the institutional church (by dividing the eight dioceses into innovative and more traditional within the four regions and further dividing the dioceses into parishes), we found that little could be concluded as to the likelihood of the existence of popular Catholicism in one diocese as opposed to another. There was a clear indication that respondents in the orthodox or cult patterns tended more often to be located in the more-traditional dioceses, as one should expect, since these dioceses continued to promote this orientation.

Regarding the social Catholicism pattern, which is the orientation of the innovative dioceses, we found that the data did not indicate that these dioceses had much influence over respondents: in general terms the relationship did not exist. After dividing the sample by region and then by class, we found that the innovative diocese in São Paulo consistently had more respondents than the traditional in the social Catholicism pattern, and although there was some indication of a possible impact in one parish each of the Northeast and Center, the relationships were very weak. Controlling for class we saw that in the Center there was a reasonable impact for the lower class. In sum, the results from all but São Paulo and possibly the lower class in the Center were not encouraging for those promoting change in the church.

What emerges from this analysis is the much higher incidence of the Spiritism pattern in the innovative dioceses than in the traditional. There were variations by region and parish but the relationships between Spiritism, innovation, and diocese were consistent. This raises a question about why this is the case. One would expect more of the orthodox Catholicism pattern in more-traditional dioceses, as indeed was found, and the likelihood of the social Catholicism pattern in the more-innovative dioceses was a matter to study. One might speculate that these innovative dioceses were innovative precisely because there were already more Spiritism adherents (and possibly fewer orthodox as well) in them than in the traditional dioceses. Most likely, however, is the explanation that Spiritists had long been present but that their number had increased because of the relatively open and innovative strategies in these dioceses, where Spiritists, in certain respects, were encouraged to state honestly their actual beliefs and practices. As a result of this openness there was no more Spiritism per se but rather an increased awareness of it and thus even more reason to innovate.

The strategies for promoting the social Catholicism pattern were still not very effective at the time of the study, except in São Paulo, where there was a history of almost three decades of fairly consistent work in this orientation. But, whereas change at the diocesan level in the early 1950s was rather unusual, today change, while retaining the same level of resources, would be even more unusual. Generally speaking, the church was not gaining new resources, personnel, or structures, and in fact, as argued in the last chapter, it is most likely that change takes place in situations of relative scarcity. In short, it is unlikely that the gradual, institutional strategy of S.P. 1 could be repeated today in any but a handful of dioceses. We are more likely to see (as in Center 1) the option for the lower classes to the detriment of the other classes.

More pointedly, we would not anticipate influence from a changing church, particularly when it was probably the perception of weak influence that stimulated change in the first instance, and as, once change has begun, old structures and groups are allowed to wither and even disappear. Largely because of this awareness by some elements in the church, a new strategy to capture influence has been developed.

8. *Comunidades Eclesiais de Base* and Other Groups

Survey of the Themes and of Descriptive Reports

More than any other current topic, the CEB has generated attention and activity at all levels of the Brazilian church as well as provoked a great deal of interest elsewhere.[1] It can be argued (as in Chapter 6) that the active adoption of CEBs as a pastoral strategy is an indication of the extent of change in a particular diocese. The CEBs presuppose an opening up to the lower classes: since the church has increased contact with these people, it will probably turn more in their direction; as the lower classes become involved with CEBs, they should develop a certain unity and sense of participation that will further change the church; and, not only will these people be inclined to generalize their experience in the church to the civil sphere, but, as the church becomes decentralized and declericalized, it will never again be able to return to a relationship of Neo-Christendom. The commitment to the CEB—if it is a real commitment and not merely the adoption of the CEB as a miniparish—has tremendous implications not only for the church but also for the sociopolitical system of Brazil. This fact is widely recognized in the country, and Rio's *Jornal do Brasil*, for example, ran a long article on the topic (14 May 1978) in which it noted that "accused of being Communists or subversives, the Basic Communities have as one of their principal functions the development of a political consciousness—nonparty and nonideological—and the awakening of the people to become aware of their rights. This unleashes a process of critical reflection on the reality of local problems and the causes of this reality." The article goes on to point out, as did many of my informants in June 1978, the importance of CEBs to politicians seeking reelection.

There are many reasons for the importance attached to the CEB, so it is to be anticipated that the resulting experiences will also vary. Among those reasons are four whose significance depends on the level of the group or structure involved. First is an increasing awareness among the hierarchy and other astute observers that the church lacks influence and is no longer actively seeking power, even if the regime were in fact willing to provide it. Thus, some new strategy for securing influence is required. However, the traditional structures or groups for relating to the laity, that is, for generating influence, are no longer dynamic or effective (if they ever were). The parish system is correctly perceived as inappropriate and cumbersome in the Brazilian context: it is too large for effective contact, generally encompasses very disparate sections of society, and is overly bureaucratic.[2] The traditional pietistic groups, such as the Apostolado de Oração and the Legião de Maria, are archaic and involve only a very small proportion of any given parish; generally the same individuals belong to a variety of these associations, none of which could be termed dynamic.

The more recent groups, such as the MFC and the cursilhos (with some notable exceptions), appeal mainly to the middle and upper classes and de-emphasize a critical sociopolitical function. The most active and important movement from the mid-1950s until the mid-1960s for linking the church to sectors of the laity and the changing environment was Catholic Action, but this association became untenable after the 1964 coup and was for the most part abolished. So, in effect, the institutional church lacks effective inter-mediary sectors for linking its new normative orientation to a changing Brazilian political context.

The continuing crisis in priestly vocations is another reason for the emergence of the CEB. The priest-to-population ratio in Brazil has never been very high and has tended to decrease even more in the past two decades. In 1970 the ratio was one priest to 7,081 persons, and by 1975 it was one priest per 8,528 persons. There is an absolute drop in the number of secular priests, on the average, of 0.20 percent per year, and the number of religious priests is falling at an even faster rate, some 0.60 percent per year. Even the willingness of some dioceses to allow nuns extensive new roles is not a solution, since their number is decreasing at the rate of about 1 percent per year.[3] In short, the historical shortage of clergy continues, and to a greater degree. It is absurd to discuss contact with the church when one priest serves ten thousand people (as is the case in much of the country); obviously some new mechanism has to be employed to relate the institution to the people.

As noted in Chapter 5, the option of the institutional church has increasingly favored the poor and those socially and economically marginalized. Clearly, none of the traditional structures were appropriate to relate to these people and thus a smaller, more flexible entity had to be found. The CEB is thought to fulfill this role because it normally brings together up to thirty individuals who reflect on the Bible and discuss their concrete problems. The CEB is considered the entity *par excellence* for relating the church to the lower classes.

Last, innovation in the form of the CEB can only be described as timely. Their formation was supported by the Second Vatican Council and the 1968 CELAM meeting in Medellín as well as by the 1979 meeting in Puebla, and they are generally legitimized by theology emanating from both Europe and Latin America. They are perfectly in tune with modern church thinking, and, as Eduardo Hoornaert argues, the CEB expresses the church ideal that has been dreamed about for so long: it is a community; it fully involves the laity; it represents a diversified ministry; it responds to the theological characteristics of the early church by emphasizing community living and expression of the Eucharist.[4]

Since so many good and valid reasons exist to stimulate the formation of CEBs, it is not surprising that they are supported at all levels. Pope Paul VI, in his apostolic exhortation of December 8, 1975, *Evangelii nuntiandi, 58,* promoted them as did the Roman Synod of 1975. At Medellín in 1968 many different sectors of the assembly encouraged CEB formation, and their formation remains a vital theme in most parts of Latin America.[5] In Brazil CEBs have been encouraged since at least 1962 and the "Plano de Emergência" and were formally adopted in the Joint Pastoral Plan of 1966-1970. In the CNBB biennial plans of 1975-1977 and 1977-1979, the CEBs remained among the four highest priorities, which is also the case in a great many dioceses, including that of São Paulo. Three national meetings have been called on this topic, the last two of which stimulated a great deal of enthusiastic participation at lower levels of the church, both in preparation and, later, in reflection on the material presented.[6]

Official support has been translated into action in some dioceses. We are told that there are some sixty thousand of these CEBs in all parts of Brazil, and it is clear that they do not emerge spontaneously but rather are the result of official church strategies and actions. For example, Carlos Mesters summarizes dozens of reports on CEBs and observes that "almost all the experiences described exist in dioceses where the bishop or the priests and nuns aid the creation of these communities . . . . It is known, on the other hand, that where the bishop or priest is against this type of renovation the process does not begin and remains blocked. This is evidence of the almost strategic importance of the ecclesiastical institution: when it aids the process, it works; when it is contrary, the process is aborted and has almost no future."[7] Furthermore, the initiative for the CEB begins with religious activities and structures such as chapels, visits, the parish system, and old associations:

In almost all the experiences described, the renovation is helped in its inception by the ecclesiastical institution. The institution takes the initiative; from the "center" the movement spreads to the bases. Using their uncommon talents the priest, nun, layman, or even bishop stimulate and unleash the process. But, to the degree in which this process takes form and begins to awaken the people so it also begins to dismantle the traditional organization of the very institution which promoted it, and the particular priest, bishop, or religious enters into an unlimited identity crisis.[8]

In effect, the formation of these entities is legitimated nationally and internationally.

However, since there are so many diverse reasons for CEB formation and such extensive justification exists for their presence, it is clearly impossible for all CEBs to be identical. This is another dimension that comes out in studies and which is certainly supported by our field work. There is a tremendous variety of CEBs: groups for evangelization, groups for reflection, Bible circles, groups for promoting awareness, groups for preparing the mass, groups for the preparation of liturgy and the sacraments, groups for human promotion, adult groups, mothers' groups, youth groups, neighborhood groups, chapel groups, cooperatives, and so forth.[9]

Some generalizations are in order, and these suggest that in the richer areas of the South the CEBs remain miniparishes and what life they may develop is only with regard to religious and not sociopolitical matters. In the poorer areas of the Northeast and Center, however, and on the periphery of cities such as São Paulo, CEBs establish more of a sociopolitical perspective, critical of the present system.

CEBs emerge from religious functions and structures and are firmly based on religious activities. They are not civil societies but rather religious associations. However, because of their very form, as decentralized communities, and because of their purpose, which is to relate the Gospel to reality, they hold great implications for both the church-as-institution and the religion it promotes. Once the process of decentralization is initiated and the people at the grass-roots level are defined as being the church, then the whole system of authority is inverted and the laity no longer has to wait for word from above but can assume responsibility on its own.[10] In this new system of involvement and decision making the archaic groups and structures in the church are superseded. If the church is based on a laity united in CEBs, then little justification remains for the rest of the institutional paraphernalia (increasingly seen as superfluous). This view is further encouraged by the emphasis in the CEBs on reading and reflecting on the Bible and making it relevant to everyday life. The layman need not depend on the priest but can, as in Protestantism, interpret God's message for himself. CEBs tend to reverse ecclesiastical authority and structure and, by bringing the church into contact with the day-to-day existence of the vast majority of its members, force a redefinition of religious goals and attitudes.

Even though the CEBs are primarily religious groupings, they have obvious sociopolitical implications. First, they offer an opportunity to participate in a society that has never encouraged participation and which does not provide channels for it. There is undoubtedly a carry-over of demands from the religious realm to the civil. Second, the various reports on the formation of the CEBs indicate that they are usually founded as a response to concrete issues such as land tenure problems and lack of transport, water, or other basic services. Thus, from the beginning at least, one of their functions has been the resolution of certain practical problems, and if they are successful with one issue there is every likelihood that they will be pressured to take up others. And, third, by making the Bible relevant to daily life, there is a tendency toward radicalization, since, depending on the selection studied, the Bible can be a utopian document indeed. In the reality of Brazil as lived by most of the lower class there is much in the Bible which is appealing, and the more utopian or radicalizing texts readily suggest themselves. A general sense emerges, both from discussions with members of these groups and from reading their texts, of a certain sociopolitical radicalization emanating from these CEBs. As Pedro Demo emphasizes, after indicating the implications for the church, "In the case of the CEB this confrontation strikes not only the dimension of the ecclesiastical hierarchy, here called to take a background role, but also affects, to a certain degree, the political activity of the traditional leaders who are considered somewhat removed from the basic necessities of the members."[11] This consequence is recognized by traditional politicians as well as newer, antiregime candidates who actively seek CEB support.

The Comunidades Eclesiais de Base are apparently very appropriate for the Brazilian church, with its history of low influence, personnel shortages, inappropriate structures, and new ideological and theological positions in conflict with those of the regime. They also have tremendous implications for both the church-as-institution and the larger society. Institutional implications are profound indeed, since the institution is so obviously understaffed that the normative commitment—in this case finding its structural component in the CEB—is a very real possibility. In my view the possibility decreases in inverse proportion to the resources the church has at its disposal in a particular area, and thus the CEB can be seen as a regional or even a class phenomenon.

Results from the Data Analysis

During the field work we gathered material on every aspect of group life in the dioceses by means of document review, participant observation, personal interviews, interviews with members of groups, and the questionnaire. The data do not fit into the same categories as those reported in the earlier discussion on CEBs, however, because the data come from the widely administered questionnaire. While questionnaires were administered to members of groups, a variety of groups was needed— both traditional and modern—and not only those that might be termed CEBs in the local context. The earlier reported material, in contrast, is drawn from reports or interpretations of reports of particular experiences. This material of necessity emphasizes the CEBs; it is intensive and regards only one particular type of group. My work is more extensive in that it deals with many types of groups. I have read hundreds of the reports on the activities of CEBs from 1973 to 1981, and although I find the concept fascinating, I feel (apparently as do many of those writing on the CEBs) that the Comunidades are still somewhat tentative ventures, albeit expanding rapidly.

Aside from a different methodology, there are a number of other reasons why the data are less than optimum to complete the categories from the earlier noted reports. There is, as noted earlier, a tremendous variety of names for these CEBs and, since little standardization exists, it is difficult to recognize what type of association qualifies as a CEB and what type does not. The reports indicate that the CEBs are found on the "margins," that is, in rural areas and the peripheral, poor areas of the cities. By the very definition of margin, it is extremely difficult to pick up these people in a survey; they are not easily found, are normally isolated, and cannot be sampled in sufficient numbers in a project such as this to produce clear results. It is, of course, for these reasons that the methodology thus far used by others relies on reports from the groups where a concentration of CEBs exists. Even the reports, and the observations on them, indicate that CEBs are a mixed bag indeed. Some are only miniparishes; others are active, but only in religious terms; some are essentially political groupings; and others are a combination of these characteristics. They vary from one region to another and can be defined at this point only by their extreme heterogeneity.

A few words about general impressions from the field work may be in order before looking at the data from the questionnaire. All of the dioceses saw a proliferation of groups but, generally speaking, the innovative dioceses can be distinguished from the more traditional by considering the balance between the older forms and those of a newer variety. For instance, the most traditional dioceses—South 2 and São Paulo 2—did have a few potentially innovative groups, such as groups for preparation of sacraments and liturgy, Bible circles, and catechismal groups. However, the overwhelming preference in both was for the traditional, pietistic groups such as the Apostolado de Oração and the Legião de Maria, for charitable organizations such as the Vicentinos, and for the religious-renewal groups such as the cursilhos. The main weight, then, was toward the more traditional, or even archaic, groups. The other two more-traditional dioceses (Northeast 2 and Center 2) as well as the two innovative ones in more-affluent areas (South 1 and São Paulo 1) still had an abundance of these more-traditional groups in all their variety, but with a greater weight toward the CEB. The latter included youth groups, human promotion groups, block coordination groups, and various types of administration groups. It is interesting that the two more-traditional dioceses in the poorer areas, Northeast 2 and Center 2, were very similar in this regard to the more-innovative ones in the richer areas—in orientation, if not in number of groups.

This was not the case, however, in the two more-innovative dioceses in the poorer areas (Northeast 1 and Center 1), probably because of the lack of resources to maintain any sort of group life at all. There remained a few pietistic groups, such as the Apostolado de Oração, but it was very clear that their days were numbered. The overwhelming orientation was toward the new groups which were following a human promotion or awareness-stimulating character. In Northeast 1 there was a bit of ambiguity, however, as there seemed too great a proliferation of these groups for any one of them to function really effectively. In Center 1 there was no doubt that the group structure was well thought out and elaborated. Generally the types broke down into evangelizing groups (that is, for stimulating awareness) in the rural areas, and on the periphery of cities, into slightly more-charitable promotional groups. It was stated (and judged accurate from the field work) that there were some two hundred evangelizing groups in the whole diocese and each contained between twenty and thirty members. The line defined and followed through at the diocesan level seemed to carry all the way down to the bases. In this diocese all the clergy and lay personnel were organized to spend most of their time in the rural areas and on the urban peripheries to assist in the formation of these potentially very significant groups.

The same cannot be said for any of the other dioceses, innovative included; group life and orientation in the other seven seemed a bit confusing. This is not to say that diocesan orientations will not be clarified with time and further definition on the part of the dioceses, but the field work for this survey did not provide the same kind of unambiguous insights suggested by some of the reports or documents on the CEB.

This report on findings, then, does not deal specifically with what might be termed CEBs, but rather with the groups in general found in the eight dioceses. It is more an extensive than an intensive coverage, and quite possibly if the survey were to be repeated today the specifically CEB-like entities would emerge more distinctly. Even so, groups approximating the ideal type of the CEB were obvious and will be discussed on the basis of the data.

The questionnaire included two large sections on groups. The first dealt with the more-traditional ones, including the Apostolado de Oração, Legião de Maria, Vicentinos, and Círculos Operários ("Workers' Circles"); with newer movements, such as the Christian Family Movement, MEB, and Catholic Action; and with institutional links, such as Catholic schools, charitable entities, cooperatives, and unions. That is, it included all group and structural connections prevalent until about the mid-1960s. There is little specific reporting on this class of group, because the primary concern here is with the newer, CEB-like associations originating from the general orientation of the Vatican Council and the CELAM meetings.

The second section included the following selection of groups: groups for preparation of sacraments (baptism, First Communion, matrimony) and liturgy; groups for reflection; groups for prayer and renewal; groups for charity (mothers' clubs and neighborhood assistance, for example); groups for promotion of awareness; Bible circles; and cursilhos, including variations such as Emáus and TLC. Since one individual may belong to more than one group, there were a total of 1,294 memberships among the 29.2 percent of the respondents who belonged to groups (see table 25). Table 26 shows the distribution of membership in religious groups for the total sample.

We see that 70.8 percent of the sample belonged to no group at all, but that the remaining 29.2 percent were members of at least one group. At first glance the membership percentage would seem unusually high, but, of course, 210 of the interviews were specifically with those belonging to groups. Our sample, then, is intentionally overrepresentative in terms of group membership. However, irrespective of this fact, the large number of multiple memberships is very interesting. It would appear that belonging to one group leads to membership in others; links are therefore multiplied. The church provides possibilities for structural links and forms of participation, since a large variety of church-related groups exists in most

Table 25
Number of Religious Groups Belonged To
(N=1,912)

Number of Groups Belonged to	% of Total Sample
0	70.8
1	10.8
2	7.3
3	5.6
4	3.1
5	1.3
6	0.9
7	0.2
Total	100.0

Table 26
Type of Religious Group Membership
(N=1,912)

Type of Group	% of Total Sample
Preparation for sacraments, liturgy	12.3
Reflection and debate	12.0
Prayer/renewal	7.4
Charity, assistance, administration	13.9
Awareness promotion	7.9
Bible circle	7.3
Cursilho and other forms of deepening faith	6.8

parishes. We found only one rural and very poor parish (in Northeast 2) with no resident priest and generally lacking in organized group life.

The same cannot be said for civil society. The questionnaire included a very large section on nonreligious groups and associations, including neighborhood associations, recreational clubs, professional associations, cultural associations, unions, student associations, and fraternal organizations such as Rotary and the Lions. Only thirteen people, or 0.7 percent of the sample, claimed membership in a group outside these seven types.

Nonmembership and multiple membership in these nonreligious groups or associations is indicated in table 27.

Table 27
Number of Civil Groups Belonged To
(N=1,912)

Number of Groups Belonged to	% of Total Sample
0	64.0
1	21.4
2	9.4
3	3.4
4	1.3
5	0.4
6	0.1
Total	100.0

Some 688 individuals, or 36 percent of the sample, belonged to civil groups, but the percentage dropped off very quickly after single membership. The drop in membership in religious groups, on the other hand, is much more gradual; those belonging to four or more religious groups comprised 5.5 percent of the sample, whereas for the civil groups this figure was only 1.8 percent.

The nature of membership in the nonreligious groups is better understood if we look more closely at the groups or associations with the highest membership percentage. The largest category, with 365 people, or 19.1 percent of the sample, is recreational clubs (such as soccer and dancing clubs), which may imply little or nothing. The second largest, with 257 members, or 13.4 percent, is the official unions, which are obligatory and largely meaningless. Those civil associations that might be compared to the religious groups in the sense of implying a decision to join and a subsequent chance for greater involvement or participation are the neighborhood associations (4.9 percent), professional associations (6.7 percent), and cultural associations (3.9 percent).

Table 28 displays the general membership profile of the sample for both religious and nonreligous groups. We see that the greatest proportion (41 percent) belonged to no group at all and that membership in only civil groups was exactly double that of membership in only religious groups. What is most striking is the low percentage (17) belonging to both civil and religious groups, which suggests, of course, very little overlap. This observation, in combination with the high percentage of nonmembership and the nature of civil groups, indicates that the general sample was not particularly rich in group affiliations. For this reason alone the involvement in religious groups assumes greater importance, particularly when these groups are CEBs, with their presumed mobilizing and awareness increasing effects.

Table 28
Group Membership Profile
(N=1,912)

Number/Type Group	% of Total Sample
None	41.0
One civil, no religious	28.0
One religious, no civil	14.0
One religious, one civil	17.0

Because of the wide variety of group names, the number of activities promoted by any one group, and multiple membership, the following analysis uses the group *activity* which the respondent indicated as the most important. Table 29 shows the distribution of these activities and table 30 indicates the distribution of religous activities by diocese.[12]

Table 29
Distribution of Activities in Religious Groups
(N=486)

Activity	%
Preparation for sacraments, liturgy	21.7
Reflection and debate	19.1
Prayer/renewal	10.6
Charity, assistance, administration	25.5
Awareness promotion	11.8
Cursilho and other forms of deepen- ing faith	11.1

A number of observations must be made regarding table 30. First, we attempted to sample specifically some thirty groups in each diocese. These responses, in combintion with the responses from the other samples, should have produced a roughly equitable distribution of activities by diocese. We found, however, that a wide range existed, from a low of 8 percent in Northeast 2 (where the rural and poor parish was located) to a high of 18 percent in Center 2.

Table 30
Distribution of Activities by Diocese
(Percentages)
(N=486)

Activity	Diocese							
	Northeast 1	Northeast 2	South 1	South 2	Center 1	Center 2	S.P. 1	S.P. 2
Preparation for sacraments, liturgy	33.0	7.0	34.0	24.0	17.0	12.0	41.0	12.0
Reflection and debate	32.0	10.0	26.0	20.0	7.0	24.0	23.0	8.0
Prayer/renewal	0.0	20.0	12.0	9.0	3.0	14.0	3.0	21.0
Charity, assistance, administration	21.0	43.0	12.0	20.0	12.0	41.0	20.0	32.0
Awareness promotion	11.0	12.0	9.0	0.0	61.0	3.0	0.0	4.0
Cursilho and other forms of deepening faith	1.0	8.0	5.0	26.0	0.0	5.0	12.0	24.0
% of N in each diocese	12.0	8.0	9.0	15.0	12.0	18.0	12.0	14.0

Second, from the description of activities in the completed question-naires, the earlier discussion on CEBs, and the variable activity distribution in the innovative and traditional dioceses, we can predict the analysis of the groups and the attitudes of their members. All of these activities presumably do not adhere to a traditional pattern; there are certainly variations. Prayer/renewal, for example, can be the basis for and involved with other activities, or may imply nothing more than prayer and renewal. With the exception of the very heavily structured diocese in the South (South 1), far more respondents in the traditional dioceses than in the progressive were involved with this activity. This was reflected most dramatically in the Northeast (0 percent in Northeast 1 versus 20 percent in Northeast 2), but held elsewhere as well.

Preparation for the sacraments and liturgy is normally associated with the CEBs, but not exclusively so, and although much more common in the innovative dioceses, it was not totally absent from the traditional ones (this would be the only explanation for its presence in South 2). And, as noted in Chapter 6, some of the traditional dioceses evidenced some aspects of change, among which this activity would certainly be included.

Reflection and debate and promotion of awareness should be combined as they are CEB-like activities. Although their distribution might be ambiguous when considered singly, when combined they were twice as common in the innovative dioceses as in the traditional. Regional variations also hold; that is, the difference between dioceses was less in the Northeast, with the traditional diocese reflecting more aspects of change than the traditional diocese in the Center.

Charity, assistance, and administration were found throughout the sample, as might be anticipated, but their lower priority in the innovative dioceses was indicated by their low frequency (an average of 16 percent in the innovative dioceses and 34 percent in the traditional).

The cursilho, and other groups aimed at deepening the faith, need not replicate the stereotypical alienating model so commonly ascribed to these groups in Latin America, but it is worth noting that they were four times as common in the traditional as in the innovative dioceses (16 percent versus 4 percent). Furthermore, there was a particular emphasis on faith-deepening activity in the richer areas of the South and São Paulo, but virtually no emphasis on this type of activity in the poorer dioceses of the Northeast and Center.

There were no completely traditional or innovative dioceses in terms of the activities of religious groups, associations, and CEBs (as we sampled them), but definite contrasts existed that might have been foreseen in light of the discussion in Chapter 6. The overall distribution may best be indicated if we combine the less-CEB-like activities (prayer and renewal, charity, assistance, and administration, and cursilhos) with the more-CEB-like activities (preparation for the sacraments and liturgy, reflection and debate, and promotion of awareness) and look at their combined distribution in the dioceses. The results of this combination are reflected in table 31.

Table 31
Innovative and Traditional Activity Distribution
in Innovative and Traditional Dioceses
(Percentages)
(N=486)

Diocese	Activity	
	Innovative	Traditional
Innovative	33.0	11.0
Traditional	19.0	36.0

Although a perfect contrast is not apparent between innovative activities in traditional dioceses, and vice versa, a substantial association does exist (Tau B of .40) and indicates that the innovative dioceses had a far greater incidence of the more-CEB-like activities than did the traditional dioceses.

We found no evidence to indicate that the CEBs were composed exclusively of members of the lower class. Statistically, in the Kendall's Tau C there is no support for the contention that these groups are essentially communities of the poor. This finding may be due in part to the sampling strategy, which could not pick up groups at the margins, but in that part of the sample which was selected precisely for its group-membership characteristic, the quota criteria of sex and education were not applied (see Appendix 1). On the other hand, these groups were not communities of the middle or higher classes either, which is significant in itself because the church's strategy could well be the politically secure one of relating primarily to the middle classes. What can now be said on the basis of our data is that the CEB as a strategy relates similarly to all social classes.

It is important to look at the internal dynamics of religious groups because it is common practice to ascribe a certain clericalism and lack of democracy to the more-traditional activities as opposed to the supposed opportunities for participation created by the CEB. This observation is, in fact, supported by the data. For example, questions about the leadership of the most important group to which the respondent belonged elicited the distribution of responses shown in table 32. What is clear from table 32 is the varied involvement of clerical personnel according to the type of activity or group. Even though again there were no completely exclusive

Table 32
Leadership of Group by Activity Type
(Percentages)
(N=483)

Activity			Group Leader			% of Activities
	Priest	Nun	Clergy-Appt. Layman	Members	Other	
Preparation for sacraments, liturgy	23.0	8.0	30.0	30.0	9.0	22.0
Reflection and debate	12.0	3.0	36.0	41.0	8.0	19.0
Prayer/renewal	25.0	14.0	39.0	17.0	5.0	11.0
Charity, assistance, administration	29.0	5.0	39.0	21.0	6.0	25.0
Awareness promotion	17.0	8.0	15.0	56.0	4.0	12.0
Cursilho and other forms of deepening faith	20.0	3.0	34.0	34.0	9.0	11.0
% of N	22.0	6.0	33.0	32.0	7.0	100.0

Table 33
Group Leaders of Innovative- and Traditional-Type Activities
(Percentages)
(N=483)

Activity		Group Leader			% of Activities
	Priest and Nun	Clergy-Appt. Layman	Members	Other	
More-CEB-like (Innovative)	24.0	29.0	40.0	7.0	53.0
Less-CEB-like (Traditional)	32.0	38.0	23.0	7.0	47.0
% of N	28.0	33.0	32.0	7.0	100.0

activities or control, the tendencies are clear. Those groups referred to as more-CEB-like had the least amount of clerical control and the greatest amount of member control. This is highlighted in table 33, where the more- and less-CEB-like activities (innovative and traditional, respectively) are combined, as are the categories of priest and nun.

The results verify the assumption that the more-traditional groups are more clerical, and presumably less democratic. We must recall that the option of a layman-run group was not an indication of participation or internal democracy, since much evidence indicates that the layman was normally appointed by the clergy and was likely to have an orientation as clerical as that of a priest or religious.[13]

Although there is a mix of groups in all the dioceses, as indicated earlier, there are clear contrasts between levels of control in traditional and in innovative dioceses. The results of the division into innovative and traditional of all the dioceses can be seen in table 34; the results for the individual dioceses appear in table 35.

Table 34
Group Leadership in Innovative and Traditional Dioceses
(Percentages)
(N=446)

Diocese	Group Leader				% of Dioceses
	Priest and Nun	Clergy-Appt. Layman	Members	Other	
Innovative	30.0	21.0	41.0	8.0	45.0
Traditional	29.0	40.0	23.0	8.0	55.0
% of N	29.0	31.0	31.0	8.0	100.0

The overall pattern is quite clear. It should be emphasized, however, that in some of the innovative dioceses, such as Northeast 1 and Center 1, religious personnel (priests and nuns) promoted the formation of groups, which could well explain why there were no striking differences between the innovative and traditional dioceses in tables 34 and 35. Throughout table 35 it is clear that the biggest contrast was between clergy-appointed laymen and the members themselves, and that the difference was greatest in precisely those two pairs of dioceses—the Center and São Paulo—where the innovative most sharply contrasted with the traditional diocese. In sum, the more-CEB-like groups and the more-innovative dioceses had higher levels of member control, or internal democracy, than the less-CEB-like groups and the more-traditional dioceses.

What are the beliefs and practices of the members of these six groups? Do the CEBs bring together the more orthodox or the more social Catholics, and do they in fact have a role in promoting one pattern or another in their membership? It is methodologically impossible here to determine whether the religious-activity group attracted those with particular beliefs and practices or whether it promoted one pattern or a combination. But, from what we do know about the goals of group organizers and about the groups' internal control and functioning, it would seem likely that the groups had at least some role in promoting particular patterns of beliefs and practices.

Table 35
Leaders of Groups by Diocese
(Percentages)
(N=449)

Diocese	Group Leader				% of Dioceses
	Priest and Nun	Clergy- Appt. Layman	Members	Other	
Northeast 1	23.0	30.0	38.0	9.0	11.0
Northeast 2	44.0	30.0	26.0	0.0	7.0
South 1	36.0	16.0	38.0	10.0	10.0
South 2	26.0	35.0	28.0	11.0	17.0
Center 1	37.0	9.0	44.0	10.0	13.0
Center 2	30.0	42.0	19.0	9.0	18.0
S.P. 1	23.0	32.0	42.0	3.0	11.0
S.P. 2	22.0	48.0	19.0	11.0	13.0
% of N	29.0	31.0	31.0	9.0	100.0

If we compare those in our sample who were involved in the six activities with those who were not, we find some interesting contrasts. There was no relationship between involvement in the activities and either the popular Catholicism or the Spiritism pattern (Kendall's Tau C of −.08 and .07, respectively). There was a mild relationship between involvement and the orthodox or cult pattern (Kendall's Tau C of .11). And, most importantly, there was a reasonably strong relationship between involvement in the activities and the social Catholicism pattern (Kendall's Tau C of .21), which indicates, of course, that those involved in the CEBs were more progressive in terms of religious beliefs and practices.

It is normal for members of any group—religious, political, or civic—to be more involved and, presumably, more aware than are nonmembers. This is, after all, one reason for their membership. So, we must compare the above findings with the results of a similar approach taken in regard to members of the more-traditional groups. These include the Christian Family Movement (MFC), the Vicentinos, the Círculos Operários, and the nowmoribund MEB and Catholic Action. Again, there was no strong association with the popular Catholicism or Spiritism patterns (Kendall's Tau C of .05 and −.07). There was a clear and reasonably strong association with the orthodox pattern (Kendall's Tau C of .23). But, in contrast to CEB members, there was almost no relationship with the social Catholicism pattern (Kendall's Tau C of .06). It is not group membership per se, then, that brings in or encourages those who are more progressive in religious terms. There are different types ofgroups and the (newer) CEBs are definitely very different in the type of activity they inspire than the more-traditional groups.

The same contrast pattern holds if we divide the six activities as before (see tables 31 and 33) and compare them on the strength of association with these same scales. The more-CEB-like activities had a negative but weak relationship with the popular Catholicism pattern (Kendall's Tau C of −.11), a weak association with the orthodox or cult pattern (Kendall's Tau C of .03) and with the Spiritism pattern (Kendall's Tau C of −.04), and a moderate relationship with the social Catholicism pattern (Kendall's Tau C of .16). Thus innovative activities are positively and markedly associated only with the social Catholicism pattern, which indicates that those in these activities do indeed have an unambiguously progressive orientation.

People's involvement in the less-CEB-like pattern is somewhat more ambiguous, but not surprising. Again, there was nothing significant with the popular Catholicism or Spiritism patterns (Kendall's Tau C of .00 and −.06, respectively); however, there was a relationship with the orthodox scale (Kendall's Tau C of .12) and with the social Catholicism scale (Kendall's Tau C of .12). In short, involvement in the more-CEB-like activities relates only to the social Catholicism scale, whereas involvement in less-CEB-like activities relates to both social and orthodox Catholicism but is weaker in the social Catholicism scale than are the more-innovative activities.

The data were reviewed in light of earlier comments on the CEB and some support was found for the general views summarized in that section, although, because survey research was used, the approaches and categories of the earlier studies could not be used. Individuals involved in the six religious

activities were much more likely than the noninvolved to fall within the social Catholicism pattern (Kendall's Tau C of .21), and also more likely
than those who belong to the more-traditional, sometimes moribund, groups
(Kendall's Tau C of .06 for the latter). More involvement in these activities
distinguished involved individuals from the remainder of the sample in terms
of a certain religious progressivism.

Despite the nature of the sampling strategy and the tremendous variety
within any one diocese (with the possible exception of Center 1), the data
support the general view based on secondary literature and studies of specific
CEBs and expressed in the first section of this chapter. The more-CEB-like
groups are found in the more-innovative dioceses and have a higher degree of
member control. The methodology for promoting progressive attitudes and
practices for both types of activity, but with an emphasis on the more-CEB-
like, would appear to work. At least in the case of these particular groups there
was an association with the social Catholicism pattern, which is more than
can be said of the church's general strategy, analyzed in the last chapter. The
specific strategy, then, would appear to be more effective than the general.

The relative success of the specific strategy over the general is much in line
with Max Weber's analysis of the role of the sects in bringing about
fundamental value changes. For him, as for us in considering a reorientation of
the church, "the problem is how does a variant ethic arise and spread in a
hostile setting, and even come to dominate that no longer hostile setting."[14]
His conclusion, as argued by Stephen Berger, is that for the new ethic to take
hold it must be institutionalized in a new structure or organization, for it does
not simply replace previously dominant ethics or cultures. The CEBs could
very well play this role, for they may become institutionalized as new
structures endowed with normative orientations. In this way the new
orientation is implemented as the groups develop.[15]

9. Conclusion

This book has attempted to describe and analyze change in the Catholic church in Brazil and evaluate the church's impact on individuals and society in general. The church has been viewed from a historical perspective as an institution related to its environment. More specifically, the framework employed to define the analysis holds as fundamental the relationships between the church and the Vatican on the one hand and the church and the Brazilian state on the other, as well as the church's perception of the general environment which it seeks to influence. Throughout the book the church's approach to influence is understood in terms of its goal in a particular context, the sectors of society which receive primary attention, and the instruments or mechanisms through which influence is exercised and commitments generated.

The church has been viewed as a large corporate entity. One can focus on its internal divisions—various groups, sectors, and strata—on progressives and conservatives, and so forth, but I have intentionally emphasized the institution as a whole. It is assumed that complete unity, let alone unanimity, is only theoretically relevant; for a long time the image of the church-as-monolith has been in disrepute. Still, enough agreement exists within the church to focus on this historic institution; although the threats of division and even schism are eternally present, the church, if anything, has shown itself historically capable of tolerating dissent and maintaining coherence—particularly during the last century. It is not, as some would have us believe, completely immobilized by internal ferment.

Thus, while different levels within the church have been dealt with— from the national level and the CNBB through the dioceses and, finally, to the parishes and CEBs—and specialized institutes and groups such as CIMI and Pastoral da Terra discussed, all have been analyzed in terms of the overall institution. There is, in my view, a dynamic for the institution as a whole that has been identified. What has been described are tendencies or trends which seem likely to continue, as opposed to completed processes. The CNBB is likely to become more emphatic and specific; CIMI has a tendency to become more critical; and the CEBs are expected to take hold and multiply. These are by no means fulfilled or terminal conditions. Indeed, in any dynamic institution there is no such thing as a completed condition: structures, processes, and goals are constantly evolving. This is particularly important to emphasize because the church, more than other institutions, is frequently assumed to possess previously worked-out strategies or programs which provide for all possible contingencies. This may have been the case in the past, and possibly holds true today in terms of exclusively religious questions, but it is certainly not the case in sociopolitical matters. Rather, the church avails itself of various strategies to deal with changing and intricate situations and processes that are often scarcely understood. We have paid particular attention to these processes and the church's response to them. There are good indications that the church tends to act in a particular manner or adopt a particular orientation not necessarily because of a prearranged agreement, nor because of a sense of unanimity, but rather because of a lack of viable alternatives. Ideology certainly does play a role in the orientation assumed or course of action taken, but alternatives are frequently imposed more by external situations than by internal conditions over which the church may have control.

It seems clear that the church today is adopting a particular approach to influence which contradicts most of its past, a situation which can be appreciated only after a brief recapitulation of the institution's history. Of particular importance is the original model of church-state and church-society relationships established in Brazil and most other Latin American countries. In this pattern, which I have termed "Christendom," the church is integrated with state and society at all levels and is not required—or encouraged—to evolve its own infrastructure or commitments. The implications of such a pattern for the church meant that the institution did not have to grow as a coherent organization and that its influence could remain untested, for it was assumed that it enjoyed a monopoly over religious belief and practice. In fact, however, religion for most of the population evolved independently of the church and church influence was illusory. This initial relationship has imposed tremendous limitations on later attempts to change, since the church is still inclined to identify influence with political power and thereby to remain allied with the state and the power it supposedly can offer.

The implications of this situation for state and society are important and reasonably clear. Because the church historically has been allied with the state, it has been unable to serve as a nexus of tension, opposition, and conflict in society, a situation which has discouraged greater pluralism. Indeed, as most students of Brazilian society have observed, there is a tremendous centralization and stability of societal structures, which has persisted and ultimately grown into a system best termed "conservative modernization." Had the church achieved a higher degree of independence, it might have played a role similar to that assigned it in Western Europe, where its opposition to the state encouraged further tension and pluralism and led to modification of the existing systems.

In addition, because of the initial religious pattern established in Brazil, combined with the church's slight influence, the generalized type of religiosity handed down to the present is in a form I have termed "popular Catholicism," which has been held up (justifiably, as the survey shows) to be a kind of pacifying agent. The most common type of religiosity, therefore, has actively militated against popular mobilization. Directly, as the church became integrated with the state, and indirectly through the type of religiosity promoted by the church, or better, permitted, the church and religion have fostered tremendous stability and continuity in Brazilian society and politics.

From its original situation of having state support but little influence, the church shifted, around the turn of this century, as a result of a republican political context and disestablishment. For the first time it entered into direct contact with the Vatican, received direction from Rome, and received resources of all sorts from the universal Church. The Brazilian church gradually developed into a modern organization resembling a model which had been expected since at least the First Vatican Council. However, as it grew organizationally and became more closely linked to the Vatican, its approach to influence became increasingly oriented toward Western Europe and, consequently, inappropriate for rural, underdeveloped Brazil. This approach included the closing of the institution to the outside world, a pastoral strategy geared to the middle and upper classes, and a general lack of concern for and attention to the particular Brazilian context. The pattern of religiosity most actively promoted—which I have termed "orthodox" or "cult" Catholicism—may not have included the same high degree of pacifying aspects as popular Catholicism but was otherworldly and, with its main focus on internal church considerations and administration of the sacraments, essentially unconcerned with sociopolitical matters or the Brazilian context. What is more, as the institution developed it became more attractive to the state; it was co-opted by the Vargas regime in the early 1930s, which developed into a relationship I have termed "Neo-Christendom." This relationship resulted in the church again receiving support and resources from the state, which in turn was legitimated by the church. Indeed, the authoritarian type of regime created by Vargas continued well into the early 1960s. Because the particularly favored stratum of society was the middle class, the rural and urban poor were largely ignored, but they persisted in their own beliefs and practices and thus reinforced traditional society and the generally low level of popular participation.

However, even this stable society began to change dramatically after the Second World War, as industrialization and urbanization increased and the possibility of a very different kind of political regime arose. In this era—Brazil's "Pre-Revolution"—everything seemed possible and the church, mainly through Catholic Action and the CNBB, became actively involved in promoting structural change in society. Support from Rome, encouragement from a changing or, at least, challenged state, and the clear perception of environmental threats favored such an approach. During this period, which lasted from approximately the mid-1950s until 1964, the church assumed a role in assisting sociopolitical change. The Pre-Revolution was aborted, however, and reaction to it resulted in the formation of a regime embodying the worst aspects of Brazil's authoritarian and socially conservative past.

Despite the church's historically conservative and largely apathetic past, it did not revert after the Pre-Revolution and has increasingly, though unevenly, assumed a role at variance with most of its past. It is adopting a commitment which negates the history of Christendom, in terms of both structures and behavior. This process is based on a number of complex, interacting factors. First of all, the pre-1964 sociopolitical commitments and orientations were not easily cast off, especially since aspects of these commitments had been legitimated internationally after Vatican II. These commitments were further specified and elaborated by a process of conflict as the regime attempted to reconsolidate a Neo-Christendom model in which the church would support the status quo. As the hierarchy, as well as other elements in the church, come to appreciate more fully the threats facing the church, in terms of both the nature of the regime and its model and the legacy of several centuries of low influence, pre-1964 commitments are further refined. The state is relentlessly withdrawing privileges the church regained during the Vargas era and has repressed priests as impartially as it has labor leaders.

These incidents, together with the fact that the regime legitimates itself in the name of national security (if economic growth alone is not sufficient), have made it clear that the church no longer occupies a privileged position in Brazilian society. The church hierarchy is finally coming to realize that the religion practiced by the majority of the population is not that promoted by the institution, a point dramatized by the rapid growth of other religious movements—particularly Protestant sects and spirit-possession cults.

And finally, as the church has adopted a new, critical role, it has increasingly become an institution where others in opposition to the regime find support; thus a certain momentum is achieved in which the church is encouraged to assume a more critical and defined position vis à vis the state. The church has become the primary institutional focus of dissidence in the country.

It is no exaggeration to state that the authoritarian and arbitrary actions of the regime have forced this role on the church. This has occurred at a time when the church has become aware of its religious weakness and seeks a new role in society. At present the church would appear to have little option but to redefine its approach to influence. The institutional problem of goal definition and coherence will arise if and when the regime is replaced by one more democratic and popular.

In the meantime the church seeks out problem areas where are found those who not only fail to benefit, but who actively suffer from the economic and social development promoted by the regime. In so doing it has redefined its approach to influence by assisting the lower classes in seeking their liberation: the church acts prophetically by means of statements denouncing and criticizing the regime and in some respects provides a countermodel. In a certain sense this is a utopian formulation, albeit with sound theological bases, which is attractive to the lower classes. The church has created and promoted groups and institutes for specific problem-areas, such as human rights, land tenure, and Indians. There is little doubt that the national church (through the CNBB and related institutes) is actively promoting a progressive social role for itself and, by backing its statements with actions, is perceived as being socially active by both supporters and opponents.

Although the church is not a monolith, sufficient unanimity concerning this new role exists among the bishops or the CNBB would not be able to issue the type of public statements it does. We find, however, that the individual dioceses do not implement national church policies evenly, and that those that fall in line do so for essentially the same reasons that caused the national church to change. In effect, there is an initial commitment by an individual or group, a certain process that involves questioning the past and seeking increased influence, and an overall encouragement caused by the awareness of weakness with regard to both structures and the church's impact. Where this new role is most actively assumed, as in S.P. 1 and

Center 1, there is an important process of specialization and complexity as the local church renegotiates its position in society.

At present, then, the church may still lack religious influence but it is not seeking power and indeed is critical of power for its role in making secure an unjust socioeconomic system. What is more, as the Basic Christian Communities expand and multiply, they tend to invert the focus of the church, a process which implies further change by bringing the institution closer to the concrete interests and problems of the population. As the church becomes less institutionalized, or redefines its role, the possibility of ever returning to a Neo-Christendom model is decreased; there will be increasingly less structure to attract the state, and it will be difficult for the church to obtain and coordinate support from the CEBs, even if it wants to.

The particular goal of the changing church—that type of religiosity I have termed "social Catholicism"—does run coterminous with general sociopolitical progressiveness, we discovered. It would be sociologically unfounded to argue that social Catholicism led to sociopolitical progressiveness, since most likely they are parallel phenomena. But it is clear that social Catholics do exist and that they do indeed hold progressive views regarding sociopolitical matters. In testing whether innovations in the dioceses lead to the social Catholicism form of religiosity, however, we find that even for our relatively closely linked sample, the evidence generally does not support this contention. In six dioceses (excluding S.P. 1 and S.P. 2) innovation, not unexpectedly, did not necessarily lead to adherence to the social Catholicism pattern. We found that in São Paulo there were significant differences holding for both parishes, and a very important exception was found in the Center, where the lower classes were more likely to adhere to this pattern in the innovative than in the more-traditional diocese.

There are a number of conclusions to be drawn from an analysis of survey results and changes in the dioceses. A general, or broad strategy to promote the social Catholicism pattern is simply not effective. Where it is effective, as in São Paulo, it is backed by almost three decades of fairly consistent work and reorientation and relatively abundant resources; the likelihood of success decreases as personnel and funds decrease. As less-wealthy dioceses adopt a more-progressive orientation, they will likely be unable to implement it effectively, since those dioceses which tend to innovate most rapidly are those which are relatively less structured and which lack resources. Those wanting to innovate the most, therefore, are least able to implement a strategy which will show actual results in terms of the social Catholicism pattern. However, the rate of change in the dioceses is generally more rapid than I had originally expected, and as the national processes continue, it may well be that most dioceses, rich as well as poor, will innovate.

In the Center there was evidence of the most consistent and active promotion of the social Catholicism pattern among the lower class, and people did, in fact, appear to be influenced by this direction. If other dioceses choose this option, it is possible that they, too, will increase their influence over this class. The implications, for the other classes and the regime they support, of increased influence over the lower class are already fairly well understood and form the basis of the conflict between church and state. Data from the Center indicate, and more general observations support, the contention that the church, by adopting a commitment to assist the poor in liberating themselves, must at least partially ignore the other classes; the lesson here is that the committed church cannot be fully catholic if it is serious in redefining its mission.

In such a context the CEBs assume great importance. Even at this rudimentary stage it is obvious that they represent a strategy which is not hindered by the paucity of resources and which can operate with the poor. By means of self-selection and the internal participation processes, there is a greater likelihood of social Catholicism among CEB members than in the more-traditional groups or in the sample in general. CEBs hold clear implications for the nature of religion, church structures and processes, and change in the larger society: for religion because they base their work on the Bible and are communally, rather than individually, oriented; for the church because they bring the institution closer to the Brazilian reality and oblige both clergy and laity to face concrete concerns; and for the larger society because they provide a model or nucleus for participation and an impetus for other groups to take root and assume roles in the larger society and polity.

Some questions may remain as to why the church is pursuing a strategy of criticizing power (as currently embodied in the authoritarian government), of seeking influence among the lower class, and of increasingly basing much of its structure on the CEB. A cynical view would have it that the church simply seeks influence and this is the quickest means of getting it. This is not sufficient reason, however, for, although the church does indeed seek influence, this strategy is not the easiest or the surest way to secure it.

Much simpler, and safer, would be to continue to base its approach on the middle class and promote pietistic and reconversion groups with minimal social content (the classic cursilhos). This strategy was adopted for a while in the early 1970s, but has now been superseded. One must give due attention to ideology in these changes, for it seems clear that a commitment to something akin to the Theology of Liberation has developed on the part of very substantial sectors of the church. Because of its pre-1964 commitment, the attempt to relate theology to Brazilian reality, the international developments in the church, and the conflict process, the predominant theological or ideological formulation clearly seeks a profound transformation in the regime and the socioeconomic model it promotes. The church's option, then, signals a reversal in structural terms of its whole history as well as of its role in society. The option is significant for society in that what remains a very central and obvious institution is intentionally trying to promote change in a regime whose best interests are served by avoiding change. Even if, in the short run, the generalized strategy of influence through the promotion of social Catholicism is unsuccessful or, at best, unworkable, the church's having opted for it—and what this implies in terms of the CEBs, groups, and institutes—is important to the underpinnings of society.

To review the contribution by the church to change in society and the regime, the following areas would have to be cited: the elaboration and promotion of models of state and society different from those officially promoted by the government and generally antagonistic to them; the use of the existing institution, and the creation of new groups and institutes when necessary, to put pressure for change on the government and other elites; the provision of a certain "space," or area, as well as support, for units like the CEBs to grow and develop, and thereby reconstruct civil society. It has been argued that the rather substantial transformation in the church took place because of the nature of the Brazilian regime. Now that the regime would appear to be opening up, will the church revert to purely religious positions and activities? In the long run this may well be the case, for the church's main function is to assist people in their quest for salvation. However, in light of the statement issued by the CNBB in August 1979 (*Subsídios para uma política social—Aids for a Social Policy*), the statement concerning the need for agrarian reform issued in February 1980, and the broad support for São Paulo strikers a few months later, it would appear that political commitment remains at the forefront of the church's concerns. A transition to an elitist or conservative democratic regime will not be enough to satisfy the demands formulated by the church during the past decade.

Obviously, the church is not going to bring on "the revolution" singlehandedly, but neither is any other single group or institution. Rather, the church is promoting a general structural change in a great many ways, and thereby is assisting a more general process. We know from historical and more-recent instances of regime change, such as in Portugal, Spain, and Nicaragua, that these structural transformations result from peculiar and unique configurations and are not the result of the actions of any one group or institution, except in the most proximate and limited sense. Furthermore, probably just as important are the changes that occur during and after structural transformations; the church in Brazil, in giving direction to a society that has yet to emerge, is preparing the people to be ready for the first time. It may well lack power and its general influence may remain shaky, but it is defining a role and position for itself fully consistent with the radical roots of the Gospel message so often voiced but so seldom carried forward.

Epilogue

The Implications of the Pope's Visit in Summer 1980

The significance of Pope John Paul II's visit to Brazil between 30 June and 11 July cannot be overemphasized. The pope's statements and actions supported the progressive sociopolitical orientation of the CNBB in specifics and in general. He did not provide the regime with material with which it might contrast the Brazilian church with the universal Church (symbolized by the papacy), and his visit generated tremendous enthusiasm, which indicated that Brazilian religiosity is very much alive.[1]

The visit was the first by any pope to Brazil. It was the longest papal trip outside Italy in modern times, a clear indication of its intended importance. The importance of the trip was also implied by its very intense nature, which saw the pope making some forty speeches and approximately two dozen homilies in thirteen cities in all parts of the country. The trip took him from Brasília, to Rio, São Paulo and other parts of the developed South, to Salvador and Recife and other parts of the underdeveloped Northeast, and finally to Manaus in the Amazon. Although some of the speeches were made to specific and somewhat restricted groups (such as diplomats, bishops, or intellectuals), most were public gatherings in which the pope came into contact with hundreds of thousands of people in a fairly direct way. It is conservatively estimated that some 15 million people attended these public appearances, and that the vast majority of the country's 120 million came into contact with him by means of television and radio. In terms of duration, distances, speeches, and contacts, the papal visit was full and important.

The stay is even more important, however, in light of the sociopolitical role of the church. We must remember that the Brazilian church is both the largest in the world and probably the most progressive in sociopolitical matters. This is significant not only within Brazil, as analyzed here, but also with regard to all of Latin America, because the Brazilian clergy have played very important roles in many instances, the CELAM meetings at Medellín in 1968 and at Puebla in 1979 being the most obvious. The Brazilians have been the leaders, and although others, such as the Nicaraguans and Salvadoreans, have moved closer to the Brazilian orientation, the executive of CELAM under Mons. López Trujillo, a Colombian, has adopted a more conservative orientation than the Brazilian. The stance the pope adopted in Brazil, then, holds continent-wide implications.

Within Brazil itself the timing of the papal visit was very important. In April and May metalworkers in the industrial area of São Paulo (the ABC region) went out on an illegal forty-one day strike, vigorously opposed and finally crushed by the government. The local church hierarchy (Dom Cláudio Humes and Cardinal Arns) and the CNBB provided moral support as well as provisions and meeting space in churches for the strikers. The regime (up to the highest levels) made clear its unhappiness with the church's involvement, and representation was made to Rome criticizing the church's support. Thus the pope's actions during his Brazilian trip would be closely scrutinized for signs of support for the striking São Paulo metalworkers.

This is not the place to attempt to analyze the personality and orientation of Pope John Paul II. There were, however, a number of indications that he might not be supportive of the progressive orientation of the Brazilian church. For example, he has strong reservations concerning Marxism and, since some of the statements from the Brazilian church have been attacked as Marxist-inspired, there was a basis for confusion on this point. His stance at the CELAM meeting in Puebla was ambiguous, but he was particularly cautious about the Theology of Liberation movement. (Some of the orientations of the Brazilian church are similar to those of the Theology of Liberation.) He has quite specifically warned against church and clerical involvement in politics, and the Vatican has emphasized orthodoxy and dogma in theological matters, as dramatized by the control over the Dutch hierarchy and in cases of theologians such as Hans Kung. All were thus watching to see whether a conservative orientation would be projected for the Brazilian church, which would serve to delegitimate its statements and actions and thereby allow the regime to use the pope's statements for its own ends. Indeed, even the question of the pope's itinerary was a political matter and it was modified four times.

The pope's words and actions during the very heavily scheduled twelve days provided unambiguous support for the progressive sociopolitical orientation of the Brazilian church, as analyzed in this book. On the very first day the pope stated that while the mission of the church is pastoral, and cannot be summed up as a sociopolitical role, the church must be concerned with society and must promote reforms aimed at a "more just society and always more in accord with the dignity of all people." Also on the first day, at the official welcoming ceremony at the presidential palace, the pope spoke out strongly in favor of human rights. It was only on the first day of the visit that he was to have these official contacts; from then on his contacts would be with either church groups (CELAM, CNBB, Eucharistic Congress) or the people (*favela* ["slum"] dwellers, workers, peasants, Indians). His contacts with government, then, were restricted from the beginning and remained formal, distant, and cold.

In his speeches the pope specifically supported the themes I have analyzed in this book. He criticized the economic model ("a dominating economism" aggravated by a "crass materialism") and supported the workers. He argued that the church had to be the church of the poor and supported liberation as the option from Medellín and Puebla. He stated that the peasants should have a right to land and the Indians a right to survive as Indians. What is more, he clearly supported the organizations and individuals by means of which the options and commitments of CELAM would be implemented: the CNBB; bishops such as Dom Helder Câmara and Cardinal Arns; and the Basic Christian Communities (whose "specific contribution for the construction of society" he noted).

All of this is not to suggest that the pope spoke only about sociopolitical matters. Indeed, his statements must be seen in the context of this book in order to be understood as emphatically supportive of the sociopolitical role of the changing church. The pope's message was primarily religious, as would be expected of a religious leader addressing sectors of the institution he heads. In religious terms the response of the people, much as in Mexico in 1979, was overwhelming. Not only were the people enthusiastic but, we are told, the pope responded to this enthusiasm by relating his speeches even more closely to their expectations.[2] His words and actions, then, were geared very much to the people; the religious theme was predominant, and the sociopolitical commitment of the Brazilian church was supported in terms of fulfilling the religious mission with the people.

This last point brings up a very important distinction between politics seen as involvement with political parties or partisan organizations and societal action which seeks to improve the plight of the people. The pope's warnings prior to the visit to Brazil discouraged party or partisan involvement but encouraged clerical involvement to help the poor.

Obviously the distinction in a society such as Brazil is not clear, but suffice it to say that the pope did support the clergy's involvement in society as defined by the Brazilian church in recent times. The church's encouragement of the CEB as one type of "intermediate social group," or pressure group, can help make society more pluralistic, and thus decrease the need for the church's direct involvement. Until that happens, however, the Brazilian clergy's work with the people can continue, with the pope's blessing.

Appendix 1: Description of the Field Study

This study grew out of my earlier book, which described and analyzed change in the Catholic church in Brazil. After having completed this first work, I began to wonder what difference it made if the church changed or not, since all observers have commented on the historical lack of influence of the Brazilian church among a population much given to "popular religiosity," forms of Spiritism, fundamental Protestant sects, and movements such as messianic cults. The only way to ascertain the impact of change in the church seemed to be a survey of some part of the population. I chose not to pursue an "anthropological" approach to the survey, for the "depth over breadth" of such an approach might be very informative about one particular area or group of people but would be completely ungeneralizable in such an enormous and heterogeneous country. I chose, instead, a general survey emphasizing breadth. As a number of problems are inherent in this approach, I will try to clarify my intentions and methodology so the study is not misrepresented and its strengths and weaknesses fully understood.

Surveys are extremely expensive because of the large number of questionnaires required and the subsequent costs of coding, key punching, and computer time. However, after an initial amount of preparation, the Canada Council agreed to fund the project and was most generous in granting a supplemental allocation when additional expenses became apparent. It was possible, therefore, to fund the full costs of the project. Although resources were not overly abundant, they were sufficient for the needs of the project. The question then became one of access.

I hoped I would be able to count on the cooperation of the church elite because I had field experience in Brazil, because the Portuguese translation of my first book had been well received, and because the study was to be designed so that the results might be employed by the church in its pastoral planning. This proved to be the case, and cooperation from elements within the church, with a few notable exceptions, was remarkable in its depth and consistency. As far as the Brazilian government was concerned, I must say that I remained in the country for ten months, traveled and interviewed constantly, and experienced no difficulty or harassment of any kind.

Both before going to the field and once in Brazil, I gave considerable thought to how the study itself, particularly the survey, would be carried out. The thorniest problem was undoubtedly the sampling strategy. As is clear throughout this book, I have been very much influenced by the ideas of the late Ivan Vallier. I agree fully with his argument for studying dioceses and emphasized this in my first book, in my 1973 article, and in Chapter 6 of the present work. Vallier stated the problem well:

The optimal strategy, (for the comparative study of religion), though entailing considerable investments of thought and time as well as the competent use of available theory, is to be found in research that (1) defines stable systemic units of intermediate complexity and that possesses salient vertical linkages (up toward the total society or international system and down to micro-units and local systems), (2) selects numerous sets or sub-sets of such units on the basis of systematic sampling plans, (3) involves observations on measurable and theoretically-significant variables referring to collective or institutional phenomena, (4) gives systematic field work (informant interviews, selective surveys, and participant-observation) a central role in data collection, and (5) builds conclusions and inferences from rigorous application of the canons of comparative analysis. Whenever these criteria are met, we not only gain a new kind of productive tension between the general and the particular, or between the micro and macro levels, but, as well, secure an empirical basis on which important variations in social structure can be identified and explained.[1]

It is the diocese, not the national church, that should demand our attention, at least if we are interested in the impact of institutional change on the population. The best strategy thus appeared to be an explicit sampling of sets of dioceses.

I selected dioceses in which serious change in terms of plans, programs, and strategies had been implemented and compared them to other dioceses similar in all respects but change. The dioceses are essential geographical units in the Catholic church, just as their bishops are key personnel. In the first instance, the question of change in the dioceses is a qualitative one. Based on my past experience, and with considerable assistance from individuals and documentation at the Instituto Nacional de Pastoral (INP), the Conferência Nacional dos Bispos do Brasil (CNBB), the Centro de Estatística Religiosa e Investigações Sociais (CERIS), and the Instituto Brasileiro de Desenvolvimento (IBRADES), we selected a possible thirty dioceses which would qualify as unequivocally changed. We had already excluded from this number those dioceses which would be impossible to match (for example, Recife), those in extremely distant and underpopulated areas (for example, the Amazon), and those which might present tricky political problems (João Pessoa, for instance). The prefield evaluation of how unequivocal the change proved to be was not crucial because research plans called for my presence in each of the dioceses finally selected. I was to look into precisely these questions of change in each diocese, where I would interview the church elite (about a dozen people in most cases, including bishop[s], clergy, and involved laity), review all available documentation, and simply observe. The results of this enquiry are presented in Chapter 6.

From this group of thirty, I selected four dioceses located in different parts of the country to give some geographical variety to the project. The selection was made also with an eye to matching the four with four other, nonchanged, dioceses. The latter were selected simultaneously with the former by employing data from CERIS on diocese size, priest/population ratios, number of parishes, and institutional presence as indicated by church-run schools, hospitals, and the like.[2]

In selecting the eight dioceses, I also took into consideration historical factors and unique characteristics which would make comparisons impossible, such as an important pilgrimage spot (Juazeiro do Norte, Bom Jesus do Lapa, for example), the predominance of a religious order, or an unusual ethnic situation. The final selection tool was extensive ecological data taken from the census and other publications of the Fundação-Instituto Brasileiro de Geografia, such as *Divisão do Brasil em micro-regiões homogêneas* (1968) and the *Subsídios à regionalização* (1968). The data included area, population density, urban/rural population, growth of urban/rural population, population distribution by age, population distribution by religion, education and literacy, extent and growth of commerce, type and extent of industry, and type and extent of agriculture. These basic data were further delimited by information provided by the micro-regions publication and observations from Brazilian contacts. A study of this type is what Donald Campbell and Julian Stanley refer to as a "static-group comparison," which is a "design in which a group which has experienced x, is compared with one which has not, for the purpose of establishing the effect of x."[3] It is, as they note, a preexperimental design, and although this may not be very high-powered in terms of optimum social science methodology, the practical problems of arranging the project up to this point were rather complicated. When the key factor is change, in a huge country with 222 ecclesiastical divisions it is no easy matter to match 8 divisions on the basis of historical and ecological variables and then to receive permission from the individual bishops to survey their dioceses. That particular stage of my life is over, and I would prefer not to relive it. With tremendous cooperation from the aforementioned organizations and several individuals, this stage was resolved, and I have no reservations concerning the choice of dioceses.

Although the diocese is the most important unit in the church and the bishop the key decision maker, the dioceses are in turn divided into parishes. In Brazil, for instance, the 222 ecclesiastical units are divided into 5,497 parishes. In order to avoid selecting unrepresentative parishes and to have better coverage, I selected 2 parishes in each diocese for the study. One was always near the center of the diocese (on the assumption that it would mirror most clearly the general diocesan orientation), while the other was located in a more outlying area (but adhered to the same general diocesan orientation). The parishes were matched, with only minor difficulties, moving from the changed diocese to the nonchanged by using the same criteria on which initial selection was based. I again conducted interviews in the parishes with the local elite, including priests and members of the laity, and in most instances, leaders, or at least members of religious groups or associations.

The selection of this study's fundamental units of analysis—the diocese and finally the parish—made it impossible to have what is known as a probability sample, primarily because the ecclesiastical divisions are not identical to those for the municipalities in the census material. The church's research institute (CERIS) does not have sampling frames and, despite a good deal of interaction with employees at the Fundação-Instituto Brasileiro de Geografia, there could be found no adequate means to define such frames in a manner which would be within our resources. Even with presumably more-complete data I would be suspicious of the reliability of any frames. In the Third World, probability samples are generally difficult, if not impossible, to devise. The most complete, thorough, and professionally executed survey was done in Brazil two years before mine by Peter McDonough and Amaury de Souza of the University of Michigan's Institute for Social Research. They restricted their sample to the six states of southeast Brazil— the most developed region of the country—an area unsuitable for my study of the church, since there were few dioceses in this region that had changed by 1974. Without an adequate sampling frame, then, a probability sample is impossible, for, as C. A. Moser and G. Kalton note, a bias can arise "if the sampling frame (list, index or other population record) which serves as the basis for selection does not cover the population adequately, completely or accurately."[4]

The sample thus had to be a "judgment," or nonprobability sample, which was, as Moser and Kalton note, "the only practicable method of sampling a population for which no suitable frame is available."[5] Since this question of types of samples is a heated issue in methodology, it is worth quoting from Moser's and Kalton's discussion dealing with the merits of the quota sample (the type we employed in the survey).

The issue of quota versus probability sampling has been a matter of controversy for many years. Some experts hold the quota method to be so unreliable and prone to bias as to be almost worthless; others think that, although it is obviously less sound theoretically than probability sampling, it can be used safely on some subjects; still others believe that with adequate safeguards quota sampling can be made highly reliable and that the extra cost of probability sampling is not worth while.[6]

They then discuss the pros and cons of quota sampling and conclude that it has some merits and in many cases is all that is possible.[7]

Isidore Chein makes a very important point in showing that studies sometimes are done for other reasons than to generalize from a sample to the whole population. As in the present case, one must determine the purpose of the study and evaluate whether probability sampling is worth the trade-off in possibly redefining the purpose of a study.[8] There are even efforts that estimate the variability of quota samples.[9]

My argument here is that, starting from the position of seeking to link attitudes to the institution, it is probably impossible to do a probability sample in any case. This linking, of course, has been one of the greatest weaknesses of survey research and caused Ivan Vallier to harshly criticize "methodological amateurism" in the study of religion and to caution us against seeking "empirical certitude through assimilating the orthodoxies of sample survey research, especially when the advocates of that approach seem to be unable to move beyond contextual analyses of behavioural reports and stated attitudes."[10] Even if the focus of inquiry here did not make a probability sample impossible, the Brazilian context of this study and the absence of data on the ecclesiastical unit would. My only option was to use a quota sample—which I probably would have done in any case because we required individuals who could be expected to be in contact with the institutional church.

The most straightforward approach to locating a sample in contact with the institutional church was to find them at mass on a Saturday evening or Sunday morning. In this way we could be sure that they attended an obligatory weekly mass, rather than rely on their word to that effect. The minimum one would expect of a person influenced by the church would be weekly mass attendance. Roughly half the sample was located in this way. We wanted a control group as well, and thus the other half of the sample was made up of people not found at mass, although they may well have attended, although less frequently, as reported in Chapter 2. In each parish we surveyed a minimum of fifty people found at mass, another fifty found elsewhere, and another dozen or so who were members of religious groups. Due to an oversampling in some areas because of further requirements of the quota sample, however, we received 1,995 questionnaires, of which 1,912 were utilized in the data analysis.

In order to ensure a cross section in terms of class and sex, the quota sample was further defined as half male and half female and half above and half below the educational mean for the region, as indicated in the census material. In the Northeast and Center this meant half were illiterate and half literate; in São Paulo and the South, half had completed primary school and half had not. If we had followed a probability sample, or had done a census of those attending mass and drawn a sample from it, we would have expected to find a preponderance of women and people above the educational mean. However, the newer church strategies are directed to men as well as women and increasingly to the lower classes. We wanted to include these target groups and did so by means of the quota method. In any parish, then, we would have at least twelve men above the educational mean, twelve below, twelve women above, and twelve below. It should be mentioned here, and will be elaborated on in Appendix 2, that level of education was used only in the sampling strategy. Class will be specified in the analysis in a much more comprehensive manner.

The questionnaire itself was formulated after a long and comprehensive process. Initially, the categories and concepts were defined according to the goals of the study, which included religious beliefs and practices, background in religious formation and education, links to the church through groups, movements, and associations, sociopolitical attitudes, information about national and local events, participation in civic groups and associations, exposure to the media, and a whole battery of controls, including education, class (salary and position), age, nationality, civil status, and migration experience. After consulting various anthologies on the subject of questionnaires, looking at others' questionnaires, and talking with Brazilian colleagues, we formulated a test questionnaire that was administered to sixty people in four areas of Minas Gerais, Estado do Rio de Janeiro, and Guanabara. The definitive questionnaire was based on the results of this application and the observations of the interviewers. The final questionnaire had sixty-five items, many of them multiple choice and several open-ended; the final computer result was 265 variables per respondent.

The questionnaires were applied under the aegis of an organization contracted for this purpose, the Centro de Estudos, Pesquisa e Planejamento (CENPLA), headed by Waldo César. I accompanied the CENPLA group to every diocese, and my assistants also cooperated with them. In each case CENPLA trained a group of young people (normally with some university education, but at least secondary) and controlled the application in the locale. Some initial problems arose because the interviewers tended to select people very much like themselves, although still within the quota requirements, and a few questionnaires had to be discarded because they appeared unreliable. The interviewers were supervised and directed to fill their quotas in different parts of the cities and rural areas. The fact that they found so many people below the educational mean indicated that they were covering the area well enough. The problem of refusals is, strictly speaking, a nonproblem in quota samples, but even so there were very few difficulties. The questionnaire included a section to be filled in by the interviewer (but uncoded) on the conduct of the interview itself. Reviewing these sections while in the field, and talking with the interviewers as well, gives me confidence that, within the limits of the quota sample strategy, the survey was properly applied. The study began in Brazil in October 1974 and was completed in June 1975. The field research was carried out between February and June, with approximately two weeks in each diocese.

The results were coded by a staff-supervised group at IBRADES. The data were punched on cards at the Pontifícia Universidade Católica in Rio de Janeiro and then transferred to magnetic tape in the computing facility there.

After returning to McGill University, I employed Mr. Edmund Horka to work with me to develop a code book from the tape, to clean the data, and to run the analyses. Various statistical techniques were used. In all instances we have followed programs in Norman Nie et al., *Statistical Package for the Social Sciences,* and have used the IBM 360-70.

A nonprobability sample survey such as this does not allow for generalization to the whole population in the country, but it is quite fascinating to see the variety of religious beliefs and practices found within even a judgment sample such as this. The data provide the evidence whereby the influence of the changing church can be evaluated within these particular ecclesiastical divisions, and Appendix 2 describes how the data were analyzed.

Appendix 2: Discussion of the Data Analysis

The use of factor analysis was briefly justified at the beginning of the final section of Chapter 2. In this instance, as in so many concerning methodology, there is a debate raging as to the utility of this technique. Its proponents, such as Richard Gorsuch and R. J. Rummel, argue strongly for its utility, but others suggest that it is all but useless. For my purposes it has proven useful in helping distill or reduce the number of variables to be used in the analysis. Even without this analysis, which is in large part a verification of historical and ethnographic evidence, it is likely that I would have selected the greater part of the questionnaire items for the scales based on the review of the cross tabulations.

PA 1, the program used, is taken from the *Statistical Package for the Social Sciences*, and consists of principal components with a varimax rotation. The twenty-nine items entered in were selected because they seemed broadest and most able to capture all possible patterns. In the case of Spiritism-related questions, they included all questions; with the orthodox Catholicism questions, they included most; and with the likelihood of a popular Catholicism pattern, they included those which seemed most specific. With regard to the questions seeking to identify a social type, there was a variety of items to attempt to capture whatever might be there since I had to rely almost exclusively on attitudinal questions. After reviewing the frequency distributions and the cross tabulations, I excluded items that were heavily skewed and sought those giving the best-possible distribution. After the factor analysis indicated the groupings, the items were reordered so that a clearer grouping could be made and those loadings not relevant for a particular factor blanked out.

In determining the number of factors to use I, of course, was influenced by the historical and ethnographic material reviewed in the first section of Chapter 2. I then followed the rule of thumb in factor analysis and retained all factors with an eigenvalue of 1.0 or above. This resulted in nine factors covering 52 percent of variance. However, following the usual approach of attempting to cover the highest amount of variance with the greatest amount of interpretability, I reduced the factors to five and then to four. Even with six factors, the popular, orthodox, and

Spiritism dimensions were clear, but the social pattern was not. The four factors then made sense and, in addition, the drop-off in percentage of variance explained was faster after four than before. Whereas one factor gave 12.3 percent of variance accounted for, two gave 9.0 percent, three gave 6.3 percent, and four gave 5.1 percent, there was a slight leveling off with five factors, to 4.1 percent. The cumulative percentage, which reached 32.6 percent with four factors, would reach 36.7 percent with five. The gain, at the cost of interpretability, did not seem appropriate.

With regard to both the number of factors and the reliability of factor analysis itself, it may be useful to present the raw material that went into the factor analysis, the correlation matrix. From the factor analysis we saw the grouping into a number of factors or patterns. The patterns were then rearranged according to the order indicated by the grouping, but not modified in any way. The association between the variables was then analyzed again by employing correlation analysis. The correlation matrix that follows is in a one-digit format and all correlations that are not significant at the .01 level are suppressed.

What is clear from the correlation matrix is the grouping into four patterns, where the first three are clearer than the fourth. The correlations within the groups are a good deal higher than with other variables not in that particular group. Further, although the 32.6 percent of variance explained by the four factors is not particularly impressive (although common for survey data of this type), the correlation matrix demonstrates that the patterns do, in fact, exist and are readily recognizable.

Although many of the variables used in the data analysis are described in the text itself, and all of the items are to be found in the questionnaire in Appendix 3, it may be useful to elaborate on some of the key variables and scales if only to avoid possible misunderstandings.

A key variable is class. In the quota sample we simplified the selection by asking only for level of education, which, of course, is a decent indicator of class all by itself. The variable as used here, however, was determined by both education and occupation. Question 54 is critical and served as the basis for our class variable. However, since the minimum salary varied from region to region in Brazil, the distinction by class (as determined by salary) also varied. Some 20 percent of the sample did not know the family income and another 4 percent would not respond. Because 24 percent missing would be too high, and because there should be and were other controls, class was also defined and delimited by occupation, as well as by education. The result for the whole sample was 1,070, or 58 percent in the lower class, 590, or 32 percent in the middle class, and 188, or 10 percent in the higher class. All but 3 percent, then, are included in the class variable. It should be noted that the proportions vary somewhat by region, as the South is clearly more middle class than the Northeast and the Center.

The scales used to define the patterns of religiosity (popular Catholicism, social Catholicism, and Spiritism) were discussed in the historical and descriptive material in Chapter 2 and further delimited later in that same chapter. The particular items used in the scales were selected because of the findings discussed in all three parts of that chapter. It should be stressed, however, that these items had the heaviest loadings in the factors (two between .30 and .40 and all the others above .40) and high communality. The scales varied in range (0-5, 0-6, 0-6, 0-4) because in some cases (such as Spiritism) there were no further items available to define this type, whereas in others (orthodox and social Catholicism) there could be an abundance. Since we are not dealing with absolute numbers but rather, with variations, the range is not particularly important.

The scales used in Chapter 7 are described in that chapter. A great many items were initially included with a view to discarding those which finally proved unclear or ambiguous. This cumbersome and inefficient procedure was the only one that seemed viable, given the disparate sample from four regions of the country and the vastly different levels of education. More than half of the items were omitted from the analysis in Chapter 7 because the responses they elicited suggested that the responses as items were unclear or unreliable. It should be immediately apparent that the relationships, although consistent and readily understandable, were not terribly strong. This was due in part to the continued use of the Tau C statistic, which is by nature a conservative ordinal measure. It was due as well to the very nature of the sample, with its great regional variations as well as class and other differences. Possibly the initial questions could have been clearer, less ambiguous, and simpler, but, even in retrospect, I cannot imagine how. It may have been possible to find a few questions that would elicit consistent and straightforward responses time after time, but at the possible cost of misrepresenting the actual attitudes of the respondent. There is, of course, considerable debate over the merits of various types of questions. It would seem that the results we obtained from the application of a great many questionnaires and from talking personally with some of the respondents merely reflected the confusion and contradictions that exist in the "real world out there." Therefore, although one could wish for stronger relationships than presented here, these were consistent, unambiguous, and hnderstandable. For present purposes these results satisfy the goals of the study.

The awareness and the control and criticism scales were selected above other possibilities (for example, questions 40, 42, 46e, and 46f) because the latter were seen to be ambiguous in my review of the cross-tab results of these questions with other items. The problem impact scale was based upon a great deal of coding of responses to open-ended questions and thus summarized a tremendous amount of data. Each segment of this scale could be run separately, but it seemed most efficient to combine the overall responses for a single scale. In these scales, and others, it is not the percentage of one particular variable that is run against another variable that is important, but rather the relationships. The goal was not to determine some absolute situation of religiosity or awareness, for example, but rather to determine how they relate to other variables also on a scale.

If one compares the abundant variety of items in the questionnaire with the items finally used in the data analysis, it would appear that I have only barely tapped what is available. This is not quite the case, for the factor analysis itself utilized twenty-nine items and the sociopolitical scales twenty-three. Furthermore, these

Table 36
Correlation Matrix

Religiosity Items

Religiosity Items	1	2	3	4	5	6	7	8	9	10	11	12	13	14	15	16	17	18	19	20	21	22	23	24	25	26	27	28	29
1	**											1	1	1	1				-1	-1		-1	-1			-1			
2	8	**										1	1	2					-1	-1	-1	-1	-1			-1	-1		
3	4	3	**									1	1	1															
4	5	5	4	**							1	1	1													-1	-1		
5	3	3	1	2	**				1			1	2	1	1	1	1			-1	-1					-1	-1		
6	2	2	1	2	2	**			-1			1	1	4	1	1			-1	-1	-1	-1	-1			-1	-1		
7							**	3	1	2	-1		3			1		1				1						1	
8							3	**	1	1	1	2	2	1	1	1	1												
9					1	-1	1	1	**	1	1	1	1	1	1	1								-1	-1	-1	-1		
10							2	1	1	**	-2	3	3	-1	-1	-1				-1									
11							-1	-1	-2	-2	**	2	2	1	1	4	1		1	2		1			1			1	
12								1	1		2	**	2	2	1	2	1				-1								
13								3			3	2	**	1	1	2	1												
14									-1		1	1	1	**	1	1	1	1							-1	-1	-1	
15									-1		1	1	1	1	**	1	2												
16							-1				4	2	2	1	1	**	2						-1			-1	-1		
17											1	1	1			2	**			-1									
18																		**	**										
19	-1	-1																	**	-1		2	1			1		1	1
20	-1	-1									2						-1		2	**	2	1	2				1	1	1
21	-1	-1			-1									-1		1		-1	1	**	**	1	2					1	1
22	-1	-1				-1						-1							1	2		**	4	1				1	1

Table 36 (continued)

23		-1							
24		-1							
25	1		-1 -1	-1 -1 -1					
26				-1 -1					
27	1	-1							
28									
29									

Religiosity Items

	1 1	4 ** 1	1 1				1 1		
		1 1 **	**						2
	-1	1		**	1				
	-1						**		
	-1 -1 -1	2			1	**			
	1 1 1	1 1 1	**						
	1 1 1 1	2						**	

16 Reliance on church
17 Prayer to our Lady
18 Reliance on church for resolution of social problems
19 Reliance on church for resolution of individuals' problems
20 Possession of Bible
21 Belief in church as agent of social change
22 Propriety of contraceptive use
23 Belief in social direction of church
24 Catholics as the People of God
25 Belief in conscience as guide
26 Belief in church's role in society and politics
27 Belief in salvation for all religions
28 Belief in ability of souls in purgatory to help those on earth
29 Belief in Christ as the Liberator

Religiosity Items
1 Making of promises
2 Making of promises to our Lady
3 Making of promises for indulgences
4 Making of money- or job-related promises
5 Benefit from miracle(s)
6 Prayer to saints
7 Attendance at Spiritist center
8 Offering to a Spiritist deity
9 Summoning of Spiritist "priest" or faith healer
10 Appropriateness of attendance at Spiritist center
11 Frequency of mass attendance
12 Closeness to church
13 Frequency of prayer
14 Attendance at mass for patron saint
15 Existence of judgment after death

fifty-two items were selected after a very extensive review of all other religious and sociopolitical items in our survey and found to be most useful for the purposes of this book. The section on groups (section III in the questionnaire) finds its way into Chapter 8. In these instances, and others, much more of the data were used than would appear at first glance. Still, not all the data were used and education, exposure to media, and migration have barely been touched as being largely inappropriate to the purposes of this book.

Appendix 3: English-Language Version of Questionnaire

The Catholic Church and Popular Religiosity in Brazil

This questionnaire is part of a study being carried out in different parts of the country about the religious beliefs and practices of Brazilians. Brazil has the largest Catholic population in the world, as well as the largest Spiritist population, with a wealth of religious beliefs and movements of all kinds. We want to understand these phenomena in relation to the Catholic church and the larger society. This study is not sponsored by the church or any government; it is financed independently with an eye to furthering the progress of science. We will not divulge the names of those involved; everything will remain anonymous. The results of the project will be published for those interested.

☐ ☐ ☐ ☐ Questionnaire Number
☐ State
☐ ☐ Municipality
☐ ☐ Parish
☐ Origin   —mass 1
                —general 2
                —group 3
☐ Type of group

I. Religious Background

To begin with, we would like to learn something about your religious background.

Q.1   Did you make your First Communion?
1. ☐ Yes
2. ☐ No
3. ☐ Don't remember   (Go on to question 2.)
9. ☐ No reply

Q.1A What do you remember most about your First Communion?
1. ☐ The party (food, many people, everything white, etc.)
2. ☐ Receiving Jesus Christ for the first time
3. ☐ The instruction received in preparation
4. ☐ Other: specify
5. ☐ Nothing
6. ☐ Don't remember
8. ☐ Not applicable (didn't make First Communion)
9. ☐ No reply

Q.2   Were you married in the church?
1. ☐ Yes
2. ☐ No
8. ☐ Not applicable (not married)   (Go on to question 3.)
9. ☐ No reply

Q.2A What impressed you most about your wedding?
1. ☐ The presence of friends and family
2. ☐ The instruction received in preparation
3. ☐ The union of two Christian people
4. ☐ The honeymoon
5. ☐ Other: specify
6. ☐ Nothing
7. ☐ Don't remember
8. ☐ Not applicable (not married)
9. ☐ No reply

Q.3   Do you go to mass?
1. ☐ More than once a week
2. ☐ Once a week
3. ☐ A few times a month
4. ☐ A few times a year
5. ☐ Never
9. ☐ No reply

Q.4 Do you go to these masses?
(Check one response on each line)

Mass:	yes	no	no reply
Seventh day after interment	1. ☐	2. ☐	9. ☐
Holy Week	1. ☐	2. ☐	9. ☐
Feast day of patron saint	1. ☐	2. ☐	9. ☐
Holy days and special days (anniversaries, graduations, etc.)	1. ☐	2. ☐	9. ☐

Q.5 Can you tell me how often your parents went to Sunday Mass when you were growing up?
(Check one response in each column)

	father	mother
Less frequently than you	1. ☐	1. ☐
More often than you	2. ☐	2. ☐
The same as you	3. ☐	3. ☐
They didn't go to mass	4. ☐	4. ☐
Don't know	5. ☐	5. ☐
Not applicable (orphan)	8. ☐	8. ☐
No reply	9. ☐	9. ☐

Q.6 Do you pray?
1. ☐ Daily
2. ☐ Sometimes
3. ☐ Rarely
4. ☐ Never   (Go on to question 7.)
9. ☐ No reply

Q.6A To whom do you pray?
(Check one response on each line)

	yes	no	not applicable	no reply
Our Lady	1. ☐	2. ☐	8. ☐	9. ☐
Saints	1. ☐	2. ☐	8. ☐	9. ☐
God	1. ☐	2. ☐	8. ☐	9. ☐
Souls	1. ☐	2. ☐	8. ☐	9. ☐
Christ	1. ☐	2. ☐	8. ☐	9. ☐
Other (specify)	1. ☐	2. ☐	8. ☐	9. ☐

Q.6B What do you usually pray for?
(Check only one response)
1. ☐ To ask for strength to face difficulties; to petition for peace or justice
2. ☐ To give thanks
3. ☐ To ask for assistance with concrete problems, such as getting a job, curing an illness, family problems, and so forth
4. ☐ Other (specify)
5. ☐ Don't know
9. ☐ No reply

Q.7   What do you expect after death?
(Check only the most important response)
1. ☐ Reincarnation
2. ☐ Salvation in heaven
3. ☐ Final judgment
4. ☐ Recompense
5. ☐ Other (specify)
6. ☐ Nothing
7. ☐ Don't know
9. ☐ No reply

Q.8   How would you characterize Jesus Christ?
(Check only the most important response)
1. ☐ Son of God who died on the cross
2. ☐ The liberator of the weak and poor
3. ☐ The most powerful of the saints
4. ☐ A person of the Holy Trinity
5. ☐ A great prophet
6. ☐ Other (specify)
7. ☐ Don't know
9. ☐ No reply

Q.9   What is the church to you?
(Check only the most important response)
1. ☐ A place where one prays or asks for something
2. ☐ The people of God
3. ☐ The priests and bishops
4. ☐ The reunion of baptized souls
5. ☐ Other (specify)
6. ☐ Don't know
9. ☐ No reply

Q.10 Do you feel that you are:
1. ☐ Close to the church?
2. ☐ More or less close?
3. ☐ Far from the church?
4. ☐ Completely disassociated from the church?
5. ☐ Don't know
9. ☐ No reply

Q.11 Was there a time when you were either closer to or farther away from the church?
1. ☐ Used to be closer
2. ☐ Used to be farther away   (Ask questions 12 and 12A.)
3. ☐ Have always been the same
4. ☐ Don't know; don't remember
9. ☐ No reply

Only for those who replied that they used to be farther away in question 11.

Q.12 Has the fact that your becoming closer to the church made any difference in your life?

1. □ Yes
2. □ No
3. □ Don't know   (Go on to question 13.)
8. □ Not applicable
9. □ No reply

Q.12A How has your life changed?
(Check one response on each line)

	yes	no	don't know	not ap- plicable	no reply
Relationship with famiy	1. □	2. □	3. □	8. □	9. □
Interest in other peoples' problems	1. □	2. □	3. □	8. □	9. □
Acceptance of hardship	1. □	2. □	3. □	8. □	9. □
Awareness of the social situation in country	1. □	2. □	3. □	8. □	9. □

Q.13 Do you think you can rely on the church to resolve these problems?
(Check one response on each line)

	yes	no	don't know	no reply
Material problems (lack of work, food, etc.)	1. □	2. □	3. □	9. □
Crisis of faith, spiritual problems	1. □	2. □	3. □	9. □
Defense of [human] rights	1. □	2. □	3. □	9. □
Personal problems	1. □	2. □	3. □	9. □

Q.14 How much influence did/do the following have over your religious life?
(Check one response on each line)

	great	some	little	none	not ap- plicable	no reply
Friends	1. □	2. □	3. □	4. □	8. □	9. □
Mother	1. □	2. □	3. □	4. □	8. □	9. □
Father	1. □	2. □	3. □	4. □	8. □	9. □
Teachers	1. □	2. □	3. □	4. □	8. □	9. □
Priests/Nuns	1. □	2. □	3. □	4. □	8. □	9. □
Books	1. □	2. □	3. □	4. □	8. □	9. □
Groups	1. □	2. □	3. □	4. □	8. □	9. □

Q.15 Do you belong to or have you ever belonged to these religious groups or associations?
(Check two responses on each line)

Religious Groups or Associations	belonged			belong		
	yes	no	no reply	yes	no	no reply
1. Devotional groups (Legion of Mary, Apostolate of Prayer, Marianos, etc.)	1. ☐	2. ☐	9. ☐	1. ☐	2. ☐	9. ☐
2. Christian Family Movement (MFC)	1. ☐	2. ☐	9. ☐	1. ☐	2. ☐	9. ☐
3. Vicentinos	1. ☐	2. ☐	9. ☐	1. ☐	2. ☐	9. ☐
4. Workers' Circles	1. ☐	2. ☐	9. ☐	1. ☐	2. ☐	9. ☐
5. Basic Education Movement (MEB)	1. ☐	2. ☐	9. ☐	1. ☐	2. ☐	9. ☐
6. Catholic Action (JEC, JUC, etc.)	1. ☐	2. ☐	9. ☐	1. ☐	2. ☐	9. ☐
7. Others (specify)	1. ☐	2. ☐	9. ☐	1. ☐	2. ☐	9. ☐

Q.16 Do you read religious magazines or newspapers or listen to radio or TV programs sponsored by the church?
1. ☐ Daily
2. ☐ Sometimes
3. ☐ Rarely
4. ☐ Never
8. ☐ Not applicable (can't read and doesn't have TV)
9. ☐ No reply

Q.17 Do you have or have you had contact with some of these church activities?
(Check two responses on each line)

	had			have		
	yes	no	no reply	yes	no	no reply
Catholic school	1. ☐	2. ☐	9. ☐	1. ☐	2. ☐	9. ☐
Basic Education Movement (MEB)	1. ☐	2. ☐	9. ☐	1. ☐	2. ☐	9. ☐
Assistance (hospitals, orphanages)	1. ☐	2. ☐	9. ☐	1. ☐	2. ☐	9. ☐
Cooperatives	1. ☐	2. ☐	9. ☐	1. ☐	2. ☐	9. ☐
Unions	1. ☐	2. ☐	9. ☐	1. ☐	2. ☐	9. ☐
Other (specify)	1. ☐	2. ☐	9. ☐	1. ☐	2. ☐	9. ☐

Q.18 Do you own religious objects?
   (Check one response on each line)

	yes	no	no reply
Statues (specify)	1. ☐	2. ☐	9. ☐
Bible	1. ☐	2. ☐	9. ☐
Crucifix	1. ☐	2. ☐	9. ☐
Picture of saint (specify)	1. ☐	2. ☐	9. ☐
Family altar	1. ☐	2. ☐	9. ☐

Q.19 Which holy day is the most important to you?
   1. ☐ Easter
   2. ☐ Feast day of your patron saint
   3. ☐ Christmas
   4. ☐ Day of a saint you are particularly devoted to
   5. ☐ Other (specify)
   6. ☐ None are particularly important
   7. ☐ All are important
   9. ☐ No reply

Q.20 Do you make promises?
   1. ☐ Yes
   2. ☐ No   (Go to question 21.)
   9. ☐ No reply

Q.20A To whom do you make promises?
   (Check one response on each line)

	yes	no	not applicable	no reply
Our Lady	1. ☐	2. ☐	8. ☐	9. ☐
Saints	1. ☐	2. ☐	8. ☐	9. ☐
God	1. ☐	2. ☐	8. ☐	9. ☐
Souls	1. ☐	2. ☐	8. ☐	9. ☐
Jesus Christ	1. ☐	2. ☐	8. ☐	9. ☐
Other (specify)	1. ☐	2. ☐	8. ☐	9. ☐

Q.20B Do you make promises in the following situations?
   (Check one response on each line)

	yes	no	not applicable	no reply
Serious illness	1. ☐	2. ☐	8. ☐	9. ☐
Lack of work or money	1. ☐	2. ☐	8. ☐	9. ☐
To obtain indulgences or pardon for sins	1. ☐	2. ☐	8. ☐	9. ☐
Moments of suffering	1. ☐	2. ☐	8. ☐	9. ☐
Other situation (specify)	1. ☐	2. ☐	8. ☐	9. ☐

Q.21 Do you think that God and the saints perform miracles?
1. □ Yes
2. □ No
3. □ Don't know   (Go on to question 22.)
9. □ No reply

Q.21A Have you ever benefited from a miracle?
1. □ Yes
2. □ No
3. □ Don't know
8. □ Not applicable (doesn't believe in miracles)
9. □ No reply

Q.22 Some people think that all beliefs and religions contain something good. Others believe that there is only one true and valid faith. Which of these ideas do you agree with?
1. □ First
2. □ Second
3. □ Don't know
9. □ No reply

Q.23 Do you go to a [Spiritist] center?
1. □ Weekly
2. □ A few times a month
3. □ A few times a year
4. □ Only went once
5. □ Never
9. □ No reply

Q.24 Have you ever made "works" or offerings?
1. □ Yes
2. □ No
9. □ No reply

Q.25 If there were a serious illness in your family, whom would you send for? (Check one response in each column)

	1st place	2nd place
Priest	1. □	1. □
Doctor	2. □	2. □
Spiritist "priest"	3. □	3. □
Faith healer	4. □	4. □
Nobody	5. □	5. □
Other (specify)	6. □	6. □
Don't know	7. □	7. □
No reply	9. □	9. □

Q.26 There are some things a Catholic is obliged to do, others which depend on the individual, and still others which are prohibited. What do you think about each of the following items?
(Check one response on each line)

	obligatory	depends on the individual	prohibited	no opinion	no reply
1. Make promises	1. ☐	2. ☐	3. ☐	4. ☐	9. ☐
2. Go to Sunday mass	1. ☐	2. ☐	3. ☐	4. ☐	9. ☐
3. Devotion to saints	1. ☐	2. ☐	3. ☐	4. ☐	9. ☐
4. Live with a person without being married in the church	1. ☐	2. ☐	3. ☐	4. ☐	9. ☐
5. Go to sessions at the [Spiritist] center	1. ☐	2. ☐	3. ☐	4. ☐	9. ☐
6. Be concerned about social problems, i.e., misery, injustice, etc.	1. ☐	2. ☐	3. ☐	4. ☐	9. ☐
7. Pray twice a day	1. ☐	2. ☐	3. ☐	4. ☐	9. ☐
8. See films or read books forbidden by the church	1. ☐	2. ☐	3. ☐	4. ☐	9. ☐
9. Be concerned with the needs of others (friends, neighbors)	1. ☐	2. ☐	3. ☐	4. ☐	9. ☐
10. Be involved in parish activities	1. ☐	2. ☐	3. ☐	4. ☐	9. ☐
11. Believe in heaven and hell	1. ☐	2. ☐	3. ☐	4. ☐	9. ☐

Q.27 I'm going to read several sentences. Some people agree with them, while others disagree. What is your opinion about each of these statements?
(Check one response on each line)

	agree completely	agree partially	neither agree nor disagree	disagree partially	disagree completely	don't know	no reply
1. Church isn't the place to resolve problems of society.	5. ☐	4. ☐	3. ☐	2. ☐	1. ☐	7. ☐	9. ☐
2. Even though he might not agree with an orientation of the church, a Catholic must obey it.	5. ☐	4. ☐	3. ☐	2. ☐	1. ☐	7. ☐	9. ☐

3. A person's con-
science is his best
guide, even though
it contradicts the
laws of the church.   1. □   2. □   3. □   4. □   5. □   7. □   9. □

4. The souls in pur-
gatory are able to
help people [on
earth].   5. □   4. □   3. □   2. □   1. □   7. □   9. □

5. "Works," the
evil eye, and curses
cannot affect peo-
ple for good or ill.   5. □   4. □   3. □   2. □   1. □   7. □   9. □

6. If a couple
doesn't want more
children, the wom-
an can take con-
traceptives.   1. □   2. □   3. □   4. □   5. □   7. □   9. □

7. The church ought
to get rid of the
statues of saints.   1. □   2. □   3. □   4. □   5. □   7. □   9. □

8. A priest is a
Catholic like all
others, with the dif-
ference that he
chose a priestly life.   1. □   2. □   3. □   4. □   5. □   7. □   9. □

9. Catholics today
receive better di-
rection from the
priests regarding
human rights.   1. □   2. □   3. □   4. □   5. □   7. □   9. □

10. A person can
be saved regardless
of the religion he
professes.   1. □   2. □   3. □   4. □   5. □   7. □   9. □

11. Spiritism has
no power to inter-
fere with peoples'
lives.   5. □   4. □   3. □   2. □   1. □   7. □   9. □

12. Salvation is
only for those who
receive the sacra-
ments of the church.   5. □   4. □   3. □   2. □   1. □   7. □   9. □

II. General Information

Q.28 Do you listen to the radio?
1. ☐ Daily
2. ☐ Sometimes
3. ☐ Rarely
4. ☐ Never
8. ☐ Not applicable   (Go on to question 29.)
9. ☐ No reply

Q.28A What sorts of programs do you listen to?
(Check one response on each line)

Programs:	a lot	little	never	not ap-plicable	no reply
Music	1. ☐	2. ☐	3. ☐	8. ☐	9. ☐
Voice of Brazil	1. ☐	2. ☐	3. ☐	8. ☐	9. ☐
National and international news	1. ☐	2. ☐	3. ☐	8. ☐	9. ☐
Sporting events	1. ☐	2. ☐	3. ☐	8. ☐	9. ☐
Educational programs	1. ☐	2. ☐	3. ☐	8. ☐	9. ☐
Soap operas, drama, etc.	1. ☐	2. ☐	3. ☐	8. ☐	9. ☐
Other (specify)	1. ☐	2. ☐	3. ☐	8. ☐	9. ☐

Q.29 Do you watch TV?
1. ☐ Daily
2. ☐ Sometimes
3. ☐ Rarely
5. ☐ Never
8. ☐ Not applicable   (Go on to question 30.)
9. ☐ No reply

Q.29A What sorts of programs do you watch?
(Check one response on each line)

Programs:	a lot	little	never	not ap-plicable	no reply
Soap operas	1. ☐	2. ☐	3. ☐	8. ☐	9. ☐
Situation comedies	1. ☐	2. ☐	3. ☐	8. ☐	9. ☐
Films	1. ☐	2. ☐	3. ☐	8. ☐	9. ☐
Soccer	1. ☐	2. ☐	3. ☐	8. ☐	9. ☐
News (national and international)	1. ☐	2. ☐	3. ☐	8. ☐	9. ☐
Other (specify)	1. ☐	2. ☐	3. ☐	8. ☐	9. ☐

Q.30 Do you know how to read?
1. ☐ Yes
2. ☐ No   (Go on to question 31.)
9. ☐ No reply

Only for those who know how to read (Questions 30A through 30D)

Q.30A Do you read the newspaper?
   1. ☐ Daily
   2. ☐ Sometimes
   3. ☐ Rarely
   4. ☐ Never
   8. ☐ Not applicable   (Go on to question 30C.)
   9. ☐ No reply

Q.30B What parts of the newspaper are you interested in?
       (Check one response on each line)

	a lot	little	not at all	not ap-plicable	no reply
Cultural news	1. ☐	2. ☐	3. ☐	8. ☐	9. ☐
National and international political news	1. ☐	2. ☐	3. ☐	8. ☐	9. ☐
Sports	1. ☐	2. ☐	3. ☐	8. ☐	9. ☐
Crime	1. ☐	2. ☐	3. ☐	8. ☐	9. ☐
Other (specify)	1. ☐	2. ☐	3. ☐	8. ☐	9. ☐

Q.30C Do you read magazines?
   1. ☐ Weekly
   2. ☐ Monthly
   3. ☐ Rarely
   4. ☐ Never
   8. ☐ Not applicable   (Go on to question 31.)
   9. ☐ No reply

Q.30D What sorts of magazines do you read?
       (Check one response on each line)

Magazines:	a lot	little	not at all	not ap-plicable	no reply
Adult comic books (*Fotonovelas*)	1. ☐	2. ☐	3. ☐	8. ☐	9. ☐
Sports magazines	1. ☐	2. ☐	3. ☐	8. ☐	9. ☐
News magazines (*Veja, Visão, Opinião*)	1. ☐	2. ☐	3. ☐	8. ☐	9. ☐
Fashion magazines (*Cláudia, Desfile, Figurinos*)	1. ☐	2. ☐	3. ☐	8. ☐	9. ☐
Other (specify)	1. ☐	2. ☐	3. ☐	8. ☐	9. ☐

Q.31 Do you know how to write?
   1. ☐ Yes
   2. ☐ No
   3. ☐ Can only sign name
   9. ☐ No reply

Q.32 Did you go, or are you going, to school?
1. ☐ Went to school
2. ☐ Did not go to school
3. ☐ Took, or is taking, MOBRAL   (Go on to question 34.)
9. ☐ No reply

Q.33 What kind of school did you attend or are you attending?
(Check one response on each line)
If you attended two kinds of school during the same course of study, indicate the one you attended longest.

	secular	Catholic	not ap- plicable	no reply
Primary	1. ☐	2. ☐	8. ☐	9. ☐
High school	1. ☐	2. ☐	8. ☐	9. ☐
Trade school	1. ☐	2. ☐	8. ☐	9. ☐
University	1. ☐	2. ☐	8. ☐	9. ☐

If only went to primary school, ask
Q.33A What year did you complete?
1. ☐ 1st
2. ☐ 2nd
3. ☐ 3rd
4. ☐ 4th
5. ☐ 5th or graduation
8. ☐ Not applicable (did not attend school)
9. ☐ No reply

III. Relationship with the Church

Q.34 Do you participate in any of these church-related activities?
(Check one response on each line)

	yes	no	no reply
1. Preparation groups (baptism, First Com- munion, liturgy, marriage, etc.)	1. ☐	2. ☐	9. ☐
2. Reflection groups	1. ☐	2. ☐	9. ☐
3. Spontaneous prayer or renewal groups	1. ☐	2. ☐	9. ☐
4. Social work groups (assistance to the poor, neighborhood associations, etc.)	1. ☐	2. ☐	9. ☐
5. Consciousness-raising groups	1. ☐	2. ☐	9. ☐
6. Bible circles	1. ☐	2. ☐	9. ☐
7. Cursilhos	1. ☐	2. ☐	9. ☐
8. Other (specify)	1. ☐	2. ☐	9. ☐

(If the answer is NO or NO REPLY for all questions, go on to question 37.)

If respondent belonged to more than one group, ask

Q.35 Which group means the most to you? (answer completely)

Q.35A Which of the following reasons were instrumental in your joining this group
(the one which means the most to you)?
(Check one response on each line)

	very im- portant	impor- tant	not im- portant	not ap- plicable	no reply
Desire to help people	1. ☐	2. ☐	3. ☐	8. ☐	9. ☐
Deepening of faith	1. ☐	2. ☐	3. ☐	8. ☐	9. ☐
Human contact	1. ☐	2. ☐	3. ☐	8. ☐	9. ☐
Looking for a purpose in life	1. ☐	2. ☐	3. ☐	8. ☐	9. ☐
Pastoral assistance	1. ☐	2. ☐	3. ☐	8. ☐	9. ☐
Other (specify)	1. ☐	2. ☐	3. ☐	8. ☐	9. ☐

Q.35B How did you come to join this group?
(Check only one response)
1. ☐ Invited by a friend or member of the group
2. ☐ Was asked to join by the priest
3. ☐ Respondent himself asked to enter group
4. ☐ Continuation of a former group
5. ☐ Other (specify)
6. ☐ Don't remember
8. ☐ Not applicable (does not belong to a group)
9. ☐ No reply

Q.35C Who directs this group?
(You may mark more than one response)
1. ☐ Priest or bishop
2. ☐ Nun
3. ☐ Lay person
4. ☐ The members themselves
5. ☐ Nobody
6. ☐ Don't know
8. ☐ Not applicable (does not belong to a group)   (Go on to question 36.)
9. ☐ No reply

Q.35D Do you help coordinate this group?
1. ☐ Yes
2. ☐ No
3. ☐ Isn't coordinated
8. ☐ Not applicable (does not belong to a group)
9. ☐ No reply

Q.36 What is the goal of this group; what do its members do?
1. ☐ Don't know
8. ☐ Not applicable (does not belong to a group)
9. ☐ No reply

Q.37 Do you belong, or have you ever belonged, to any of the following groups?

| Group: | belonged | | | belong | | |
	yes	no	don't re-member	yes	no	don't re-member
Neighborhood associations	1. ☐	2. ☐	9. ☐	1. ☐	2. ☐	9. ☐
Recreational club (sports, dance, etc.)	1. ☐	2. ☐	9. ☐	1. ☐	2. ☐	9. ☐
Professional association	1. ☐	2. ☐	9. ☐	1. ☐	2. ☐	9. ☐
Cultural association	1. ☐	2. ☐	9. ☐	1. ☐	2. ☐	9. ☐
Union	1. ☐	2. ☐	9. ☐	1. ☐	2. ☐	9. ☐
Rotary Club, Lions, etc.	1. ☐	2. ☐	9. ☐	1. ☐	2. ☐	9. ☐
Student associations	1. ☐	2. ☐	9. ☐	1. ☐	2. ☐	9. ☐
Other (specify)	1. ☐	2. ☐	9. ☐	1. ☐	2. ☐	9. ☐

IV. General Information

Now, we would like to have your opinion about the society in which we live.

Q.38 Can you tell me:
(Check one response on each line)

	answer	don't know	no reply
1. Who is the president of Brazil?	C: 1 ☐ E: 2 ☐	3. ☐	9. ☐
2. Who was the president before him?	C: 1 ☐ E: 2 ☐	3. ☐	9. ☐
3. Who is the mayor of this city?	C: 1 ☐ E: 2 ☐	3. ☐	9. ☐
4. Who is the bishop of this diocese?	C: 1 ☐ E: 2 ☐	3. ☐	9. ☐
5. Which party won the last elections here?	C: 1 ☐ E: 2 ☐	3. ☐	9. ☐
6. What does MOBRAL do?	C: 1 ☐ E: 2 ☐	3. ☐	9. ☐
7. What does INPS do?	C: 1 ☐ E: 2 ☐	3. ☐	9. ☐

Q.39 Which of the two parties is more in line with your way of thinking?
1. ☐ ARENA
2. ☐ MDB
3. ☐ Neither
4. ☐ Both
5. ☐ Don't know
9. ☐ No reply

Q.40 In your opinion, what is the principal obligation of a Brazilian citizen? (Check only the most important response)
1. ☐ Pay your taxes on time
2. ☐ Work
3. ☐ Look for solutions to the country's problems
4. ☐ Other (specify)
5. ☐ Don't know
9. ☐ No reply

Q.41 In your opinion, what is the biggest problem in Brazil today?
1. ☐ Don't know
2. ☐ There aren't any major problems   (Go on to question 42.)
3. ☐ No reply

Q.41A Has this problem had any effect on people like yourself?
1. ☐ A great effect
2. ☐ Some effect
3. ☐ A slight effect
4. ☐ No effect
5. ☐ Don't know
8. ☐ Not applicable (indicated no problem)   (Go on to question 42.)
9. ☐ No reply

Q.41B How has this problem affected the lives of people like you?
1. ☐ Don't know
8. ☐ Not applicable (indicated no problem or no ill effects)
9. ☐ No reply

Q.42 Whom do you feel you can count on to defend the interests of people such as yourself? (The interviewer should range these from a low of 0 to a high of 5. Check one response on each line).

	0 to 5	don't know	not ap-plicable	no reply
Unions	☐	7. ☐	8. ☐	9. ☐
Boss	☐	7. ☐	8. ☐	9. ☐
Government	☐	7. ☐		9. ☐
Church	☐	7. ☐		9. ☐
Armed Forces	☐	7. ☐		9. ☐
ARENA politicians	☐	7. ☐		9. ☐
MDB politicians	☐	7. ☐		9. ☐
Other (specify)	☐	7. ☐		9. ☐

Q.43 In your opinion, what is the most serious problem in the place (city or county) where you live?
1. ☐ Don't know
2. ☐ There aren't any serious problems   (Go on to question 44.)
9. ☐ No reply

Q.43A Who ought to resolve this problem? (can check more than one response)
1. ☐ The inhabitants themselves
2. ☐ The local government
3. ☐ The state government
4. ☐ The federal government
5. ☐ The church, i.e., the priests
6. ☐ There's no solution
7. ☐ Don't know
8. ☐ Not applicable (indicated no problem)   (Go on to question 44.)
9. ☐ No reply

Q.44 I'm going to read a few sentences. Some people agree with them; others disagree. What is your personal opinion about each of these statements?

	Agree com-pletely	Agree par-tially	Neither agree nor dis-agree	Disagree par-tially	Disagree com-pletely	Don't know	No reply
1. People can't be considerate of others if they want to get ahead in this world.	1. ☐	2. ☐	3. ☐	4. ☐	5. ☐	7. ☐	9. ☐
2. It wouldn't do to reform present-day society as it would likely create confusion.	5. ☐	4. ☐	3. ☐	2. ☐	1. ☐	7. ☐	9. ☐

3. The church shouldn't become
involved in social and
political matters.   5. □   4. □   3. □   2. □   1. □   7. □   9. □
4. Generally, the government bu-
reaucrats don't pay attention
to what the people really want. 1. □   2. □   3. □   4. □   5. □   7. □   9. □
5. If the government listened to
the people the country would
end up in a mess.   5. □   4. □   3. □   2. □   1. □   7. □   9. □

Q.45 Up to now have you been able to realize most of your plans, or have you had to
be content with less?
1. □ Realized most of plans
2. □ Is in the process of realizing plans
3. □ Has had to be content with less (Go on to question 45A.)
6. □ Don't know
8. □ Not applicable (doesn't make plans)
9. □ No reply

Q.45A What things caused you to fall short of your plans?
1. □ Bad luck
2. □ Didn't fight enough to get ahead
3. □ Didn't have any opportunity
4. □ Problems of illness
5. □ Other reason (specify)
6. □ Don't know
8. □ Not applicable (has already or is in process of realizing plans)
9. □ No reply

Q.46 What do you think of the following statements? Do you agree or disagree?
a) It's better for people to be satisfied with what little they have than constantly to
struggle to get more.
0 □ Agree   1 □ Don't know   2 □ Disagree   9 □ No reply
b) When I make plans, I generally feel I will fulfill them.
2 □ Agree   1 □ Don't know   0 □ Disagree   9 □ No reply
c) Poor people don't improve their lives almost always because they don't want to.
0 □ Agree   1 □ Don't know   2 □ Disagree   9 □ No reply
d) One's destiny is already determined.
0 □ Agree   1 □ Don't know   2 □ Disagree   9 □ No reply
e) People ought to struggle to get ahead.
2 □ Agree   1 □ Don't know   0 □ Disagree   9 □ No reply
f) Every person has the right to decide for himself what's best.
2 □ Agree   1 □ Don't know   0 □ Disagree   9 □ No reply
g) Voting is the best way to choose politicians.
2 □ Agree   1 □ Don't know   0 □ Disagree   9 □ No reply
h) The government knows best how to choose good politicians.
0 □ Agree   1 □ Don't know   2 □ Disagree   9 □ No reply

Q.47 What class would you say you belonged to?
1. ☐ Upper
2. ☐ Upper-middle
3. ☐ Middle
4. ☐ Lower-middle
5. ☐ Lower
6. ☐ Don't know
9. ☐ No reply

Q.48 Are you working at present?
1. ☐ Yes   -Ask ALTERNATIVE "A" of question 49.
2. ☐ No   -Ask ALTERNATIVE "B" of question 49.
3. ☐ Housewife   -Ask ALTERNATIVE "C" of question 49.
9. ☐ No reply   -Ask ALTERNATIVE "B" of question 49.

Q.49 Alternative "A": What sort of work do you do?
Alternative "B": What sort of work did you do during most of your life?
Alternative "C": What sort of work does your husband do? (If the husband is unemployed, ask what he did when he was working.)
01 ☐ Farming
02 ☐ Business
03 ☐ Industry
04 ☐ Civil servant
05 ☐ Teaching and research
06 ☐ Professional (doctor, lawyer, etc.) (specify)
07 ☐ Transport
08 ☐ Banker
09 ☐ Armed Forces
10 ☐ Landlord
11 ☐ Repair service, mechanic
12 ☐ Other (specify)
88 ☐ Not applicable (has never worked)
99 ☐ No reply

Q.50A) For those who are working at present: What position do you hold?
B) For those who aren't working: What position did you hold longest?
C) For housewives: What is your husband's present position? (If husband is unemployed, ask which position he held longest.)
1. ☐ Employee
2. ☐ Partner or owner
3. ☐ Self-employed
4. ☐ Jack of all trades
5. ☐ Other (specify)
8. ☐ Not applicable (has never worked)
9. ☐ No reply

Q.51A) For those who are working at present: Can you describe just what it is you do at work?
  B) For those who aren't working: Can you describe what it was you used to do at work?
  C) For housewives: Can you describe just what your husband does at work? (If husband is unemployed, describe what he used to do.)

DESCRIPTION OF JOB
  1. □ Don't know
  8. □ Not applicable (has never worked)
  9. □ No reply

Q.52 *The following is to be completed without questioning the respondent.*

The questions about work refer to:
  1. □ The present job of the respondent. (YES to question 48)
  2. □ A former job (NO to question 48)
  3. □ The husband's present job (if respondent is a housewife)
  4. □ The husband's former job
  5. □ The respondent has never worked
  6. □ The respondent did not reply to the questions about employment

Q.53 *For those who aren't working (NO to question 48) and for the housewives whose husbands are unemployed:*
Why aren't you (or your husband) working?
  1. □ Student
  2. □ Doing military service
  3. □ Retired
  4. □ Sick for over a month
  5. □ Unemployed because can't find work
  6. □ Unemployed because doesn't want to work
  7. □ Other (specify)
  8. □ Not applicable (is working)
  9. □ No reply

Q.54 What is the monthly income of your family? (Family =group of people which the respondent supports—wife, children—or group which supports him—father, mother, brothers, etc.)
  Cr $_____
  77.777 __ Don't know
  99.999 __ Don't want to answer

Q.55 Sex: (note)
  1. □ Male
  2. □ Female

Q.56 Color: (note)
  1. ☐ White
  2. ☐ Mulatto
  3. ☐ Black
  4. ☐ Other (specify)

Q.57 How old are you? _____ years
  97. ☐ Don't know
  99. ☐ No reply

Q.58 Are you:
  1. ☐ Born in Brazil?
  2. ☐ Foreign-born? Specify:_____

(If foreign-born, ask:)
Q.58A How old were you when you came to Brazil?_____ years
  88. ☐ Not applicable (native-born)
  99. ☐ No reply

Q.59 Do you get together with members of any foreign colony?
  1. ☐ Yes   Which one:_____
  2. ☐ No
  9. ☐ No reply

Q.60 *(For Brazilians only:)*
  What state were you born in? What county?
    ☐ State: _____
  77. ☐ Don't know
  99. ☐ No reply

  County: _____
  77. ☐ Don't know
  99. ☐ No reply

Q.61 Were you born in a rural or urban area?
  1. ☐ Rural
  2. ☐ Urban
  3. ☐ Don't know
  9. ☐ No reply

Q.62 Have you ever lived in any other place?
  1. ☐ Yes
  2. ☐ No   (Go on to question 63.)
  9. ☐ No reply

Q.62A In what state?
   ☐ State: _____
   77. ☐ Don't know
   88. ☐ Not applicable (has always lived in the same place)
   99. ☐ No reply

Q.62B In what county?
      ☐ County: _____
   7777. ☐ Don't know
   8888. ☐ Not applicable (has always lived in the same place)
   9999. ☐ No reply

Q.62C For how long?
      ☐ _____ years
   77. ☐ Don't know
   88. ☐ Not applicable (has always lived in the same place)
   99. ☐ No reply

Q.63 Are you:
   1. ☐ Married
   2. ☐ Widowed
   3. ☐ Single
   4. ☐ Live with another person
   5. ☐ Separated (legally or informally)
   9. ☐ No reply

Q.64 Do you have any children?
   1. ☐ Yes
   2. ☐ No
   9. ☐ No reply

Q.64A How many children?
   ☐ _____ Number
   ☐ No reply

Q.65 Have you ever been interviewed before?
   1. ☐ Yes
   2. ☐ No
   3. ☐ Don't remember
   4. ☐ No reply

Control
(To be completed after the interview.)

Address of the respondent: _____

1. Note the characteristics of respondent's house (construction, size, furniture, etc.) and make an evaluation as to his probable class:
   1. ☐ Upper
   2. ☐ Upper-middle
   3. ☐ Middle
   4. ☐ Lower-middle
   5. ☐ Lower

2. How long did the interview last? _____hours

3. Was the interview carried out in the presence of others?
   1. ☐ Yes   Who:_____
   2. ☐ No

4. What degree of interest did the respondent manifest before being interviewed?
   1. ☐ No interest
   2. ☐ Little interest
   3. ☐ Some interest
   4. ☐ Great interest
   5. ☐ Extreme interest

5. Did the respondent have any difficulty in understanding the questions?
   1. ☐ No difficulty
   2. ☐ Little difficulty
   3. ☐ Some difficulty
   4. ☐ Great difficulty
   5. ☐ Extreme difficulty

6. How much explanation did you have to give about the questions?
   1. ☐ Didn't explain anything
   2. ☐ Explained a few questions
   3. ☐ Explained about half of the questions
   4. ☐ Explained most of the questions
   5. ☐ Explained all the questions

7. In order of importance, which were the three questions which the respondent had the most difficulty in understanding?
   ☐ 1st_____
   ☐ 2nd_____
   ☐ 3rd_____

8. At the end of the interview what degree of interest did the respondent manifest?
   1. ☐ No interest
   2. ☐ Little interest
   3. ☐ Some interest
   4. ☐ Great interest
   5. ☐ Extreme interest

9. Other observations:_____

Abbreviations

ACB	Ação Católica Brasileira; Brazilian Catholic Action
ARENA	Aliança Nacional Renovadora; National Renovating Alliance
CEAS	Centro de Estudos e Ação Social; Center of Studies and Social Action
CEB	Comunidade Eclesial de Base; Basic Christian Community
CEBRAP	Centro Brasileiro de Planejamento; Center of Brazilian Planning
CEHILA	Comissão de Estudos de História da Igreja na América Latina; Commission for the Study of the History of the Church in Latin America
CELAM	Conferência do Episcopado Latino-Americano; Latin American Episcopal Conference
CENPLA	Centro de Estudos, Pesquisa e Planejamento; Center of Studies, Research and Planning
CERIS	Centro de Estatística Religiosa e Investigações Sociais; Center of Religious Statistics and Social Investigation
CIMI	Conselho Indigenista Missionário; Native Missionary Council
CNBB	Conferência Nacional dos Bispos do Brasil; National Conference of Brazilian Bishops
COPEI	Comité de Organización Política Electoral Independiente; Social Christian Party (Venezuela)
FUNAI	Fundação Nacional do Indio; National Indian Foundation
IBGE	Instituto Brasileiro de Geografia e Estatística; Brazilian Institute of Geography and Statistics
IBRADES	Instituto Brasileiro de Desenvolvimento; Brazilian Institute for Development
INP	Instituto Nacional de Pastoral; National Pastoral Institute
INPS	Instituto Nacional de Providência Social; National Institute for Social Security
ITER	Instituto de Teologia do Recife; Institute of Theology of Recife

MDB	Movimento Democrático Brasileiro; Brazilian Democratic Movement
MEB	Movimento de Educação de Base; Basic Education Movement
MFC	Movimento Familiar Cristão; Christian Family Movement
MOBRAL	Movimento Brasileiro de Alfabetização; Brazilian Literacy Movement
MPLA	Movimento Popular para Libertação de Angola; Popular Movement for the Liberation of Angola
PLC	Peregrinação de Líderes Cristãos; Pilgrimage of Christian Leaders
SNI	Serviço Nacional de Informação; National Information Service
SPI	Serviço de Proteção dos Indios; Indian Protection Service
SUDAM	Superintendência do Desenvolvimento de Amazônia; Superintendency for the Development of Amazônia
SUDENE	Superintendência do Desenvolvimento do Nordeste; Superintendency for the Development of the Northeast
TLC	Treinamento de Liderança Cristã; Christian Leadership Training

Notes

Introduction

1. Centro de Estatística Religiosa e Investigações Sociais (CERIS), *Primeiro relatório da coordenação do programa de pesquisas do plano de pastoral de conjunto* describes the research projects. See also Pedro A. Ribeiro de Oliveira, "Catolicismo popular no Brasil" (unpublished CERIS report), for an extremely well-done study on popular Catholicism, but one in which beliefs and practices are not related to structures.

2. See John L. McKenzie, *The Roman Catholic Church*, esp. p. 22, for a description of the structure and dynamic of the church.

3. Charles Y. Glock and Phillip E. Hammond (eds.), *Beyond the Classics? Essays in the Scientific Study of Religion*, p. 417. For suggestions on research strategies, see Thomas C. Bruneau, "Power and Influence: Analysis of the Church in Latin America and the Case of Brazil," *Latin American Research Review* 8, no. 2 (Summer 1973):25-51; and Ivan Vallier, "Comparative Studies of Roman Catholicism: Dioceses as Strategic Units," *Social Compass* 16, no. 2 (1969):147-184.

4. On voting, see Arend Lijphart, "Class Voting and Religious Voting in the European Democracies: A Preliminary Report"; John Meisel, "Religious Affiliation and Electoral Behaviour," *Canadian Journal of Economics and Political Science* 22 (1956):481-496; and John H. Whyte, "The Catholic Factor in the Politics of Democratic States," in *The Church and Modern Society*, ed. Leo Moulin, pp. 23-37. On Christian Democracy, see Giles Wayland-Smith, *The Christian Democratic Party in Chile*; and Edward J. Williams, *Latin American Christian Democratic Parties*. For an example of survey research on religion, see Kenneth P. Langton and Ronald Rapoport, "Religion and Leftist Mobilization in Chile," *Comparative Political Studies* 9, no. 3 (October 1976):277-308.

5. Lucy C. Behrman, "The Political and Social Impact of the Peoples' Priests in Chile," in *Religion and Political Modernization*, ed. Donald E. Smith, pp. 183-201; Thomas G. Sanders and Brian H. Smith, "The Chilean Catholic Church During the Allende and Pinochet Regimes," *AUFS Fieldstaff Reports* 23, no. 1

(March 1976); George W. Grayson, "The Church and Military in Peru," in *Religion and Political Modernization*, ed. Donald E. Smith, pp. 303-324; Thomas G. Sanders, "The Church in Latin America," *Foreign Affairs* 48, no. 2 (January 1970):285-299; Carlos Astiz, "The Catholic Church in Latin American Politics: A Case Study of Peru," in *Latin American Prospects for the 1970's*, ed. David H. Pollock and Arch Ritter, pp. 131-148; Michael Dodson, "Religious Innovation and the Politics of Argentina," (Ph.D. dissertation); and Emanuel de Kadt, *Catholic Radicals in Brazil.*

6. For content analyses, see Frederick C. Turner, *Catholicism and Political Development in Latin America;* and Hubert Schwan and Antonio Ugalde, "Orientations of the Bishops of Colombia Toward Social Development, 1930-1970," *Journal of Church and State* 16, no. 3 (1974):473-492. For surveys, see Thomas G. Sanders, *Catholic Innovation in a Changing Latin America;* and Daniel H. Levine, "Church Elites in Venezuela and Colombia: Context, Background, and Beliefs," *Latin American Research Review* 14, no. 1 (Spring 1979):51-79.

7. Luigi Einaudi et al., "Latin American Institutional Development: The Changing Catholic Church"; David E. Mutchler, *The Church as a Political Factor in Latin America with Particular Reference to Colombia and Chile.*

8. Rowan Ireland, "The Catholic Church and Social Change in Brazil: An Evaluation," in *Brazil in the Sixties*, ed. Riordan Roett, pp. 345-371; Daniel H. Levine, "Democracy and the Church in Venezuela," *Journal of Interamerican Studies and World Affairs* 18, no. 1 (February 1976):3-23; Lars Schoultz, "The Roman Catholic Church in Colombia: Revolution, Reform, and Reaction," *América Latina* 14, no. 3 (1971):90-107; Brian Smith, "Religion and Social Change: Classical Theories and New Formulations in the Context of Recent Developments in Latin America," *Latin American Research Review* 10, no. 2 (Summer 1975):3-34; and Kenneth Westhues, "The Established Church as an Agent of Change," *Sociological Analysis* 34, no. 2 (Summer 1973):106-124.

9. Ernst Troeltsch, *The Social Teaching of the Christian Churches*, 2:999-1000.

10. Thomas C. Bruneau, *The Political Transformation of the Brazilian Catholic Church*; idem, "Power and Infuence"; Daniel H. Levine and Alexander W. Wilde, "The Catholic Church, 'Politics,' and Violence: The Colombian Case," *Review of Politics* 39, no. 2 (April 1977):220-239; and the Ph.D. dissertation by Brian Smith, "The Catholic Church and Political Change in Chile." The latest and best statements within this approach, including the preceding articles, are Daniel H. Levine, (ed.), *Churches and Politics in Latin America*; and Ivan Vallier, *Catholicism, Social Control and Modernization in Latin America*; idem, "Comparative Studies of Roman Catholicism"; idem, "Extraction, Insulation, and Re-Entry: Toward a Theory of Religious Change," in *The Church and Social Change in Latin America*, ed. Henry Landsberger, pp. 9-35.

11. For extensive discussion on the relationship of regimes to patterns of modernization, see Guillermo O'Donnell, "Reflections on the Patterns of Change

in the Bureaucratic-Authoritarian State," *Latin American Research Review* 13, no. 1 (1978):3-39; and the volume edited by David Collier, *The New Authoritarianism in Latin America.*

12. Troeltsch, *Social Teaching*, 1:32. On Theology of Liberation, see, for example, Gustavo Gutiérrez, *A Theology of Liberation*; the very good reviews by Phillip E. Berryman, "Latin American Liberation Theology," *Theological Studies* 34, no. 3 (September 1973):357-395; and T. Howland Sanks and Brian H. Smith, "Liberation Ecclesiology: Praxis, Theory, Praxis," *Theological Studies* 38, no. 1 (March 1977):3-38.

13. Phillip Selznick, *Leadership in Administration*; idem, "Foundations of a Theory of Organizations," *American Sociological Review* 13 (1948):25-35; Daniel Katz and Robert Kahn, *The Social Psychology of Organizations*; James Thompson, *Organizations in Action.* In this same general approach, see Chester Barnard, *The Functions of the Executive*; and Wolf V. Heydebrand, "The Study of Organizations," *Social Science Information* 6, no. 5 (October 1967):59-86.

14. James Thompson and William McEwen, "Organizational Goals and Environment," *American Sociological Review* 23 (1958):23-31.

15. Thomas F. O'Dea, *The Catholic Crisis.*

16. Troeltsch, *Social Teaching*, 1:86.

17. See McKenzie, *Roman Catholic Church*, pp. 63-96; and René Metz, *What is Canon Law?*

Chapter 1: History of the Church in Brazil

1. The new literature since the publication of my earlier book includes Riolando Azzi, *O episcopado do Brasil frente o catolicismo popular*; idem, "O início da restauração católica no Brasil, 1920-1930," *Síntese* 4, no. 10 (May-August 1977):61-91; idem, "O episcopado brasileiro frente à Revolução de 1930," *Síntese* 5, no. 12 (January-March 1978):47-97; Comissão de Estudos de História da Igreja na América Latina (CEHILA), *História da igreja no Brasil: Primeira época*; Eduardo Hoornaert, *Formação do catolicismo brasileiro, 1550-1800*; and João Alfredo Montenegro, *Evolução do catolicismo no Brasil.*

2. Pe. Júlio Maria, *O catolicismo no Brasil*, p. 25.

3. As summarized by Hoornaert, *Formação do catolicismo brasileiro*, p. 34.

4. J. Lloyd Mecham, *Church and State in Latin America*, p. 36.

5. Comissão de Estudos de História da Igreja na América Latina (CEHILA), *História da igreja no Brasil*, pp. 35-38.

6. Hoornaert, *Formação do catolicismo brasileiro*, p. 18.

7. Sérgio Buarque de Hollanda, *Raizes do Brasil*, p. 44.

8. On the nature of society, see Gilberto Freyre, *The Masters and the Slaves*; Paulo Prado, *Retrato do Brasil*; and Francisco de Oliveira Vianna, *Populações meridionais do Brasil*, vols. 1 and 2.

9. For a general characterization of the pattern of evangelization, see Robert Ricard, "Comparison of Evangelization in Portuguese and Spanish America," *The Americas* 14 (1957):444-454. For extensive and detailed comments on the

church's insertion in the society, see Hoornaert, *Formação do catolicismo brasileiro*, pp. 66-87.

10. Basílio Magalhães, *Estudos de história do Brasil*, p. 152.

11. For elaboration on these regulations, see Magalhães, *Estudos de História*, p. 104; and Maria, *Catolicismo no Brasil*, pp. 142-148.

12. Maria, *Catolicismo no Brasil*, p. 211.

13. On the Religious Question, see especially Sister Mary Crescentia Thornton, *The Church and Freemasonry in Brazil 1872-1875*.

14. For data on institutional growth, see Winfredo Plagge, *A igreja no Brasil*; and Gustavo Pérez et al., *O problema sacerdotal no Brasil*.

15. The "Romanization" was first characterized by Roger Bastide, "Religion and the Church in Brazil," in *Brazil: Portrait of Half a Continent*, ed. T. Lynn Smith and A. Marchant, pp. 334-355. See also a more detailed analysis by Pedro Assis Ribeiro de Oliveira, "Catolicismo popular e romanização do catolicismo brasileiro," *Revista Eclesiástica Brasileira* 36, no. 141 (March 1976):131-142.

16. Maria, *Catolicismo no Brasil*, pp. 250-251.

17. For a discussion of church involvement in politics and privileges won, see Azzi, "O episcopado brasileiro," pp. 47-97.

18. The constitutional measures, in historical perspective, are detailed in Pe. Geraldo Fernandes, "A religião nas constituições republicanas do Brasil," *Revista Eclesiástica Brasileira* 8 (December 1948):830-858.

19. For a more extensive discussion of "Christendom" and "Neo-Christendom," see chaps. 1 and 2 of my earlier book.

Chapter 2: Religious Beliefs and Practices

1. Thales de Azevedo, *O catolicismo no Brasil*, p. 26.

2. Gilberto Freyre, *Casa grande e senzala*, p. 122, cited in René Ribeiro, *Religião e relações raciais*, p. 42.

3. Instituto de Teologia do Recife (ITER), *A fé popular no Nordeste*.

4. Renato Ortiz, "La morte blanche du sorcier noir," (Ph.D. dissertation), p. 7.

5. Riolando Azzi, "Elementos para a história do catolicismo popular," *Revista Eclesiástica Brasileira* 36, no. 141 (March 1976):98, 97.

6. Eduardo Hoornaert, *Formação do catolicismo brasileiro, 1550-1800*, p. 17.

7. L. F. Tonellare, "Notas dominicais," *Revista do Instituto Archeológico e Geográfico Pernambucano* 11, no. 61, cited in Ribeiro, *Religião e relações raciais*, pp. 89-90.

8. Fernão Cardim, *Tratados da terra e gente do Brasil*, p. 294, cited in Ribeiro, *Religião e relações raciais*, p. 42.

9. Hoornaert, *Formação do catolicismo brasileiro*, p. 78.

10. José Comblin, "Situação histórica do catolicismo no Brasil," *Revista Eclesiástica Brasileira* 26 (September 1966):583-584.

11. Donald Warren, "Portuguese Roots of Brazilian Spiritism," *Luso-Brasilian Review* 5, no. 2 (December 1968):13.

12. Ribeiro, *Religião e relações raciais*, p. 58.

13. Azzi, "Elementos para a história," p. 99.

14. Maria Madeleine Govaers, "Aspects du syncrétisme religieux brésilien dans le cadre de son acculturation," (M.A. thesis), p. 73.

15. Francisco Cartaxo Rolim, "Diocese de Nova Iguaçu: Protestanismo-espiritismo: Uma perspectiva sociológica," (unpublished report); and Eduardo Hoornaert, *Verdadeira e falsa religião no Nordeste,* p. 72.

16. Pedro Assis Ribeiro de Oliveira, "Catolicismo popular e romanização do catolicismo brasileiro," *Revista Eclesiástica Brasileira* 36, no. 141 (March 1976):131-142.

17. Azevedo, *Catolicismo no Brasil,* p. 27. This is the same distinction elaborated by Hoornaert, *Verdadeira e falsa religião,* pp. 7-11.

18. Alberto Antoniazzi, "Várias interpretações do catolicismo popular no Brasil," *Revista Eclesiástica Brasileira* 36, no. 141 (March 1976):84.

19. Maria Isaura Pereira de Queiroz, *O campesinato brasileiro,* p. 73. For extensive bibliography, see Pedro Assis Ribeiro de Oliveira, "Catolicismo popular no Brasil-Bibliografia," *Revista Eclesiástica Brasileira* 36, no. 141 (March 1976):272-280; and idem., "Bibliografia sobre religiosidade popular," *Religião e Sociedade,* no. 1 (May 1977), pp. 181-194.

20. Queiroz, *Campesinato brasileiro,* p. 73. See also Bernardino Leers, *Religiosidade rural;* and Shepard Forman, *The Brazilian Peasantry,* chapter 6.

21. See Rolim, "Diocese de Nova Iguaçu"; idem, "Expansão protestante em Nova Iguaçu," *Revista Eclesiástica Brasileira* 33, no. 131 (September 1973):660-675.

22. William R. Read and Frank A. Ineson, *Brazil 1980,* p. 165.

23. See Conferência Nacional dos Bispos do Brasil (CNBB), Secretariado Regional Leste 1, *Macumba: Cultos afro-brasileiros* for the contributions of Frei Raimundo Cintra and Frei Boaventura Kloppenburg. There is now a great deal of material on various forms of Spiritism, and in addition to that of Ortiz, cited in note 4 above, see also his "Du syncrétisme à la synthèse: Umbanda, une religion brésilienne," *Archives de Sciences Sociales des Religions,* no. 40 (1975), pp. 89-97; and his article, with Paula Montero, "Contribuição para um estudo quantitativo da religião umbandista," *Ciência e Cultura* 28, no. 4 (October 1975):407-416. Diana Brown now has a number of excellent papers, including "Umbanda e classes sociais," *Religião e Sociedade,* no. 1 (May 1977), pp. 31-43. Rather than citing the extensive bibliography on this topic, it is best to note that *Religião e Sociedade,* no. 1 (May 1977) includes a bibliography, pp. 181-194.

24. Marco Aurélio Luz and George Lapassade, *O segredo da Macumba,* pp. 10-18.

25. Seth Leacock and Ruth Leacock, *Spirits of the Deep,* p. 85.

26. From a mimeo document produced by the Instituto Nacional de Pastoral in 1974. That particular section is by Prof. Martien Maria Groetelaars and Pe. Dagmar Pereira Nóbrega.

27. For the catechist, see Laís Mourão, "O camponês e a colonização missionária," *Revista de Vozes* 68, no. 7 (September 1974):49-58.

28. Thales de Azevedo, *Cultura e situação racial no Brasil,* p. 184.

29. Pedro Assis Ribeiro de Oliveira, "Catolicismo popular no Brasil," (unpublished report).

30. "Pesquisa-aspectos psico-sociais da religiosidade no estado da Guanabara," *Síntese* 2, no. 3 (January 1975):49-105.

31. For a good compilation of these studies, see Godofredo J. Deelen, *A sociologia a serviço da pastoral*.

32. Francisco Cartaxo Rolim, "Catolicismo no Brasil," *Lumiar*, no. 26 (April 1970), pp. 93-154. These typologies are also reviewed in Oliveira, "Catolicismo popular no Brasil," pp. 4-16.

33. Pedro Assis Ribeiro de Oliveira, "Catolicismo popular e pastoral: Notas para discussão," (unpublished report).

34. Leers, *Religiosidade rural*, p. 36.

35. Emanuel de Kadt, "Religion, the Church, and Social Change in Brazil," in *The Politics of Conformity in Latin America*, ed. Claudio Véliz, p. 197.

36. Data provided by Peter McDonough and Amaury de Souza of the Center for Political Studies, Institute for Social Research, the University of Michigan, Ann Arbor, Michigan, July 1979.

37. See Godofredo Deelen, passim. Also, for the argument on class, see Francisco Cartaxo Rolim, "Quelques aspects de la pratique dominicale au Brésil," *Social Compass* 14 (May-June 1967):457-468.

38. There is a substantial difference between the attendance sample (with 72 percent attending mass once a week or more), and those in the general sample (with 47 percent attending this frequently); however, we should also note that some 85 percent of our group sample attend at least once a week. On the other hand, among those in the attendance sample, 6 percent attend "sometimes a year or never"; in the general sample the figure is 22 percent, and in the group sample it is only 2 percent. In short, while the group sample is the most "orthodox" and the attendance sample the next, even the general sample does attend mass although not nearly as frequently.

39. That religion does have many "dimensions" is now widely accepted, but probably most important in initiating this view was the work of Glock and Stark. See, for example, Rodney Stark and Charles Glock, *American Piety*. For factor analysis techniques in the study of religion, see the following indicative articles: Morton King and Richard A. Hunt, "Measuring the Religious Variable," *Journal for the Scientific Study of Religion* 14 (1975):13-22; Victor Cline and James Richard, "A Factor-Analytic Study of Religious Belief and Behavior," *Journal of Personality and Social Psychology* 1, no. 6 (1965):569-578; Morton King et al., "Measuring the Religious Variable: Alternative Factor Analyses."

40. R. J. Rummel, "Understanding Factor Analysis," *Journal of Conflict Resolution* 2 (December 1967):466.

41. These findings support the conclusions of Morton King and Richard A. Hunt in *Measuring Religious Dimensions*. See, in this same orientation, Cline and Richard, "A Factor Analytic Study." In contrast, see Richard Clayton and James Gladden, "The Five Dimensions of Religiosity: Toward Demythologizing a Sacred

Artifact," *Journal for the Scientific Study of Religion* 13 (1974):135-143.

Chapter 3: Initiation of a New Approach to Influence
1. Some of the material in this chapter was dealt with in my earlier book. Since its publication there have been a number of new studies. There is now a fairly complete study on the constitutional and theological characteristics and implications of the Conferência Nacional dos Bispos do Brasil. Pe. Gervásio Fernandes de Queiroga, *Conferência Nacional dos Bispos do Brasil.* For a discussion on Ação Popular, the radical movement coming out of Catholic Action, see José Luiz Sigrist, "Fenomenologia de consciência universitária Cristã no Brasil," (Ph.D. dissertation). For the church's role in the important education law of 1961, which I dealt with in the Portuguese edition of my first book, but not the English, see Danilo Martins de Lima, "Educação, igreja, ideologia: Uma análise sociológica das influências da Igreja Católica na elaboração da Lei no. 4.024/61 de Diretrizes e Bases da Educação Nacional" (M.A. thesis).
2. See, for instance, Dom João Becker, *A religião e a pátria em face das ideologias modernas*, especially p. 34.
3. For an especially competent characterization of this period, see Thomas Skidmore, *Politics in Brazil, 1930-1964.*
4. This sense of drama is conveyed nicely in Antônio Callado, *Tempo de Arraes.* See also his novel *Quarup.*
5. Conferência Nacional dos Bispos do Brasil (CNBB), *Plano de Emergência*, p. 9.
6. Michel Schooyans, *O comunismo e o futuro da igreja no Brasil*, p. 90.
7. See chapter 4 of my first book and the bibliography cited there.
8. In addition to Lima on the Law of 1961, see also the Centro de Estatística Religiosa e Investigações Sociais (CERIS) study on church involvement in social welfare, "Recursos sociais da igreja no Brasil."
9. The purposes and processes concerning the Conferência Nacional dos Bispos do Brasil (CNBB) are dealt with in great detail in Gervásio Fernandes de Queiroga and, analytically, in chapter 5 of my first book.
10. A stimulating analysis of the change in the church in which the social is emphasized over the organizational and social which I provide, is found in Luiz Gonzaga de Souza Lima, *Evolução Política dos católicos e da igreja no Brasil.* This book also reprints many of the most important documents which indicate change.
11. There is a new analysis of the conflicts which employs a rather abstract, if stimulating perspective, and touches on a myriad of topics; see Roberto Romano, *Brasil: Igreja contra estado.* See also my earlier book, in which I provide a detailed description of the process of conflict between church and state and point out how this process has increasingly forced the church to remove itself and its approach to influence from the regime.

Chapter 4: The Brazilian Regime: 1964-1980
1. Of particular utility in formulating this chapter were the following: Fernando

Henrique Cardoso, *Autoritarismo e democratização;* David Collier (ed.), *The New Authoritarianism in Latin America*; Pedro Demo, *Desenvolvimento e política social no Brasil*; Kenneth Paul Erickson, *The Brazilian Corporate State and Working Class Politics;* Peter Evans, *Dependent Development*; Georges-André Feichter, *O regime modernizador do Brasil, 1964/1972*; Peter Flynn, *Brazil: A Political Analysis*; Celso Furtado, *Análise do "modelo" brasileiro*; Fernando Pedreira, *Brasil política;* Riordan Roett, *Brazil: Politics in a Patrimonial Society*; idem (ed.), *Brazil in the Seventies*; Ronald M. Schneider, *The Political System of Brazil*; Gláucio Ary Dillon Soares, "After the Miracle," *Luso-Brazilian Review* 15, no. 2 (Winter 1978):278-302; Nelson Werneck Sodré, *Brasil: Radiografia de um modelo*; Alfred Stepan (ed.), *Authoritarian Brazil*; André Gustavo Stumpf and Merval Pereira Filho, *A Segunda Guerra: Sucessão de Geisel.* Material was also used from the following journals: Instituto Universitário de Pesquisas do Rio de Janeiro, *Dados;* Civilização Brasileira, *Encontros com a Civilização Brasileira* (since July 1978); and Centro Brasileiro de Pesquisa (CEBRAP), *Estudos CEBRAP.*

2. Ray S. Cline, *World Power Assessment*, p. 130, as cited in Ronald M. Schneider, *Brazil: Foreign Policy of a Future World Power*, p. xviii.

3. Schneider, *Brazil: Foreign Policy*, p. 1.

4. For the best classical interpretation of the lack of autonomous groups, see Francisco de Oliveira Vianna, *Populações meridionais do Brasil*, vols. 1 and 2. For a more recent analysis of the centralizing state, see R. A. Amaral Vieira, *Intervencionismo e autoritarismo no Brasil.*

5. Alfred Stepan gave a good deal of attention to this ideology in *The Military in Politics.* Dom Cândido Padin has updated his earlier writing on the ideology: see "A doutrina da segurança nacional," *Revista Eclesiástica Brasileira* 37, no. 146 (June 1977):331-342. José Comblin has stated his most succinct description and analysis in "The National Security Doctrine," and elaborated on it in *A ideologia da segurança nacional.* The most recent statement is by Mike Burgess and Daniel Wolf, "Brazil: The Concept of Power in the Brazilian Higher War College (ESG)."

6. Comblin, "The National Security Doctrine," p. 36.

7. Pedreira, *Brasil política*, pp. 34-35, quoting.

8. Comblin, "The National Security Doctrine," p. 47.

9. Ibid., p. 61.

10. Quoted in Padin, "A doutrina da segurança nacional," pp. 338-339.

11. Unlike the relative scarcity of political science literature on Brazil, there is a tremendous amount by economists. See the complete and well-organized review by William G. Tyler, "Brazilian Industrialization and Industrial Policies: A Survey," *World Development* 4, nos. 10 and 11 (1976):863-882. Particular attention should be paid to two very different interpretations: Edmar Bacha, *Os mitos de uma década*; and Stefan H. Robock, *Brazil: A Study in Development Progress.* A recent general survey by Werner Baer is particularly useful: *The Brazilian Economy.*

12. Werner Baer, "The Brazilian Growth and Development Experience: 1964-1975," in *Brazil in the Seventies*, ed. Riordan Roett, p. 43.

13. Tyler, "Brazilian Industrialization," p. 867.

14. On the theme of the state's role in the economy, there is now a tremendous amount of good literature. See, for instance, Werner Baer et al., "The Changing Role of the State in the Brazilian Economy," *World Development* 1, no. 11 (November 1973):23-35; Carlos Estevam Martins (ed.), *Estado e capitalismo no Brasil;* and José Roberto Mendonça de Barros and Douglas H. Graham, "The Brazilian Economic Miracle Revisited: Private and Public Sector Initiative in a Market Economy" *Latin American Research Review* 13, no. 2 (1978):5-39.

15. Werner Baer, "The Brazilian Boom 1968-72: An Explanation and Interpretation," *World Development* 1, no. 8 (August 1973):1-17. A contrasting view can be found in Bacha, *Os mitos,* and his *Issues and Evidence on Recent Brazilian Economic Growth.*

16. Schneider, *Brazil: Foreign Policy,* p. 16.

17. Bacha, *Os mitos,* argues, as do those in the dependency school, that Brazil is more dependent, whereas Robert Packenham ("Trends in Brazilian National Dependency Since 1964," in *Brazil in the Seventies,* ed. Riordan Roett, pp. 89-115) argues that it is less.

18. Concerning the surplus of unskilled labor, see Bacha, *Os mitos,* pp. 15-16, as well as William G. Tyler, *Manufactured Export Expansion and Industrialization in Brazil,* pp. 62-64.

19. Again, there is a tremendous amount of literature on this topic. See, for instance, Ricardo Tolipan and Arthur Carlos Tinelli, *A controvérsia sobre distribuição de renda e desenvolvimento;* and the special number of Instituto Universitário de Pesquisas do Rio de Janeiro, *DADOS,* on this topic, no. 11, 1973. The "official" position is defended in Carlos Geraldo Langoni, *Distribuição da renda e desenvolvimento econômico do Brasil.*

20. Tyler, "Brazilian Industrialization," p. 874; see Baer, "Brazilian Growth," on tax incentives; and Robock, *Brazil,* pp. 57-85. For the social implications of this situation, see Pedro Demo, "Política social no Brasil após 1964"; and World Bank (IBRD), *Brazil: Human Resources Special Report.* For further analysis of the distribution of income, see Guy Pfeffermann and Richard Webb, *The Distribution of Income in Brazil.*

21. Mário Henrique Simonsen and Roberto de Oliveira Campos, *A nova economia brasileira,* passim. The competing evidence is summarized by Tyler, "Brazilian Industrialization," p. 874.

22. The continuing misery is documented frequently in the articles of any of the weekly newsmagazines, such as *Veja, Movimento,* and *Isto é.* For particularly strong evidence on São Paulo, the richest state and the richest city, see a study done for the Justice and Peace Commission of the Archdiocese of São Paulo, Cândido Procópio Ferreira de Camargo (ed.), *São Paulo 1975: Crescimento e pobreza.* For a thorough and responsible analysis of the Amazon projects which shows that they can lead to misery, see Dennis J. Mahar, *Desenvolvimento econômico da Amazônia.* It should be noted that IPEA (Institute for Applied Economic Research) is part of the government, and it seems remarkable that such a telling document could have been published. Interviews in June 1978 in Brasília indicated that there are

documents for internal circulation only which note in very grave terms the populace's situation in this sociopolitical regime.

23. As yet there is no integrated analysis of the current liberalization in Brazil or in other Latin American and southern European countries. The processes, however, are being closely observed and material is becoming available. This theme was the basis of a series of workshops at the Latin American Program of the Woodrow Wilson International Center for Scholars in September of 1979; there was a panel on it at the American Political Science Association meeting in August 1980; and there were a series of presentations on this theme at the Centre for Developing-Area Studies of McGill University in the spring of 1980. The book arising from the McGill series is Thomas C. Bruneau and Philippe Fauchers (eds.), *Authoritarian Capitalism: The Contemporary Economic and Political Development of Brazil.*

Chapter 5: Current Church Responses and Strategies

1. Bispos e Superiores Religiosos do Nordeste, *Eu ouvi os clamores do meu povo*; and Bispos do Centro-Oeste, *Marginalização de um povo.* These can also be found in Luiz Gonzaga de Souza Lima, *Evolução Política dos católicos e da igreja no Brasil.*

2. For coverage of the visit and editorials on its implications, see *O Estado de São Paulo*, 9-11 July 1974.

3. For details on censorship relating to the church, see *Jornal do Brasil*, 18 June 1978.

4. This is stated clearly by Dom Paulo Evaristo Arns in *Em defesa dos direitos humanos, encontro com o Reporter*, p. 114.

5. Conferência Nacional dos Bispos do Brasil (CNBB), *Diretrizes gerais da ação pastoral da igreja no Brasil, 1975/1978*, pp. 9-10, 16. There was even a series of articles in the influential *O Estado de São Paulo* on various aspects of the weakness of the church, the varieties of religiosity, and the growth of Spiritism and Protestantism (9-18 January 1973, under the general title, "Brazilian Catholicism in Crisis"). These articles have been published as a book: Fausto Cupertino, *As muitas religiões do brasileiro.*

6. Conferência Nacional dos Bispos do Brasil (CNBB), *Diretrizes Gerais.*

7. Ibid.

8. Ibid.

9. Ibid.

10. Cândido Procópio Ferreira de Camargo, *São Paulo 1975: Crescimento e pobreza.* By 1978 this book had seen four editions.

11. Documents indicating both the facts and the awareness of them by elements in the church can be found in the monthly *Serviço de Documentação (SEDOC)*, published by Editora Vozes of Petrópolis. See, for instance, no. 101 on Indians and no. 105 on the situation in the rural areas. Also of importance are the studies published in Centro de Estudos e Ação Social, *Cadernos do CEAS* in Salvador, and Centro Brasileiro de Análise e planejamento, *Cadernos do CEBRAP* in São Paulo; both are critical of the economic model.

12. The "Package of April" was a set of measures intended to keep the opposition MDB (Movimento Democrático Brasileiro—Brazilian Democratic Movement) out of power by means of indirect elections and control over the use of the media for political propaganda. In this way the military, with President Geisel at the head, would maintain control. For details on the "Package" and a very good discussion on the autocratic power of President Geisel, power far greater than that of Getúlio Vargas and his Constitution of 1937, see Walder de Góes, *O Brasil do General Geisel*. For church reactions to the divorce law, see *Serviço de Documentação (SEDOC)*, no. 107 (December 1977).

13. For background information on these incidents and others, see *Veja* of 29 December 1976, and *Extra* of February 1977, "Igreja e governo." The incidents, and general repression of the church, became so common that Cardinal Arns of São Paulo and Bishop Balduino of Goiás commissioned a study of the overall situation. This came out as a thirty-eight page document entitled "Repressão à igreja no Brasil: Reflexo de uma situação de opressão (1968-1978)," published by the Centro Ecumênico de Documentação e Informação in Rio de Janeiro in December 1978. It was translated into English in Austin, Texas, in March 1979, but apparently has not been published yet.

14. "Comunicação pastoral ao povo de Deus," November 1976. This document can be found in Lima, *Evolução política*.

15. Ibid.

16. This new orientation is found in all the church organizations of any importance, including the Conferência dos Religiosos do Brasil and the Associação de Educação Católica do Brasil. It is interesting to note that the Centro de Estatística Religiosa e Investigações Sociais (CERIS) is doing less purely religious research and more social-involvement types of projects.

17. *O Estado de São Paulo*, 2 December 1975.

18. "Comunicação pastoral ao povo de Deus," November 1976, in Lima, *Evolução política*.

19. Ibid.

20. Conferência Nacional dos Bispos do Brasil (CNBB), *Exigências cristãs de uma ordem política*. Translated and reproduced in *LADOC* 8, no. 3 (January/February 1978):1-14.

21. Ibid.

22. See, for instance, the interview with Dom Ivo Lorscheider on this point in *O Estado de São Paulo*, 17 May 1978.

23. Conferência Nacional dos Bispos do Brasil (CNBB), "Subsídios para Puebla" (unpublished report). See also the many analyses on the initial Puebla statement in *Revista Eclesiástica Brasileira* 38, no. 149 (March 1978), and J. B. Libânio, "A III conferência geral do episcopado latino-americano," *Síntese* 5, no. 12 (January-March 1978):95-105.

24. Conferência Nacional dos Bispos do Brasil (CNBB), *Subsídios para uma política social*.

25. The literature on this topic includes popularized versions of the international statement by Pe. Jocy Rodrigues, *Declaração universal dos direitos humanos*; a

number of journal issues dedicated specifically to the theme, including *Revista Eclesiástica Brasileira* 37, no. 145 (March 1977), and *CEI* supplement, no. 15 (September 1976). Serious studies include Arns, *Em defesa dos direitos humanos*; Antônio Fragoso (ed.), *A firmeza permanente*; Hubert Lepargneur, *A igreja e o reconhecimento dos direitos humanos na história*; and Hubert Lepargneur et al., *Direitos humanos*. For a general review in English, see Pro Mundi Vita, "The Brazilian Church and Human Rights," *Dossiers* (September-October 1977).

26. This very important series of documents can be obtained from the Conferência Nacional dos Bispos do Brasil (CNBB) in Brasília or the Secrétariat d'appui des Journées Internationales, 14 rue Saint-Benoit 75006 Paris.

27. This case provides some insight into the limits imposed on a national church by the Vatican when the latter is specifically concerned with an issue. Still, the Brazilians took the initiative in starting the project and it can probably continue on its own. The details of the progress and then demise of the project were provided by interviews in June 1978 in São Paulo and Brasília. The documents have been published from the first stage and are available from the Paris office in Portuguese, Spanish, French, and English. See, for the Portuguese version, Conferência Nacional dos Bispos do Brasil (CNBB), *Por uma sociedade superando as dominações*. A newsletter is published also which provides information on the various national and international groups involved in the project. From the documents it would appear to be very active still at the international level.

28. Probably the still most useful single source on the agrarian situation in Brazil is the very-difficult-to-obtain Pan American Union, *Posse e uso da terra e desenvolvimento sócio-econômico do setor agrícola: Brasil*. See also two very good sources: Antônio Barros de Castro, *7 ensaios sobre a economia brasileira*; and José de Souza Martins, *Capitalismo e tradicionalismo*.

29. On the low absorption of labor, see Dennis J. Mahar, *Desenvolvimento econômico da Amazônia*, pp. 67, 127, 128. The general situation in the Amazon area is described and analyzed in "Amazônia," *Cadernos do CEAS*, no. 28 (December 1973), pp. 1-82. The general situation in the rural areas, and the conflicts it has caused, are discussed in Conferência Nacional dos Bispos do Brasil (CNBB), *Pastoral da terra*, nos. 11 and 13. The means for the incentives are described in Banco da Amazônia, *Amazônia: Legislação desenvolvimentista*.

30. Mahar, *Desenvolvimento econômico*, p. 152. See also a very excellent monograph in which this point is further elaborated: Jean Hébette and Rosa E. Acevedo Marín, *Colonização espontânea, política agrária e grupos sociais*, pp. 22-23, 28-29.

31. 1971 (n.p.). See also Dom Pedro Casaldáliga, *Yo creo en la justicia y en la esperanza*, for insights into his view of the area's problems and the church's responsibilities.

32. Comissão Pastoral da Terra, *Boletim*, and the works cited in note 28.

33. For the statements, see *Serviço de Documentação (SEDOC)* 10, no. 105 (October/November 1977).

34. Conferência Nacional dos Bispos do Brasil (CNBB), *Igreja e problemas da terra*.

35. The most recent book on this subject is Sheldon H. Davis, *Victims of the Miracle*. A very good review of much of the new literature concerning this problem is A. R. Gross, "Getting to the Frontier: Recent Books on the Development of the Brazilian Amazon," *Journal of Development Studies* 16, no. 1 (1979): 99-112.

36. Cited in *Boletim do CIMI* (Conselho Indigenista Missionário), no. 41 (October 1977). Also cited there is Law no. 01/N of 25 January 1971, which states "Assistance to the Indian . . . does not anticipate and cannot obstruct national development, not even the fronts of penetration for the integration of the Amazon" (p. 13).

37. The monthly bulletin is a wealth of information and for a short statement of activities, see *Serviço de Documentação (SEDOC)* 9, no. 101 (May 1977):1181-1185. I have verified the accuracy of the document through interviews in Brasília, Goiás, Mato Grosso, and São Paulo. Even as CIMI was being formed, several involved individuals issued a provocative document (in December 1973) entitled *Y-Juca-Pirama: O Indio—Aquele que deve morrer (Y-Juca-Pirama: The Indian—He Who Must Die)*, which detailed the appalling situation of the Indians.

38. Quoted in *Serviço de Documentação (SEDOC)* 9, no. 101 (May 1977):1186.

39. Ibid.

40. Most of the information in this section was obtained in interviews in São Paulo in June 1978. For the main characteristics of the pastoral, see also "Arquidiocese de São Paulo, 1 plano bienal de pastoral: 1976-1977." The cardinal's thinking on any number of issues can be found in the many books he has published and in the interviews granted to the media. See especially, Arns, *Em defesa dos direitos humanos*.

41. No. 3 on the list was Cardinal Arns's book on human rights; no. 4 was Dom Pedro Casaldáliga's book about his experiences; no. 5 was Sobral Pinto's work dealing with liberty; and no. 10 was Comblin's book about national security.

Chapter 6: Innovations in the Dioceses

1. Conferência Nacional dos Bispos do Brasil (CNBB), *Diretrizes gerais da ação pastoral da igreja no Brasil, 1975/1978*, p. 96.

2. For 1980-1984 the orientation of the church in Brazil is to be inspired by the conclusions of the Latin American Episcopal Conference (CELAM) meeting in Puebla. The main lines to be implemented concern Brazilian society in transformation; evangelization beginning from an option in favor of the poor; seeking the complete liberation of man; an increasing participation and communion, with a view toward the construction of a fraternal society, and, in this way, the announcing of the final kingdom. For elaboration on these and details on activities, see Conferência Nacional dos Bispos do Brasil (CNBB) 5 *plano bienal dos organismos nacionais, 1979/1980*. The current activities and priorities of the CNBB can be easily appreciated from a review of some of its publications, including *Notícias* (weekly), *Comunicado Mensal* (monthly), *Documentos da CNBB* (on official activities), and *Estudos da CNBB* (on topics such as agrarian reform, CEBs, and the pastoral for labor).

212 Notes to pages 97-116

3. The four regions from which the eight dioceses were selected are indicated on the map on p. 2. South includes Rio Grande do Sul, Santa Catarina, and Paraná; S.P. is the state of São Paulo; Center is Goiás; and Northeast includes the states of Ceará, Rio Grande do Norte, Paraiba, and Pernambuco. In all cases "1" means those that were selected because initial evidence indicated they were changing and had already adopted a progressive sociopolitical orientation; "2" means that initial evidence suggested a more-or-less static situation and the continuation of a conservative sociopolitical orientation.

4. Throughout I cite frequently from documents collected in the dioceses (normally pastoral plans). I cannot, however, specify the dioceses for fear of causing problem.

5. Francisco Cartaxo Rolim, "Estrutura da igreja no Brasil" (unpublished research report).

6. This point is widely appreciated concerning education. For information regarding other church institutions, such as hospitals and orphanages, see Centro de Estatística Religiosa e Investigações Sociais (CERIS), "Relatório final: Recursos sociais da igreja no Brasil" (unpublished report).

7. Data from Centro de Estatística Religiosa e Investigações Sociais (CERIS), with the most recent figures for 1975.

8. Data from Centro de Estatística Religiosa e Investigações Sociais (CERIS), 1975, show that of the 5,947 parishes, secular priests had responsibility for 52 percent and religious priests for 40 percent (the missing 8 percent is due to a number of reasons unimportant here). The latter figure has been steadily increasing, from 30 percent in 1963, to 36 percent in 1969, to 40 percent in 1975. Further, in 1975, while 76 percent of the secular priests were Brazilian nationals, 47 percent of the religous priests were.

9. On returning to Brazil in June 1978, after three years away, I found that Center 1 had gone far beyond what I had anticipated and had assumed a much more clearly defined political option. In general, for most of the country, the process seemed well advanced in comparison with three years earlier, and the options much more clearly defined. This was even more the case on my visit in 1981.

10. Cândido Procópio Ferreira de Camargo (ed.), *São Paulo 1975: Crescimento e pobreza.*

Chapter 7: Patterns of Religiosity, Sociopolitical Attitudes, and Change in the Dioceses

1. Most useful in this regard was the anthology of questionnaire items edited by John P. Robinson and Phillip R. Shaver, *Measures of Social Psychological Attitudes.* Of some utility was William M. O'Barr (ed.), *Survey Research in Africa.* The questionnaire and suggestions from the Institute for Social Research (Ann Arbor) and the Instituto Universitário de Pesquisas (Rio de Janeiro) team were also very useful in formulating our survey items, and of course they were pretested before being included in our questionnaire.

2. This scale is composed of the seven items in question 38 of the questionnaire, which may be found in Appendix 3.

3. This scale is composed of the five items in question 44 of the questionnaire, which concern attitudes toward the government and society. To these are added items a-d and g-h in question 46, which seek to ascertain the respondent's attitudes on control and criticism.

4. This scale is composed of open-ended questions 41, 41b, and 43, as well as closed questions 41a and 43a. Each series has been coded in order to ascertain the respondent's attitudes on problems, whom problems affect, and what may be done about them. The local and national aspects have been combined to form this scale.

5. See Hubert M. Blalock, Jr., *Causal Inferences in Nonexperimental Research*. We should take Blalock's discussion on causality seriously. Since all variables cannot be imagined, let alone controlled, simplifying assumptions are made. "We first assume that all other variables explicitly included in the causal model have been controlled or do not vary" (p. 19). The many possible types of variables cannot, however, all be dealt with by such methods as randomization and thus, "no matter how elaborate the design, certain simplifying assumptions must always be made" (p. 26). What emerges from Blalock's discussion is the precariousness of making causal inferences under any conditions. I am aware of these strictures and they inform my discussion and data analysis. Given the fundamental nature of these strictures, one wonders whether other sampling methods giving a probability sample could move us very much farther along in attaining closure on an analytical problem.

Chapter 8: *Comunidades Eclesiais de Base* and Other Groups

1. The quantity and diversity of literature on the topic indicates this. A partial bibliography would include the following: Alvaro Barreiro, *Comunidades eclesiais de base e evangelização dos pobres;* Raimundo Caramurú de Barros, *Comunidade eclesial de base;* Pe. Afonso Gregory (ed.), *Comunidades eclesiais de base;* F. A. Pastor, "Paróquia e comunidade de base," *Síntese* 4, no. 10 (May-August 1977):21-45. There have now been three national meetings on the topic. Results of the first two have been published in *Serviço de Documentação (SEDOC)* 7, no. 81 (May 1975), and 9, no. 95 (October 1976). Some of the international literature includes Pro Mundi Vita, "Basic Communities in the Church," no. 62 (September 1976), and "Basic Christian Communities," *LADOC 'Keyhole' Series* 4 (1976).

2. For a review of the general literature on this "crisis of the parish," see Pastor, *Paróquia*, pp. 25-30. See also Pe. Afonso Gregory (ed.), *Pastoral de grandes cidades;* and idem, *A paróquia ontem, hoje e amanhã.*

3. Data from Centro de Estatística Religiosa e Investigações Sociais (CERIS), with the most recent statistics from 1975. The absolute numbers are secular priests, 4,990; religious priests, 7,634; and nuns, 38,517.

4. From unpublished notes by Eduardo Hoornaert, January 1975, in Vitória, Espírito Santo.

5. For papal support, see Pro Mundi Vita, "Basic Communities," pp. 4-6; for

Latin America, see Gregory, *Comunidades*, pp. 76-81. In general see Pastor, *Paróquia*, pp. 21-45. In the Latin American Episcopal Conference (CELAM) meeting of January and February 1979, held in Puebla, Mexico, the CEBs were supported in clear and forthright terms. See Conferência do Episcopado Latino-Americano (CELAM), *III General Conference of Latin American Bishops, Puebla*, items 96-100.

6. As noted earlier, the first meeting resulted in the *Serviço de Documentação (SEDOC)* publications. The last one was held in João Pessoa in late July 1978, and was preceded by meetings in the regions for at least a year. See, for example, *O São Paulo*, 21-27 January 1978.

7. Carlos Mesters, "O futuro do nosso passado," *Serviço de Documentação (SEDOC)* 7, no. 81 (1975):1137.

8. Ibid.

9. Claudio Perani, in a manuscript to be published in the Centro de Estudos e Ação Social's *Cadernos do CEAS*, makes the point well: "Today the term CEB does not necessarily define a renovating tendency in the Brazilian church but does indicate the various orientations that diversify the present tendencies within the church." One of the most constant observers of the CEBs, Jether Ramalho, raises the question of whether they are a real change and commitment to the people or just another technique for exercising traditional religious influence ("Algumas notas sobre duas perspectivas de pastoral popular," *Cadernos do ISER*, 6 [March 1977]:34).

10. The argument on inversion is made in Leonardo Boff, "Eclesiogênese: As comunidades eclesiais de base re-inventam a igreja," *Serviço de Documentação (SEDOC)* 9, no. 95 (1976):393-438.

11. Pedro Demo, *Comunidade: Igreja na base*, p. 37. The political aspect in terms of awareness and participation is recognized in the latest study on the growing CEB phenomenon: Conferência Nacional dos Bispos do Brasil (CNBB), *Comunidades eclesiais de base no Brasil: Experiências e perspectivas*, especially pp. 67-75.

12. One may note that whereas there are 558 members of groups, we have in this distribution 486 activities. The decrease is due to the increased rigor between the question on membership and the question on activity, thereby forcing any ambiguous membership from the count. Further, the activity question is open-ended and, in some cases, ambiguous responses were eliminated. In this instance, as in others, rounding causes the percentages to add up to less than 100.

13. See, for example, Francisco Cartaxo Rolim, "Estrutura da igreja no Brasil," passim. This is one of the key themes in Gianfranco Poggi, *Catholic Action in Italy: The Sociology of a Sponsored Organization*.

14. Stephen D. Berger, "The Sects and the Breakthrough into the Modern World: On the Centrality of the Sects in Weber's Protestant Ethic Thesis," *Sociological Quarterly* 12 (Autumn 1971):491.

15. I am grateful to Professor Heinrich Krumweide of Mannheim University for bringing Berger's excellent article to my attention and for indicating how it related

to my work. I have also attempted to develop Ivan Vallier's insight regarding "extraction, insulation, and re-entry" to the CEBs. See my "The Catholic Church and Development in Latin America: The Role of the Basic Christian Communities," *World Development* 8, nos. 7 and 8 (July and August 1980):535-544.

Epilogue: The Implications of the Pope's Visit in Summer 1980
    1. A complete collection of the papal pronouncements and letters is found in *Pronunciamentos do Papa no Brasil.* Selected texts with commentary situating the pronouncements and actions are found in Adair Leonardo Rocha and Luiz Alberto Gomes de Souza, *O povo e o Papa.*
    2. *O povo e o Papa*, p. 83.

Appendix 1: Description of the Field Study
    1. Ivan Vallier, "Comparative Studies of Roman Catholicism: Dioceses as Strategic Units," *Social Compass* 16, no. 2 (1969):149.
    2. For a description and analysis of church-run institutions, see Centro de Estatística Religiosa e Investigações Sociais (CERIS), "Relatório final: Recursos sociais da igreja no Brasil."
    3. Donald T. Campbell and Julian C. Stanley, *Experimental and Quasi-Experimental Designs for Research*, p. 12.
    4. C. A. Moser and G. Kalton, *Survey Methods in Social Investigation,* p. 79.
    5. Ibid., p. 135.
    6. Ibid., p. 127.
    7. Ibid., pp. 133-137.
    8. Isidore Chein, "An Introduction to Sampling," in *Research Methods in Social Relations*, ed. Claire Selltiz et al., pp. 536-537.
    9. Frederick F. Stephan and Philip J. McCarthy, *Sampling Opinions,* chapter 10.
    10. Vallier, "Comparative Studies," p. 149. Vallier was extremely concerned in his research with questions of methodology. He developed courses in this area and published a book of original essays which included two by practitioners of survey research, Robert H. Somers and Sidney Verba. See Vallier, *Comparative Methods in Sociology.*

Bibliography

Alves, Márcio Moreira. *A igreja e a política no Brasil.* São Paulo: Editora Brasiliense, 1979.

"Amazônia." *Cadernos do CEAS,* no. 28 (December 1973), pp. 1-82.

Antoniazzi, Alberto. "Várias interpretações do catolicismo popular no Brasil." *Revista Eclesiástica Brasileira* 36, no. 141 (March 1976):82-95.

Arns, Dom Paulo Evaristo. *Em defesa dos direitos humanos, encontro com o Reporter.* Rio de Janeiro: Editora Brasília, 1978.

"Arquidiocese de São Paulo, 1 plano bienal de pastoral: 1976-1977." São Paulo.

Astiz, Carlos. "The Catholic Church in Latin American Politics: A Case Study of Peru." In *Latin American Prospects for the 1970's: What Kinds of Revolutions,* edited by David H. Pollock and Arch Ritter. New York: Praeger, 1973.

Azevedo, Thales de. *O catolicismo no Brasil.* Rio de Janeiro: Ministério de Educação e Cultura, 1955.

———. *Cultura e situação racial no Brasil.* Rio de Janeiro: Editora Civilização Brasileira, 1966.

Azzi, Riolando. "Elementos para a história do catolicismo popular." *Revista Eclesiástica Brasileira* 36, no. 141 (March 1976):95-131.

———. "O episcopado brasileiro frente à Revolução de 1930." *Síntese* 5, no. 12 (January-March 1978):47-97.

———. *O episcopado do Brasil frente o catolicismo popular.* Petrópolis: Editora Vozes, 1977.

———. "O início da restauração católica no Brasil, 1920-1930." *Síntese* 4, no. 10 (May-August 1977):61-91.

Bacha, Edmar. *Issues and Evidence on Recent Brazilian Economic Growth.* Development Discussion Paper, no. 12. Cambridge, Mass.: Harvard Institute for International Development, February 1976.

———. *Os mitos de uma década.* Rio de Janeiro: Paz e Terra, 1976.

Baer, Werner. "The Brazilian Boom 1968-72: An Explanation and Interpretation."

218   Bibliography

World Development 1, no. 8 (August 1973):1-17.
————. *The Brazilian Economy: Its Growth and Development.* Columbus, Ohio: Grid Publishing, 1979.
————. "The Brazilian Growth and Development Experience: 1964-1975." In *Brazil in the Seventies*, edited by Riordan Roett, pp. 41-62. Washington, D.C.: American Enterprise Institute, 1976.
————; Isaac Kerstenetsky; and Annibal V. Villela. "The Changing Role of the State in the Brazilian Economy." *World Development* 1, no. 11 (November 1973):23-35.
Banco da Amazônia. *Amazônia: Legislação desenvolvimentista.* Belém-Pará: Departamento de Estudos Econômicos, 1969.
Barnard, Chester. *The Functions of the Executive.* Cambridge, Mass.: Harvard University Press, 1938.
Barreiro, Alvaro. *Comunidades eclesiais de base e evangelização dos pobres.* São Paulo: Edições Loyola, 1978.
Barros, Raimundo Caramurú de. *Comunidade eclesial de base: Uma opção pastoral decisiva.* Petrópolis: Editora Vozes, 1967.
"Basic Christian Communities." *LADOC 'Keyhole' Series* 4 (1976).
Bastide, Roger. "Religion and the Church in Brazil." In *Brazil: Portrait of Half a Continent*, edited by T. Lynn Smith and A. Marchant. New York: Dryden Press, 1951.
Becker, Dom João. *A religião e a pátria em face das ideologias modernas.* Porto Alegre: Typographia do Centro, 1939.
Behrman, Lucy C. "The Political and Social Impact of the Peoples' Priests in Chile. In *Religion and Political Modernization*, edited by Donald E. Smith. New Haven, Conn.: Yale University Press, 1974.
Benkö, Antonius. "Pesquisa-aspectos psico-sociais da religiosidade no estado da Guanabara." *Síntese* 2, no. 3 (January 1975):49-105.
Berger, Peter L. *Pyramids of Sacrifice.* New York: Basic Books, 1974.
Berger, Stephen D. "The Sects and the Breakthrough into the Modern World: On the Centrality of the Sects in Weber's Protestant Ethic Thesis." *Sociological Quarterly* 12 (Autumn 1971):486-499.
Berryman, Phillip E. "Latin American Liberation Theology." *Theological Studies* 34, no. 3 (September 1973):357-395.
Bispos do Centro-Oeste. *Marginalização de um povo: Grito das igrejas.* Goiânia, May 1973.
Bispos e Superiores Religiosos do Nordeste. *Eu ouvi os clamores do meu povo.* Salvador: Editora Beneditina, 1973.
Blalock, Hubert M., Jr. *Causal Inferences in Nonexperimental Research.* New York: W. W. Norton, 1972.
Bloom, David. "The State and Conservative Modernization: The Brazilian Case." M. A. thesis, McGill University, 1976.
Boff, Clodovis. *Comunidade eclesial: Comunidade política.* Petrópolis: Editora Vozes, 1978.
Boff, Leonardo. "Eclesiogênese: As comunidades eclesiais de base re-inventam a

igreja." *Serviço de Documentação (SEDOC)* 9, no. 95 (1976):393-438.

Boulard, F., and J. Remy. "Urban Cultural Regions and Religious Practice in France." *Social Compass* 15 (June 1968):453-469.

Brown, Diana. "Umbanda e classes sociais." *Religião e Sociedade*, no. 1 (May 1977), pp. 31-43.

Bruneau, Thomas C. "The Catholic Church and Development in Latin America: The Role of the Basic Christian Communities." *World Development* 8, nos. 7 and 8 (July and August 1980):535-544.

———. *O Catolicismo brasileiro em época de transição*. São Paulo: Edições Loyola, 1974.

———. "Obstacles to Change in the Church: Lessons from Four Brazilian Dioceses." *Journal of Interamerican Studies and World Affairs* 15, no. 4 (November 1973):395-414.

———. *The Political Transformation of the Brazilian Catholic Church*. Cambridge: At the University Press, 1974.

———. "Power and Influence: Analysis of the Church in Latin America and the Case of Brazil." *Latin American Research Review* 8, no. 2 (Summer 1973): 25-51.

———, and Philippe Faucher, eds. *Authoritarian Capitalism: The Contemporary Economic and Political Development of Brazil*. Boulder, Col.: Westview Press, 1981.

Buarque de Hollanda, Sérgio. *Raizes do Brasil*. Rio de Janeiro: Livraria José Olympio Editora, 1936.

Burgess, Mike, and Daniel Wolf. "Brazil: The Concept of Power in the Brazilian Higher War College (ESG)." Latin American Research Unit, doc. 27. Toronto, 1979.

Callado, Antônio. *Quarup*. Translated by Barbara Shelby. New York: Knopf, 1970.

———. *Tempo de Arraes: Padres e comunistas na revolução sem violência*. Rio de Janeiro: José Alvaro Editora, 1965.

Camargo, Cândido Procópio Ferreira de, ed. *São Paulo: Growth and Poverty*. London: Bowerdean Press, 1978.

———. *São Paulo 1975: Crescimento e pobreza*. São Paulo: Edições Loyola, 1975.

Campbell, Donald T., and Julian C. Stanley. *Experimental and Quasi-Experimental Designs for Research*. Chicago: Rand McNally, 1963.

Campos, Renato Carneiro. *Igreja política e região*. Recife: Instituto Joaquim Nabuco de Pesquisas Sociais, 1967.

Cardim, Fernão. *Tratados da terra e gente do Brasil*. 2nd ed. Rio de Janeiro: Editora Nacional, 1939.

Cardoso, Fernando Henrique. *Autoritarismo e democratização*. Rio de Janeiro: Paz e Terra, 1975.

———. *O modelo político brasileiro*. São Paulo: Difusão Européia do Livro, 1973.

Casaldáliga, Dom Pedro. *Yo creo en la justicia y en la esperanza*. Bilbao:

220   Bibliography

Desclée de Brouwer, 1975.
Castro, Antônio Barros de. *7 ensaios sobre a economia brasileira*. 2 vols. Rio de Janeiro: Forense, 1969.
Centro Brasileiro de Análise e Planejamento (CEBRAP). *Cadernos do CEBRAP*, São Paulo, 1973-1978.
————. *Estudos CEBRAP*, São Paulo, 1973-1978.
Centro de Estatística Religiosa e Investigações Sociais (CERIS). *Primeiro relatório da coordenação do programa de pesquisas do plano de pastoral de conjunto*. Rio de Janeiro: CERIS, 1966.
————. "Recursos sociais da igreja no Brasil." Rio de Janeiro: CERIS, 1975.
————. "Relatório final: Recursos sociais da igreja no Brasil." Unpublished CERIS report. Rio de Janeiro, 1975.
Centro de Estudos e Ação Social (CEAS). *Cadernos do CEAS*, Salvador.
Centro Dom Vital. *A Ordem*, Rio de Janeiro, 1922-1960.
Centro Ecumênico de Documentação e Informação (CEDI). *Presença*, Rio de Janeiro, 1975-1980.
————. "Repressão à igreja no Brasil: Reflexo de uma situação de opressão (1968-1978)." Rio de Janeiro: CEDI, 1978.
Chein, Isidore. "An Introduction to Sampling." In *Research Methods in Social Relations*, by Claire Selltiz; Lawrence Wrightsman; and Stuart Cook. 3rd edition. New York: Holt, Rinehart and Winston, 1976.
Civilização Brasileira. *Encontros com a Civilização Brasileira*, July 1978-present.
Clayton, Richard, and James Gladden. "The Five Dimensions of Religiosity: Toward Demythologizing a Sacred Artifact." *Journal for the Scientific Study of Religion* 13 (1974):135-143.
Cline, Ray S. *World Power Assessment: A Calculus of Strategic Drift*. Boulder, Col.: Westview Press, 1975.
Cline, Victor, and James Richard. "A Factor-Analytic Study of Religious Belief and Behavior." *Journal of Personality and Social Psychology* 1, no. 6 (1965):569-578.
Collier, David, ed. *The New Authoritarianism in Latin America*. Princeton, N.J.: Princeton University Press, 1979.
Comblin, José. *A ideologia da segurança nacional: Poder militar na América Latina*. Translated by A. Veiga Filho. Rio de Janeiro: Civilização Brasileira, 1977.
————. "The National Security Doctrine." Latin American Research Unit, doc. 3, no. 2. Toronto, 1976.
————. "Situação histórica do catolicismo no Brasil." *Revista Eclesiástica Brasileira* 26 (September 1966):583-584.
Comissão de Estudos de História da Igreja na América Latina (CEHILA). *História da igreja no Brasil: Primeira época*. Petrópolis: Editora Vozes, 1977.
Comissão Pastoral da Terra. *Boletim*, Goiânia, 1975-1980.
Conferência do Episcopado Latino-Americano (CELAM). *III General*

Conference of Latin American Bishops. Puebla. Washington, D.C.: National Conference of Catholic Bishops, 1979.

Conferência Nacional dos Bispos do Brasil (CNBB). *Comunicado Mensal,* São Paulo.

―――. *Comunidades eclesiais de base no Brasil: experiencias e perspectivas.* São Paulo: Edições Paulinas, 1979.

―――. *Diretrizes gerais da ação pastoral da igreja no Brasil, 1975/1978.* São Paulo: Edições Paulinas, 1975.

―――. *Documentos da CNBB,* São Paulo.

―――. *Estudos da CNBB,* São Paulo.

―――. *Exigências cristãs de uma ordem política.* São Paulo: Edições Paulinas, 1978.

―――. *Igreja e problemas da terra.* São Paulo: Edições Paulinas, 1980.

―――. *Notícias.* São Paulo, 1977-1980.

―――. *Pastoral da terra.* São Paulo: Edições Paulinas, 1976 and 1977.

―――. *Plano de emergência.* Rio de Janeiro: Livraria Dom Bosco Editora, 1962.

―――. *Por uma sociedade superando as dominações.* Vol. 1. São Paulo: Edições Paulinas, 1978.

―――. *5 plano bienal dos organismos nacionais, 1979/1980.* São Paulo: Edições Paulinas, 1980.

―――. "Subsídios para Puebla." Unpublished report. Itiaci, S.P.: CNBB, 1978.

―――. *Subsídios para uma política social.* São Paulo: Edições Paulinas, 1979.

―――. Secretariado Regional Leste 1. *Macumba: Cultos afro-brasileiros: Candomblé, Umbanda, observações pastorais.* São Paulo: Edições Paulinas, 1972.

Conselho Indigenista Missionário (CIMI). *Boletim do CIMI,* Goiânia, 1975-1980.

Cupertino, Fausto. *As muitas religiões do brasileiro.* Rio de Janeiro: Civilização Brasileira, 1976.

Davis, Sheldon H. *Victims of the Miracle: Development and the Indians of Brazil.* Cambridge: At the University Press, 1977.

Deelen, Godofredo J., SS. C. C. *A sociologia a serviço da pastoral.* Petrópolis: Editora Vozes, 1966.

Della Cava, Ralph. "Igreja e estado no Brasil do século XX: Sete monografias recentes sobre o catolicismo brasileiro, 1916/64." *Estudos CEBRAP* 12 (April-June 1975):5-53.

Demerath, N. J., III, and Phillip E. Hammond. *Religion in a Social Context.* New York: Random House, 1969.

Demo, Pedro. *Comunidade: Igreja na base.* São Paulo: Edições Paulinas, 1974.

―――. *Desenvolvimento e política social no Brasil.* Rio de Janeiro: Editora Universidade de Brasília, 1978.

―――. "Política social no Brasil após 1964." Mimeographed. CEPAL, 1979.

Dodson, Michael. "Religious Innovation and the Politics of Argentina: A Study of the Movement of Priests for the Third World." Ph.D. dissertation, Indiana University, 1973.

Dussel, Enrique. *History and the Theology of Liberation.* Translated by John

Drury. New York: Orbis Books, 1976.

Einaudi, Luigi; Michael Fleet; Alfred Stepan; and Richard Maulin. "Latin American Institutional Development: The Changing Catholic Church." Memorandum RM-6136-DOS. Santa Monica, Cal.: The Rand Corporation, October 1969.

Erickson, Kenneth Paul. *The Brazilian Corporate State and Working Class Politics.* Berkeley and Los Angeles: University of California Press, 1977.

O Estado de São Paulo, 1974-1979.

Evans, Peter. *Dependent Development: The Alliance of Multinational, State, and Local Capital in Brazil.* Princeton, N.J.: Princeton University Press, 1979.

Extra, São Paulo.

Faucher, Philippe. "Croissance et répression, la double logique de l'état dépendent: le cas du Brésil."*Revue Canadienne de Science Politique* 12, no. 4 (December 1979):747-774.

Fernandes, Pe. Geraldo. "A religião nas constituições republicanas do Brasil." *Revista Eclesiástica Brasileira* 8 (December 1948):830-858.

Fiechter, Georges-André. *O regime modernizador do Brasil, 1964/1972.* Rio de Janeiro: Fundação Getúlio Vargas, 1974.

Flora, Cornelia Butler. "Mobilizing the Masses: The Sacred and the Secular in Colombia." Ph.D. dissertation, Cornell University, 1970.

Flynn, Peter. *Brazil: A Political Analysis.* London: Ernest Benn, 1978.

Forman, Shepard. *The Brazilian Peasantry.* New York: Columbia University Press, 1975.

Fragoso, Antônio, ed. *A firmeza permanente.* São Paulo: Coedição Loyola-Vega, 1977.

Freyre, Gilberto. *Casa grande e senzala.* 6th ed. Rio de Janeiro: José Olympio Editora, 1950.

―――. *The Masters and the Slaves.* Translated by Samuel Putnam. New York: Knopf and Co., 1946.

Fundação Instituto Brasileiro de Geografia. *Divisão do Brasil em microregiões homogêneas 1968.* Rio de Janeiro: Instituto Brasileiro de Geografia e Estatística (IBGE), 1970.

Furtado, Celso. *Análise do "modelo" brasileiro.* Rio de Janeiro: Editora Civilização Brasileira, 1972.

Glock, Charles Y., and Phillip E. Hammond, eds. *Beyond the Classics? Essays in the Scientific Study of Religion.* New York: Harper & Row, 1973.

―――, and Rodney Stark. *Religion and Society in Tension.* Chicago: Rand McNally & Co., 1965.

Góes, Walder de. *O Brasil do General Geisel.* Rio de Janeiro: Editora Nova Fronteira, 1978.

Gorsuch, Richard I. *Factor Analysis.* Philadelphia: W. B. Saunders Co., 1974.

Govaers, Maria Madeleine. "Aspects du syncrétisme religieux brésilien dans le cadre de son acculturation." M.A. thesis, Université Catholique de Louvain, 1969.

Grayson, George W. "The Church and Military in Peru." In *Religion and Political Modernization,* edited by Donald E. Smith. New Haven, Conn.: Yale University Press, 1974.

Gregory, Pe. Afonso, ed. *Comunidades eclesiais de base: Utopia ou realidade.* Petrópolis: Editora Vozes, 1973.

————. *A paróquia ontem, hoje e amanhã.* Petrópolis: Editora Vozes, 1967.

————. *Pastoral de grandes cidades.* Petrópolis: Editora Vozes, 1967.

Gross, A. R. "Getting to the Frontier: Recent Books on the Development of the Brazilian Amazon." *Journal of Development Studies* 16, no. 1 (1979):99-112.

Gutiérrez, Gustavo. *A Theology of Liberation.* Maryknoll, N.Y.: Orbis Books, 1973.

Haller, Archibald O., ed. *Socioeconomic Change in Brazil. Luso-Brazilian Review* 15, no. 2 (Winter 1978).

Hébette, Jean, and Rosa E. Acevedo Marín. *Colonização espontânea, política agrária e grupos sociais.* Belém-Para: Núcleo de Altos Estudos Amazônicos, 1976.

Heydebrand, Wolf V. "The Study of Organizations." *Social Science Information* 6, no. 5 (October 1967):59-86.

Hoornaert, Eduardo. *Formação do catolicismo brasileiro, 1550-1800.* Petrópolis: Editora Vozes, 1974.

————. *Verdadeira e falsa religião no Nordeste.* Salvador, Bahia: Editora Beneditina, 1972.

Instituto de Planejamento Econômico e Social (IPEA). *Brasil: 14 anos de revolução.* Rio de Janeiro: IPEA/INPES, 1978.

Instituto de Teologia do Recife (ITER). *A fé popular no Nordeste.* Salvador, Bahia: Editora Beneditina, 1974.

Instituto Universitário de Pesquisas do Rio de Janeiro, *Dados,* 1972-1978.

Ireland, Rowan. "The Catholic Church and Social Change in Brazil: An Evaluation." In *Brazil in the Sixties,* edited by Riordan Roett. Nashville, Tenn.: Vanderbilt University Press, 1972.

Isto E, São Paulo, 1975-1978.

Jornal do Brasil, Rio de Janeiro, 1974-1978.

Kadt, Emanuel de. *Catholic Radicals in Brazil.* London: Oxford University Press, 1970.

————. "Religion, the Church, and Social Change in Brazil." In *The Politics of Conformity in Latin America,* edited by Claudio Véliz. London: Oxford University Press, 1967.

Kalverkamp, Frei Desidério, O.F.M., and Frei Boaventura Kloppenburg, O.F.M. *Ação pastoral perante o espiritismo.* Petrópolis: Editora Vozes, 1961.

Katz, Daniel, and Robert Kahn. *The Social Psychology of Organizations.* New York: Wiley, 1966.

King, Morton B. "Measuring the Religious Variable: Nine Proposed Dimensions." *Journal for the Scientific Study of Religion* 6, no. 2 (Fall 1967):173-190.

————, and Richard A. Hunt. *Measuring Religious Dimensions.* Studies in Social

Science, no. 1. Dallas, Tex.: Southern Methodist University, 1972.

—— and ———. "Measuring the Religious Variable." *Journal for the Scientific Study of Religion* 14 (1975):13-22.

———; David Arno; and Richard Hunt. "Measuring the Religious Variable: Alternative Factor Analyses." Paper presented at joint RRA and SSSR meeting, 28 October 1977.

Krischke, Paulo José. *A igreja e as crises políticas no Brasil.* Petrópolis: Editora Vozes, 1979.

LADOC 'Keyhole' Series, Office of International Justice and Peace, United States Catholic Conference, 1975-1980.

Lalive D'Epinay, Christian. "Changements sociaux et développement d'une secte: le Pentecostisme au Chili." *Archives de Sociologie des Religions* 23 (January-June 1967).

Langoni, Carlos Geraldo. *Distribuição da renda e desenvolvimento econômico do Brasil.* Rio de Janeiro: Editora Expressão e Cultura, 1973.

Langton, Kenneth P., and Ronald Rapoport. "Religion and Leftist Mobilization in Chile." *Comparative Political Studies* 9, no. 3 (October 1976):277-308.

Leacock, Seth, and Ruth Leacock. *Spirits of the Deep: A Study of an Afro-Brazilian Cult.* Garden City, N.Y.: Doubleday, 1972.

Leers, Frei Bernardino, O.F.M. *Religiosidade rural: Uma contribuição local.* Petrópolis: Editora Vozes, 1967.

Lepargneur, Hubert. *A igreja e o reconhecimento dos direitos humanos na história.* São Paulo: Cortez e Moraes, 1977.

—— et al. *Direitos humanos.* São Paulo: Edições Paulinas, 1978.

Levine, Daniel H. "Church Elites in Venezuela and Colombia: Context, Background, and Beliefs." *Latin American Research Review* 14, no. 1 (Spring 1979):51-79.

———, ed. *Churches and Politics in Latin America.* Beverly Hills, Cal.: Sage Publications, 1980.

———. "Democracy and the Church in Venezuela." *Journal of Interamerican Studies and World Affairs* 18, no. 1 (February 1976):3-23.

———, and Alexander W. Wilde. "The Catholic Church, 'Politics,' and Violence: The Colombian Case." *Review of Politics* 39, no. 2 (April 1977):220-239.

Libânio, J. B. "A III conferência geral do episcopado latino-americano." *Síntese* 5, no. 12 (January-March 1978):95-105.

Lijphart, Arend. *Class Voting and Religious Voting in the European Democracies: A Preliminary Report.* Survey Research Center Occasional Paper, no. 8. Glasgow: University of Strathclyde, 1971.

Lima, Danilo Martins de. "Educação, igreja, ideologia: Uma análise sociológica das influências da Igreja Católica na elaboração da Lei no. 4.024/61 de Diretrizes e Bases da Educação Nacional." M.A. thesis, Pontifícia Universidade Católica do Rio de Janeiro, 1975.

Lima, Luis Gonzaga de Souza. *Evolução política dos católicos e da igreja no Brasil.* Petrópolis: Editora Vozes, 1979.

Luz, Marco Aurélio, and Georges Lapassade. *O segredo da Macumba.* Rio de Janeiro: Paz e Terra, 1972.

McKenzie, John L. *The Roman Catholic Church.* Garden City, N.Y.: Image Books, 1969.

Magalhães, Basílio. *Estudos de história do Brasil.* Rio de Janeiro: Companhia Editora Nacional, 1940.

Mahar, Dennis J. *Desenvolvimento econômico da Amazônia: Uma análise das políticas governamentais.* Rio de Janeiro: Instituto de Planejamento Econômico e Social, 1978.

Margolis, Maxine L., and William E. Carter, eds. *Brazil. Anthropological Perspectives: Essays in Honor of Charles Wagley.* New York: Columbia University Press, 1979.

Maria, Pe. Júlio. *O catolicismo no Brasil.* 1900. Reprint. Rio de Janeiro: Livraria AGIR, 1950.

Martins, Carlos Estevam, ed. *Estado e capitalismo no Brasil.* São Paulo: Editora de Humanismo, Ciência e Tecnologia-CEBRAP, 1977.

Martins, José de Souza. *Capitalismo e tradicionalismo.* São Paulo: Pioneira, 1975.

Marx, Gary T. *Protest and Prejudice.* New York: Harper & Row, 1967.

Mecham, J. Lloyd. *Church and State in Latin America.* Rev. ed. Chapel Hill: University of North Carolina Press, 1966.

Medina, C. A. de. *Participação e trabalho social.* Petrópolis: Editora Vozes, 1977.

Meisel, John. "Religious Affiliation and Electoral Behaviour." *Canadian Journal of Economics and Political Science* 22 (1956):481-496.

Mendonça de Barros, José Roberto; and Douglas H. Graham. "The Brazilian Economic Miracle Revisited: Private and Public Sector Initiative in a Market Economy." *Latin American Research Review* 13, no. 2 (1978):5-39.

Mesters, Carlos. "O futuro do nosso passado." *Serviço de Documentação (SEDOC)* 7, no. 81 (1975):1133-1191.

Metz, René. *What Is Canon Law?* Translated by Michael Derrick. New York: Hawthorne Books, 1960.

Montenegro, João Alfredo. *Evolução do catolicismo no Brasil.* Petrópolis: Editora Vozes, 1972.

Moser, C. A., and G. Kalton. *Survey Methods in Social Investigation.* London: Heinemann Educational Books, 1971.

Mourão Laís. "O camponês e a colonização missionária." *Revista de Vozes* 68, no. 7 (September 1974):49-58.

Movimento, São Paulo, 1978.

Mutchler, David E. *The Church as a Political Factor in Latin America: With Particular Reference to Colombia and Chile.* New York: Praeger, 1971.

Netto, Pe. José, S. J. "O cursilho de Cristandade." Mimeographed. Instituto Nacional de Pastoral, October 1972.

Nie, Norman H.; C. Hadlai Hull; Jean G. Jenkins; Karen Steinbrenner; Dale H.

226 Bibliography

Bent. *Statistical Package for the Social Sciences*. 2nd ed. New York: McGraw-Hill, 1975.

O'Barr, William M.; David Spain; and Mark Tessler, eds. *Survey Research in Africa: Its Applications and Limits*. Evanston, Ill.: Northwestern University Press, 1973.

O'Dea, Thomas F. *The Catholic Crisis*. Boston: Beacon Press, 1968.

O'Donnell, Guillermo. "Reflections on the Patterns of Change in the Bureaucratic-Authoritarian State." *Latin American Research Review* 13, no. 1 (1978):3-39.

Oliveira, Pedro Assis Ribeiro de. "Bibliografia sobre religiosidade popular." *Religião e Sociedade*, no. 1 (May 1977), pp. 181-194.

―――. "Catolicismo popular e pastoral: Notas para discussão." Unpublished Centro de Estatística Religiosa e Investigaçãoes Sociais (CERIS) report. Rio de Janeiro, 1975.

―――. "Catolicismo popular e romanização do catolicismo brasileiro." *Revista Eclesiástica Brasileira* 36, no. 141 (March 1976):131-142.

―――. "Catolicismo popular no Brasil." Unpublished Centro de Estatística Religiosa e Investigações Sociais (CERIS) report, no. 9. Rio de Janeiro, 1970.

―――. "Catolicismo popular no Brasil-Bibliografia." *Revista Eclesiástica Brasileira* 36, no. 141 (March 1976):272-280.

―――― et al. *Evangelização e comportamento religioso popular*. Petrópolis: Editora Vozes, 1978.

Ortiz, Renato. "Du syncrétisme à la synthèse: Umbanda, une religion brésilienne." *Archives de Sciences Sociales des Religions*, no. 40 (1975), pp. 89-97.

―――. "La morte blanche du sorcier noir." Ph.D. dissertation. Ecole des Hautes Etudes en Sciences Sociales, Paris, 1975.

――――, and Paula Montero. "Contribuição para um estudo quantitativo da religião umbandista." *Ciência e Cultura* 28, no. 4 (October 1975):407-416.

Packenham, Robert. "Trends in Brazilian National Dependency Since 1964." In *Brazil in the Seventies*, edited by Riordan Roett, pp. 89-115. Washington, D.C.:American Enterprise Institute, 1976.

Padin, Dom Cândido. "A doutrina da segurança nacional." *Revista Eclesiástica Brasileira* 37, no. 146 (June 1977):331-342.

Pan American Union. *Posse e uso da terra e desenvolvimento sócio-econômico do setor agrícola: Brasil*. Washington, D.C.: Comitê Inter-Americano de Desenvolvimento Agrícola, 1966.

Pastor, F. A. "Paróquia e comunidade de base." *Síntese* 4, no. 10 (May-August 1977):21-45.

Peacock, James L. "Religion, Communications, and Modernization: A Weberian Critique of Some Recent Views." *Human Organization* 28, no. 1 (Spring 1969): 35-41.

Pedreira, Fernando. *Brasil Política*. São Paulo: Difusão Européia do Livro, 1975.

Pérez, Gustavo; Afonso Gregory; and François Lepargneur. *O problema sacerdotal no Brasil*. Rio de Janeiro: Centro de Estatística Religiosa e Investigações Sociais

(CERIS), 1965.
Perlman, Janice E. *Rio's Favelados and the Myths of Marginality*. Institute of Urban and Regional Development Working Paper, no. 223. Berkeley and Los Angeles: University of California Press.
Pfeffermann, Guy, and Richard Webb. *The Distribution of Income in Brazil*. World Bank Staff Working Paper, no. 356. Washington, D.C.: World Bank, 1979.
Plagge, Winfredo. *A igreja no Brasil*. Rio de Janeiro: Centro de Estatística Religiosa e Investigações Sociais (CERIS), 1965.
Poggi, Gianfranco. *Catholic Action in Italy: The Sociology of a Sponsored Organization*. Stanford, Cal.: Stanford University Press, 1967.
Prado, Paulo. *Retrato do Brasil*. São Paulo: Editora Brasiliense, 1944.
Pro Mundo Vita. "Basic Communities in the Church." no. 62 (September 1976).
———. "The Brazilian Church and Human Rights." *Dossiers* (September-October 1977).
———. *Bulletin and Special Notes*, Brussels, 1974-1980.
Pronunciamentos do Papa no Brasil: Textos apresentados pela CNBB. Petrópolis: Editora Vozes, 1980.
Queiroga, Pe. Gervásio Fernandes de. *Conferência Nacional dos Bispos do Brasil. Comunhão e corresponsabilidade*. São Paulo: Edições Paulinas, 1977.
Queiroz, Maria Isaura Pereira de. *O campesinato brasileiro*. Petrópolis: Editora Vozes, 1973.
Ramalho, Jether. "Algumas notas sobre duas perspectivas de pastoral popular." *Cadernos do ISER* 6 (March 1977):31-39.
Read, William R., and Frank A. Ineson. *Brazil 1980: The Protestant Handbook*. Monrovia, Cal.: Missions Advanced Research & Communications Center, 1973.
Les religions au Brésil. Archives de Sciences Sociales des Religions 47, no. 1 (January-March 1979):1-164.
Ribeiro, René. *Religião e relações raciais*. Rio de Janeiro: Ministério da Educação e Cultura, 1956.
Ricard, Robert. "Comparison of Evangelization in Portuguese and Spanish America." *The Americas* 14 (1957):444-454.
Robinson, John P., and Phillip R. Shaver. *Measures of Social Psychological Attitudes*. Rev. ed. Ann Arbor, Mich.: Survey Research Center for Social Research, 1973.
Robock, Stefan H. *Brazil: A Study in Development Progress*. Lexington, Mass.: Lexington Books, 1975.
Rocha, Adair Leonardo, and Luiz Alberto Gomes de Souza. *O povo e o Papa: Balanço crítico da visita de João Paulo II ao Brasil*. Rio de Janeiro: Civilização Brasileira, 1980.
Rodrigues, Pe. Jocy. *Declaração universal dos direitos humanos*. Petrópolis: Vozes de Petrópolis, 1977.
Roett, Riordan, ed. *Brazil in the Seventies*. Washington, D.C.: American

Enterprise Institute, 1976.

————. *Brazil: Politics in a Patrimonial Society.* Rev. ed. New York: Praeger, 1978.

Rolim, Francisco Cartaxo. "Catolicismo no Brasil." *Lumiar,* no. 26 (April 1970) pp. 93-154.

————. "Diocese de Nova Iguaçu: Protestantismo-espiritismo: Uma perspectiva sociológica." Unpublished report. Rio de Janeiro: Sociedade de Pesquisas e Estudos Sócio-Eclesiais, 1973.

————. "Estrutura da igreja no Brasil." Unpublished research report, no. 1.2 of Plano de Pastoral de Conjunto of Conferência Nacional dos Bispos do Brasil. Rio de Janeiro: Centro de Estatística Religiosa e Investigações Sociais (CERIS), 1968.

————. "Expansão protestante em Nova Iguaçu." *Revista Eclesiástica Brasileira* 33, no. 131 (September 1973):660-675.

————. "Quelques aspects de la pratique dominicale au Brésil." *Social Compass* 14 (May-June 1967):457-468.

Romano, Roberto. *Brasil: Igreja contra estado.* São Paulo: Kairós Livraria e Editora, 1979.

Rummel, R. J. "Understanding Factor Analysis." *Journal of Conflict Resolution* 2 (December 1967):444-479.

Sanders, Thomas G. *Catholic Innovation in a Changing Latin America.* Cuernavaca, Mexico: Centro Intercultural de Documentación, 1970.

————. "The Church in Latin America." *Foreign Affairs* 48, no. 2 (January 1970):285-299.

————, and Brian H. Smith. "The Chilean Catholic Church during the Allende and Pinochet Regimes." *AUFS Fieldstaff Reports* 23, no. 1 (March 1976).

Sanks, T. Howland, and Brian H. Smith, S. J. "Liberation Ecclesiology: Praxis, Theory, Praxis." *Theological Studies* 38, no. 1 (March 1977):3-38.

Santos, Benedito Beni dos; José Carlos Sebe Bom Heihy; Francisco Cartaxo Rolim; Oscar de Figueiredo Lustosa; Riolando Azzi; Pedro A. Ribeiro de Oliveira; Hubert Lapargneur; Roberto Mascarenhas Roxo; Raimundo Cintra; and Geraldo Majella Agnelo. *A religião do povo..* São Paulo: Edições Loyola, 1978.

O São Paulo, 1974-1979.

Schmitter, Philippe. *Interest Conflict and Political Change in Brazil.* Stanford, Cal.: Stanford University Press, 1971.

Schneider, Ronald M. *Brazil: Foreign Policy of a Future World Power.* Boulder, Col.: Westview Press, 1976.

————. *The Political System of Brazil.* New York: Columbia University Press, 1971.

Schooyans, Michel. *O comunismo e o futuro da igreja no Brasil.* São Paulo: Editora Herder, 1963.

Schoultz, Lars. "The Roman Catholic Church in Colombia: Revolution, Reform, and Reaction." *América Latina* 14, no. 3 (1971):90-107.

Schwan, Hubert, and Antonio Ugalde. "Orientations of the Bishops of Colombia toward Social Development, 1930-1970." *Journal of Church and State* 16, no. 3 (1974):473-492.

Selznick, Phillip. "Foundations of a Theory of Organizations." *American Sociological Review* 13 (1948):25-35.

———. *Leadership in Administration.* Evanston, Ill.: Rowe, Peterson & Co., 1975.

Serviço de Documentação (SEDOC), Petrópolis, 1974-1978.

Sigrist, José Luiz. "Fenomenologia de consciência universitária Cristã no Brasil." Ph.D. dissertation, Rio Claro University, 1973.

Simonsen, Mário Henrique, and Roberto de Oliveira Campos. *A nova economia brasileira.* Rio de Janeiro: Editora José Olympio, 1974.

Skidmore, Thomas. *Politics in Brazil, 1930-1964.* New York: Oxford University Press, 1967.

Smith, Brian. "The Catholic Church and Political Change in Chile." Ph.D. dissertation. Yale University, 1979.

———. "Religion and Social Change: Classical Theories and New Formulations in the Context of Recent Developments in Latin America." *Latin American Research Review* 10, no. 2 (Summer 1975):3-34.

Soares, Gláucio Ary Dillon. "After the Miracle." *Luso-Brazilian Review* 15, no. 2 (Winter 1978):278-302.

———. *Sociedade e política no Brasil.* São Paulo: Difusão Européia do Livro, 1973.

Sodré, Nelson Werneck. *Brasil: Radiografia de um modelo.* Petrópolis: Editora Vozes, 1974.

Stark, Rodney, and Charles Glock. *American Piety: The Nature of Religious Commitment.* Berkeley and Los Angeles: University of California Press, 1968.

Stepan, Alfred, ed. *Authoritarian Brazil.* New Haven, Conn.: Yale University Press, 1973.

———. *The Military in Politics: Changing Patterns in Brazil.* Princeton, N.J.: Princeton University Press, 1971.

Stephan, Frederick F., and Philip J. McCarthy. *Sampling Opinions.* New York: John Wiley & Sons, 1958.

Stumpf, André Gustavo, and Merval Pereira Filho. *A Segunda Guerra: Sucessão de Geisel.* São Paulo: Editora Brasiliense, 1979.

Thompson, James. *Organizations in Action.* New York: McGraw Hill, 1967.

———, and William McEwen. "Organizational Goals and Environment." *American Sociological Review* 23 (1958):23-31.

Thornton, Sister Mary Crescentia. *The Church and Freemasonry in Brazil 1872-1875: A Study in Regalism.* Washington, D.C.: The Catholic University of America Press, 1948.

Tolipan, Ricardo, and Arthur Carlos Tinelli. *A controvérsia sobre distribuição de renda e desenvolvimento.* Rio de Janeiro: Zahar Editores, 1975.

Tonellare, L. F. "Notas dominicais." Translated by Alfredo de Carvalho. In

Revista do Instituto Arqueológico e Geográfico Pernambucano 11, no. 61 (1904).

Troeltsch, Ernst. *The Social Teaching of the Christian Churches.* Translated by Olive Wyon. 2 vols. 1931. Reprint. New York: Harper Torchbooks, 1960.

Turner, Frederick C. *Catholicism and Political Development in Latin America.* Chapel Hill: University of North Carolina Press, 1971.

Tyler, William G. "Brazilian Industrialization and Industrial Policies: A Survey." *World Development* 4, nos. 10 and 11 (1976):863-882.

———. *Manufactured Export Expansion and Industrialization in Brazil.* Tubingen: JCB Mohr (Paul Siebeck), 1976.

Vallier, Ivan. *Catholicism, Social Control and Modernization in Latin America.* Englewood Cliffs, N.J.: Prentice-Hall, 1970.

———. *Comparative Methods in Sociology.* Berkeley and Los Angeles: University of California Press, 1971.

———. "Comparative Studies of Roman Catholicism: Dioceses As Strategic Units." *Social Compass* 16, no. 2 (1969):147-184.

———. "Extraction, Insulation, and Re-Entry: Toward a Theory of Religious Change." In *The Church and Social Change in Latin America,* edited by Henry Landsberger. Notre Dame, Ind.: University of Notre Dame Press, 1970.

Veja, São Paulo, 1974-1980.

Véliz, Claudio, ed. *The Politics of Conformity in Latin America.* London: Oxford University Press, 1967.

Vianna, Francisco de Oliveira. *Populações meridionais do Brasil.* Vols. 1 and 2. Rio de Janeiro: Livraria José Olympio Editora, 1938.

Vieira, R. A. Amaral. *Intervencionismo e autoritarismo no Brasil.* São Paulo: Difusão Européia do Livro, 1975.

Warren, Donald. "Portuguese Roots of Brazilian Spiritism." *Luso-Brazilian Review* 5, no. 2 (December 1968):3-33.

Wayland-Smith, Giles. *The Christian Democratic Party in Chile.* Cuernavaca, Mexico: Centro Intercultural de Documentación, 1969.

Westhues, Kenneth. "The Established Church as an Agent of Change." *Sociological Analysis* 34, no. 2 (Summer 1973):106-124.

Whyte, John H. "The Catholic Factor in the Politics of Democratic States." In *The Church and Modern Society,* edited by Leo Moulin. Beverly Hills, Cal.: Sage Publications, 1977.

Willems, Emilio. *Followers of the New Faith.* Nashville, Tenn.: Vanderbilt University Press, 1967.

Williams, Edward J. *Latin American Christian Democratic Parties.* Knoxville: University of Tennessee Press, 1967.

World Bank (IBRD). *Brazil: Human Resources Special Report.* World Bank Country Study. Washington, D.C., October 1979.

Index